The Urban Transformation

For the first time in history, half of the world's population lives in urban areas and it is expected that, by 2050, that figure will rise to above two-thirds. A large proportion of this urban growth will be taking place in the cities of the developing world, where the provision of adequate health, shelter, water and sanitation and climate change adaptation efforts for rapidly-growing urban populations will be an urgent priority. This transition to an urban world could be a negative transformation; but, if well-planned, it could also offer an unprecedented opportunity to improve the lives of some of the world's poorest people.

This volume brings together some of the world's foremost experts in urban development with the aim of approaching these issues as an opportunity for real positive change. The chapters focus on three strategically critical aspects of this transformation:

- public health
- shelter, water and sanitation
- climate change adaptation.

These are considered using an integrated approach that takes account of the many different sectors and stakeholders involved, and always in terms of the solutions rather than the problems. The book offers a blueprint for action in these sectors and will be of great interest to academics and policy-makers in all aspects of urban development and planning.

Elliott D. Sclar is Director of the Center for Sustainable Urban Development (CSUD) at the Earth Institute at Columbia University and Professor of Urban Planning in the university's Graduate School of Architecture, Planning and Preservation.

Nicole Volavka-Close is Associate Director of the Center for Sustainable Urban Development (CSUD) at Columbia University's Earth Institute.

Peter Brown is an independent editorial consultant.

The Urban Transformation

Health, shelter and climate change

Edited by
Elliott D. Sclar,
Nicole Volavka-Close
and Peter Brown

Routledge
Taylor & Francis Group
LONDON AND NEW YORK

from Routledge

First published 2013
by Routledge
2 Park Square, Milton Park, Abingdon, Oxon, OX14 4RN

Simultaneously published in the USA and Canada
by Routledge
711 Third Avenue, New York, NY 10017

Routledge is an imprint of the Taylor & Francis Group, an informa business

British Library Cataloguing in Publication Data
A catalogue record for this book is available from the British Library

Library of Congress Cataloging-in-Publication Data
The urban transformation : health, shelter and climate change / edited by Elliott D. Sclar, Nicole Volavka-Close and Peter Brown.
p. cm.
Includes bibliographical references and index.
1. Urban ecology (Sociology) 2. Sustainable urban development. 3. Urban health. 4. Urban poor. 5. City planning. 6. Urbanization—Environmental aspects. I. Sclar, Elliott. II. Volavka-Close, Nicole. III. Brown, Peter (Peter G.), 1948-
HT241.U7284 2012
307.76 – dc23
2012003296

ISBN13: 978-1-84971-215-6 (hbk)
ISBN13: 978-1-84971-216-3 (pbk)
ISBN13: 978-0-203-10768-3 (ebk)

Typeset in Sabon
by Swales & Willis Ltd, Exeter, Devon

MIX
Paper from
responsible sources
FSC
www.fsc.org   FSC® C004839

Printed and bound by CPI Group (UK) Ltd, Croydon, CR0 4YY

Contents

List of illustrations

Figures

Tables

Boxes

Notes on contributors

Editors

Elliott D. Sclar is Director of the Center for Sustainable Urban Development (CSUD) at the Earth Institute, Columbia University and Professor of Urban Planning at Columbia's Graduate School of Architecture, Planning and Preservation. An economist and urban planner, Sclar was co-coordinator of the Taskforce on Improving the Lives of Slum Dwellers, one of ten United Nation's Millennium Project taskforces created to implement the Millennium Development Goals. Sclar is an economist and Urban Planner. His book *You Don't Always Get What You Pay For: The Economics of Privatization* (2000), a critique of overreliance on market mechanisms, has won two major academic prizes.

Nicole Volavka-Close is Associate Director of the Center for Sustainable Urban Development (CSUD) at Columbia University's Earth Institute. She recently co-authored the paper 'Traffic impacts on $PM_{2.5}$ air quality in Nairobi, Kenya' (2011) as well as the book chapter 'Improving Population Health in a Rapidly Urbanizing World' for the volume, *Urban Health: A Global Perspective* (2011). She is interested in the interdependent issues of urban health, transport and land use, and climate change.

Peter Brown began his career as a senior editor at *Scientific American*, served as managing editor of *Physics Today*, and was named editor-in-chief of *The Sciences* in 1989. He remained at *The Sciences* until that magazine was closed in 2001. Shortly thereafter, he and his partners purchased *Natural History* magazine from the American Museum of Natural History, and he became editor-in-chief of that magazine. He now works as an independent editorial consultant.

Contributors

Waleska Teixeira Caiaffa, MD, MPH, PhD, is Professor of Epidemiology and Public Health at the School of Medicine, Federal University of Minas Gerais, Brazil. She is co-founding President of the Observatory for Urban

Health in Belo Horizonte, President of the International Society for Urban Health and a research consultant for the National Council for Scientific and Technological Development (Brazil). Her research and publications focus on urban health, including infectious and non-transmissible diseases, as well as on multiple collaborative projects with population-based designs on the individual, environmental and social level determinants of health.

Rachel Cardone is a Program Officer at the Bill and Melinda Gates Foundation, where she focuses on sustainable urban sanitation service delivery models. Her portfolio invests in developing new methodologies, models and financing arrangements that increase cost effectiveness and impact of aid funding, and leverage private funds for service delivery. Prior to the Foundation, she worked on strategy development, policy and implementation with organizations including the World Bank, the UK's Department for International Development, World Economic Forum, African Development Bank and leading non-governmental organizations (NGOs). She has an MPA from Columbia University's School of International and Public Affairs.

Catarina Fonseca is a senior programme officer and the WASHCost Director (2008–12) at the International Water and Sanitation Centre (IRC) in the Netherlands. She has 12 years of experience at the IRC. She has been coordinating the IRC theme on financing, supervising innovative action research with multidisciplinary teams in multiple countries and providing technical support to several foundations, development banks, international organizations and governments in developing countries. Fonseca holds an MA in Development Studies (The Hague, Netherlands) and was originally trained as an Economist (MA, Lisbon, Portugal). She is currently working on her PhD (Cranfield, UK).

Stephen Hammer, PhD, is a Lecturer in Energy Planning at the Massachusetts Institute of Technology, and co-Director of the Urban Climate Change Research Network. He is a member of New York City's Energy Policy Task Force and from 2009 to 2010 he led the Energy Smart Cities Initiative. Hammer taught at Columbia University's School of International and Public Affairs (SIPA) and served as Director of the Urban Energy Program at SIPA's Center for Energy, Marine Transportation and Public Policy. Hammer holds a PhD from the London School of Economics and an MPP from the Kennedy School of Government at Harvard University.

Trudy Harpham, PhD, is Emeritus Professor at London South Bank University and Honorary Professor at the London School of Hygiene and Tropical Medicine. She specializes in urbanization in developing countries and its impact on well-being. She has over 100 journal publications, has produced five books, including *In The Shadow of The City: Community*

Health and the Urban Poor (1988, Oxford Medical Publications, with Tim Lusty and Patrick Vaughan) and *Urbanization and Mental Health in Developing Countries* (1995, Avebury, with Ilona Blue) and has studied the environmental and social determinants of health in sub-Saharan Africa, Asia and Latin America.

Kirsten Havemann, MD, PhD, is a social and public health specialist with interest and expertise in health and social sector analysis, design and systems development. She has extensive knowledge and skills in participatory and action-oriented research and operations. After more than 20 years of field experience in Africa and Asia, where she held posts such as Senior Adviser for the Danish Government, she moved to the World Bank's Social Development Department and then to the World Health Organization (WHO). Havemann is currently with the Danish Government, where she served as Senior Adviser for Health in Copenhagen before being posted to Maputo, Mozambique.

Gordon McGranahan, PhD, is Principal Researcher in the Human Settlements Group at the International Institute for Environment and Development. He works on a range of urban environmental issues, with an emphasis on addressing poverty and environmental problems in and around the home, and researching how the critical scale of urban environmental burdens changes as cities become wealthier. Co-authored publications include: *The Citizens at Risk: From Urban Sanitation to Sustainable Cities* (2001, Earthscan), 'Are the debates on water privatization missing the point' (2003, *Environment and Urbanization*) and 'The rising tide: assessing the risks of climate change and human settlements in low-elevation coastal zones' (2007, *Environment and Urbanization*).

Shagun Mehrotra, PhD, is an Assistant Professor at Milano School of International Affairs, Management, and Urban Policy. His research, teaching and policy advice focus on climate change, infrastructure economics and finance, and poverty reduction in cities, particularly in large developing-country slums. Mehrotra established Climate and Cities, an international policy advisory facility jointly housed at The Earth Institute, Columbia University, and the US National Aeronautics and Space Administration (NASA) Goddard Institute for Space Studies. Previously, he was on the staff of the World Bank, leading infrastructure reform of public utilities in Africa with a focus on expanding services to the urban poor.

Susan Mercado, MD, MPH, is Team Leader of the WHO's Tobacco-Free Initiative at the Western Pacific Regional Office and is trained as a tobacco dependence treatment specialist. She has been with the WHO for more than ten years and has served as Team Leader for Urbanization and Health Equity Research and head of the Knowledge Network on Urban Settings for the WHO Commission on Social Determinants of

Health at the WHO Centre for Health Development in Kobe, Japan and Acting Regional Adviser for Health Promotion at the Western Pacific Regional Office.

Diana Mitlin, PhD, is an economist and social development specialist who works at the International Institute for Environment and Development (London) and the Institute for Development Policy and Management at the University of Manchester. Her major focus is on urban poverty reduction, particularly in the areas of secure tenure, basic services and housing, and shelter finance. For the last ten years, Mitlin has worked closely with Shack/Slum Dwellers International. Publications include *Empowering Squatter Citizen* (2004, Earthscan, with David Satterthwaite*)* and *Rights-based Approaches to Development: The Pitfalls and Potentials* (2008, Kumarian Press, with Sam Hickey).

John C. Mutter, PhD, is jointly appointed in the Department of Earth and Environmental Sciences with a specialty in seismology and in the School of International and Public Affairs (SIPA), and is a member of the faculty of the Earth Institute at Columbia University. He is Director of Graduate Studies for the PhD in Sustainable Development at SIPA and Director of the Earth Institute's post-doctoral Fellows program. He researches the role of natural disasters in supporting the global inequality in development status and particularly in suppressing development opportunities for the poorest.

Keiko Nakamura, MD, PhD, is the Head of International Health and Medicine at the Graduate School of Tokyo Medical and Dental University. She works on research and education in the areas of public health and urban policy. Nakamura has served as the Head of the Secretariat of the Alliance for Healthy Cities since its inauguration in 2004; this consists of 168 cities and research institutions from ten countries in Asia and the Pacific. She conducts public health research in Afghanistan, Cambodia, Fiji, India, Japan, Lao PDR, Mongolia, Philippines, Thailand and Vietnam, and teaches young public health leaders from these and others countries.

Cynthia Rosenzweig, PhD, is a Senior Research Scientist at the US National Aeronautics and Space Administration's Goddard Institute for Space Studies and a Professor at Barnard College. Her research involves the development of interdisciplinary methodologies to assess the potential impacts of and adaptations to global environmental change. She has organized and led large-scale interdisciplinary studies including the New York City Panel on Climate Change and Metropolitan East Coast Regional Assessment. She was a coordinating lead author of the 'Observed changes in climate and their effects' chapter (Working Group II) of the IPCC Fourth Assessment Report, and served on the IPCC Task Group.

William Solecki, PhD, is the Director of the City University of New York's (CUNY) Institute for Sustainable Cities and a Professor at Hunter College, CUNY. His research includes urban environmental change, and climate impacts and adaptation. He is a founding member of the Urban Climate Change Research Network and the International Human Dimensions Programme on Global Environmental Change, has served as the co-leader of the New York City Panel on Climate Change and the Metropolitan East Coast Assessment, and is currently a lead author of the chapter on urban areas (Working Group II) for the IPCC Fifth Assessment Report.

Sophie Trémolet has worked as a consultant in the water and sanitation sector for the last 15 years. She holds a Master's in Economics and Business from the Institute of Political Studies (Paris) and a Master's in International Affairs from Columbia University (New York). Trémolet runs an independent consulting practice (www.tremolet.com) focusing on providing high-level advice on the design of optimal water sector reform strategies, including financing and regulatory strategies. Her clients include donor agencies, governments, public and private service providers, foundations and NGOs. She is the Chair of the Technical Advisory Committee of the Global Sanitation Fund.

David Vlahov, RN, PhD, is Dean of the School of Nursing at the University of California, San Francisco. He previously served as Director for the Center for Urban Epidemiologic Studies at the New York Academy of Medicine and Professor of Clinical Epidemiology at the Columbia University Mailman School of Public Health. Professor Vlahov was the first President of the International Society for Urban Health, host of the 2nd and 9th International Conferences on Urban Health, and has published extensively on this topic.

Acknowledgments

This book would not have been possible without the visionary leadership and support of the Rockefeller Foundation. We particularly wish to thank Judith Rodin, the Foundation's President, and Darren Walker, former Vice-President of Foundation Initiatives. They understood the importance of taking a global approach to the urban challenge. We also wish to thank all of the contributors for lending their expert knowledge and experience to this volume. The Center for Sustainable Urban Development, where we are based, is one of the eight global centers of excellence supported by the Volvo Research and Education Foundations.

Elliott Sclar and Nicole Volavka-Close
Center for Sustainable Urban Development
Earth Institute, Columbia University
New York, New York
May 15, 2012

Abbreviations and acronyms

AAG	Adaptation Assessment Guidebook
ACHR	Asian Coalition for Housing and Rights
ACTED	Agency for Technical Cooperation and Development, France
ADB	Asian Development Bank
AFCSR	Asian Forum on Corporate Social Responsibility
AHC	Alliance for Healthy Cities
AIDF	Asian Infectious Disease Project
BARR	Building assessment and rubbish removal
CapEx	capital expenditures
CapManEx	capital maintenance expenditures
CBO	community-based organization
CLACC	Capacity Strengthening in Least Developed Countries for Adaptation to Climate Change
CMP	Community Mortgage Program
CMU	contract management unit
CNG	compressed natural gas
CO_2	carbon dioxide
CoC	cost of capital
CODI	Community Organization Development Institute, Thailand
COMFORÇA	a committee intended to give citizens a voice at the municipal level in the participatory budgeting process, Brazil
COP17	17th Conference of the Parties to the United Nations Framework Convention on Climate Change
CRS	Catholic Relief Services
CVCCCM	Mexico City's Virtual Center on Climate Change
DAC	Development Assistance Committee
DEP	Department of Environmental Protection, US
DHS	Demographic and Health Survey
DRR	disaster risk reduction
FAP	flexible adaptation pathways
FEMA	Federal Emergency Management Agency, US
FHC	family health center
FUPROVI	Foundation for Housing Promotion, Costa Rica
GAR	global assessment report
GDP	gross domestic product
GHG	greenhouse gas
GIS	geographic information systems
GLAAS	Global Annual Assessment of Sanitation and Drinking Water
GNI	gross national income
GNP	gross national product
GRET	Groupe de Recherche et d'Echanges Technologiques, France
HCP	Healthy City Project
HDI	Human Development Index

HUDCO	Housing and Urban Development Corporation, India	NHB	National Housing Bank, India
HVAC	heating, ventilation and air conditioning	NHMFC	National Home Mortgage Finance Corporation, Philippines
ICICI	Industrial Credit and Investment Corporation of India Bank	NOx	nitrogen oxide
ICLEI	International Council for Local Environmental Initiatives (Local Governments for Sustainability)	NPCC	New York City Panel on Climate Change
		NYCDEP	New York City Department of Environmental Protection
IFI	international financial institution	O&M	operations and maintenance
		ODA	official development assistance
ILO	International Labour Organization	OECD	Organisation for Economic Co-operation and Development
IMR	infant mortality rate		
IPCC	Intergovernmental Panel on Climate Change	ONEA	National Water and Sanitation Office, Burkina Faso
JMP	Joint Monitoring Program	OPP	Orangi Pilot Project, Pakistan
JNNURM	Jawaharlal Nehru National Urban Renewal Mission, India	OPP-RTI	Orangi Pilot Project Research and Training Institute (OPP-RTI) of Karachi
KIP	Kampung Improvement Programme, Indonesia	PHP	People's Housing Process, South Africa
LDCs	least developed countries		
LECZ	low-elevation coastal zone	PLANASA	National Water Supply and Sanitation System, Brazil
LWUA	Local Water Utilities Administration, Philippines	PPAG	Plano Plurianual de Ação Governamental, multi-year plan, Brazil
MAUC	Mongolian Association of Urban Centres		
MDF	Municipal Development Fund	PPI	public–private infrastructure
MDGs	Millennium Development Goals of the UN	PRODEL	Local Development Programme, Nicaragua
		RBI	Reserve Bank of India
MEC	Metropolitan East Coast Regional Assessment of Climate Variability and Change, USA	RWSA	Rural Waterworks and Sanitation Association
		SDFN	Shack Dwellers Federation of Namibia
MFI	microfinance institution	SDI	Shack/Slum Dwellers International
MIREP	mini drinking water networks programme (French acronym)	SEWA	Self-Employed Women's Association, India
MoU	memorandum of understanding	SOFELES	Sociedades Financieras de Objeto Limitado, Mexico
MRGO	Mississippi River Gulf Outlet, US	SOx	sulphur oxide
		SPARC	Society for the Promotion of Area Resources Centres, India
NBFC	non-banking financial company		
NGO	non-governmental organization	SSIP	small-scale independent provider
NHAG	Namibian Housing Action Group	Sida	Swedish International Development Cooperation Agency

SUD-Net	Sustainable Urban Development Network	UNEP	United Nations Environment Programme
TDR	transferable development rights	UNFCCC	United Nations Framework Convention on Climate Change
UCDO	Urban Community Development Office	UNISDR	United Nations International Strategy for Disaster Reduction
UCLG	United Cities and Local Governments		
UHI	urban heat island	UQLI	urban quality of life index
UHLP	Unified Home Lending Program, Philippines	WHO	World Health Organization
UN	United Nations	WSS	water and sanitation systems
UNDP	United Nations Development Programme		

Chapter 1

Understanding the twenty-first century urban transformation

A Global South perspective

Elliott Sclar and Nicole Volavka-Close

Urbanization in the twenty-first century

The year 2009 marked the first time that over half of the world's population (3 billion plus people) resided in urban areas. By 2050, the world's population is expected to increase from approximately 6 billion at the turn of the millennium to 9 billion. By then, over two-thirds of the population, or more than 6 billion people, will live in urban areas. The majority of urban population growth in the next 40 years will occur in the urbanizing areas of the low- and middle-income countries commonly referred to as the Global South – countries mainly located in sub-Saharan Africa and Southern Asia. Urban populations in these regions will more than double, from 2.5 billion in 2009 to over 5 billion in 2050, as rural population growth will continue to slow and then begin to contract in these areas in the next decade (United Nations, Department of Economic and Social Affairs, Population Division 2010). Most of the Global South's demographic transformation will occur in small- and medium-sized cities, not the mega cities of 10 million plus people that typically grab global headlines.

This urban transformation holds great promise in terms of making the world's cities places where people can live healthy, productive and secure lives. However, it also holds the potential to make this a planet of cities divided by great affluence for a few and crushing poverty for the many, a scenario that is borne out by the paradigmatic images of vast swaths of slums juxtaposed against modern high-rise buildings in the cities of the developing world. However, neither outcome is inevitable. Whether the rapid, twenty-first century urban transformation turns out to be a blessing or a curse depends on choices: choices made by community groups in cities across the Global South, choices made by local, regional and national officials in these places and choices made by international lenders and donors, to name the most obvious.

As the contributors to this volume demonstrate, we know a great deal about the scope of the challenge, the options the various actors have and the steps needed to foster positive outcomes, as well as the obstacles that they must overcome. One of the most important issues that the world faces with regard to this difficult decision-making process is enhancing the capacity of those who must act to do so both wisely and effectively. Urbanization, because of the high degree of social interdependency that it engenders and upon which it depends, presents an added degree of complexity in addressing its several challenges in piecemeal fashion. And that is where the contributors to this volume play an important role. All of them have looked long and hard at the scope of the individual problems in the context of the complex political, social and environmental realities that form the on-the-ground conditions in the world's cities. In the papers collected here, they offer their expert judgments on effective ways to improve the urban condition in this context. To cite but one instance, Vlahov and Caiaffa, in their chapter on improving health outcomes in Belo Horizonte, Brazil, clearly make the connection between local governance and health status using the example of participatory budgeting and its impact on the operational effectiveness of local health centers.

Expanding urbanization is the essential story of human society. Ancient cities and their accompanying institutions of civilization sprung up across the planet often in isolation from one another. City building is thus a characteristic of the innately social nature of the human species. There were times when urbanization appeared as an inevitable trajectory, such as in the heydays of ancient Greece and Rome. There were times when it began disappearing, as in the era of the European Dark Ages after the fall of Rome or during the era of the bubonic plague. But even when urbanization was contracting in one place such as Europe, it was thriving and expanding in others such as Asia and America. With the coming of the industrial revolution and the emergence of the factory, urbanization accelerated extensively and intensively in Western Europe and North America. Industrialization transformed cities from places largely dominated by consumption and trade into major loci of production, consumption and trade.

The specific urban transformation that is the central focus of this volume, the urbanization presently sweeping the Global South, must be appreciated as the next phase of this longer sweep of history when more than two of every three people living anywhere in the world will be urban residents. Despite urbanization's historic trend, until comparatively recently – mainly the last decade – extreme global poverty has typically and predominantly been associated with life in rural areas. Development efforts at international, national and regional levels over the past six decades have more or less reflected this notion in their policy prescriptions. It is noteworthy that the eight United Nations Millennium Development Goals (MDGs) adopted by the world's heads of state at the UN General Assembly in September 2000, along with their 18 specific targets, make only one passing reference (target 11 of goal 7) to the world's urban condition and the specific plight of the urban poor, calling for the improvement in the lives of 100 million slum dwellers by 2020. Yet, it was estimated in 2003 that almost one billion people – or one out of three urban dwellers – were already living in slums (1.7 billion people; UN-HABITAT, 2003). There was clearly a disconnect between the scope of the problem and the relatively small number of lives targeted for improvement.

Narratives and scale

One part of the explanation for the long neglect of the issue of urban poverty relates to the narratives and metrics used to comparatively describe urban and rural life. Urban averages, because they are weighted by the affluence at the top of the wealth distribution, tend to distort the on-the-ground urban reality: a reality that is best illuminated by the people who are too often excluded from the aggregated data relied on by governments and international institutions as they make policy and funding decisions. Living in settlements that are often deemed illegal by government authorities, the urban poor are frequently not included in census data and the lands they live on are left off official maps. It is difficult to solve problems that do not officially exist. Making the invisible visible is key in any effort towards equitable and sustainable urban development. Creating such social visibility comes through a range of efforts. The most important of these have been the self-organized efforts of urban community groups, through engagement in processes such as community mapping, that are forcing the rest of the world to take notice of its new urban reality with all its challenges and to view overcoming them as a global responsibility. Our contributors do a good job of documenting the extent of these efforts.

A second part of the explanation for this neglect is the complexity of the situation itself. As the contributors to this volume make clear, there is extensive interdependence and connection among the various individual manifestations of the severe social costs of urban poverty. For example, the proper and timely distribution of anti-retroviral medications to HIV-positive individuals will make little difference in terms of health outcomes if these people live in places lacking access to safe drinking water. Hence, the challenge is comprised not only of medical service delivery but of municipal infrastructure creation and maintenance as well.

A final element of this explanation is perhaps the most uncomfortable of all to confront. For many of those in positions of power there is a strong desire to see the urban poor simply disappear. City and metropolitan plans too often project a desire on the part of decision-makers to rebuild their cities for people who are not there and whom they hope will somehow appear at the expense of the displacement of the people who are actually living there. Indeed, as one of our authors, Dr. John Mutter, demonstrates (Chapter 9), in the aftermath of Hurricane Katrina it was not that the urban poor who suffered greatly were not acknowledged: it was that they were simply not a priority in either the immediate aftermath or the long-term efforts to rebuild the city. As with the case of New Orleans, too often planning for cities in the Global South does not include the needs of the current residents, but rather is aimed towards accommodating more affluent population groups that it is hoped will appear.

While human gregariousness in part explains the emergence of cities, it is only the necessary condition. The sufficient condition is the fact that high-density living and efficient locational proximity – the prime characteristics of urban life – are also the prime spatial generators of economic opportunity and human innovation. For the world's poor, an urban life holds out a powerful promise of a chance at a significant improvement in the condition not just of their lives but, perhaps more importantly, of the lives of their progeny. But the benefits of density and proximity only deliver on their promises when they are accompanied by access to a range of basic urban necessities that make it possible to enjoy a decent quality of life lived in close proximity to vast numbers of socially diverse people and activities.

Many of these necessities are so obvious that they dissolve into invisibility for urban dwellers in the Global North. To take but two simple examples, consider toilets and running water, a topic of concern to some of our contributors. Urban residents in the Global North take both of these for granted to the point that they hardly ever give them a second thought. Yet if they did think about them, they would be hard-pressed to understand how the lives they lead might continue if these suddenly disappeared. Flip that around and ask how might the urban lives of these newly expanding poor urban populations fulfill their promise if they do not have similar access to such simple necessities as safe drinking water and effective systems of sanitation?

Put succinctly, one of the great urban challenges of the present century is one of urban population growth running significantly ahead of the urban infrastructure and urban services needed to sustain it. The result is a steady observable degradation of urban life, the burden of which is carried by the poorest urban residents. Existing problems, such as lack of access to health care, clean water and decent sanitation services are multiplied, because the challenges of rapid urban growth are not addressed. Adding to this complexity are the effects of climate change, which further exacerbate existing threats to social and economic development, as well as to national and international security. Unless these issues are addressed in a comprehensive manner, by mid-century, urban poverty will be the essential face of global poverty with all the social and political instability inherent in this trend. These problems cannot solve themselves because of all the complex interdependencies of urban life. Active steps by competent governments that are accountable to *all* the populations they serve must be taken to ensure that, at the very least, this growing global urban population has access to the basic public services necessary for a decent life.

The two questions that follow from that last observation are how do competent governments evolve and what are the necessary active steps? These concerns motivated the production of this volume as well as all of the volume's contributors. Each of them address key underlying questions about next steps with respect to their areas of expertise. We term the issues addressed here as part of answering what we call the 'how' question. How do we take innovations that promise effective solutions for various elements of the urban challenge in key areas of governance and programmatic action, and bring them up to a scale of application of sufficient scope so that they make a significant improvement in the lives of the vast numbers of the urban poor?

Thinking back on the long swings of history, we start from the assumption that problems of urbanization facing cities in the present century are really not terribly different in character from the ones that faced cities that urbanized during the era of the industrial revolution, though the geographic and demographic extent is considerably larger. The lesson of that history is that we solved problems such as these once before. While any analogy between past and present is never perfect, there is sufficient similarity that we can take heart from previous experience and know that we are capable of doing it again. At this juncture, while we know a great deal about the general dimensions of the challenge, the papers in this volume provide us with the detail we need to develop successful solutions to the specific twenty-first century iterations of these challenges.

Most importantly, these contributions demonstrate that we do not lack for specific innovative ideas in addressing the 'how' question. The larger question is really the 'scale' question. How do we take the innovative solutions discussed here up to a sufficient scale to meaningfully improve the situation?

Complexity and the modern urban context

Changing the course of development will not only depend on building capacity of grassroots groups to articulate the needs of the urban poor, but also on the process through which effective forms of urban governance emerge out of community-based organizations (CBOs) and other civil society groups as well as via the organs of formal government. Social innovations only go to scale and endure when they are institutionalized in some form of governance. A crucial first step in this regard is ensuring that community-based inputs and innovations become embedded in the planning and decision-making processes at the local and regional levels of governance. At these levels, the urban poor are able to be active and effective agents of their own development. That said, it is important to also stress that the burden of change cannot rest solely upon their shoulders. The public sector too must be transformed as part of the urbanization process. It must be rendered capable of taking an active, competent and positive role in guiding the development process in the public interest, rather than only serving the private interests of various privileged groups. Decision-makers, planners, designers, engineers and other urban professionals must be trained to see these new urban forms in ways that reflect the needs of *all* populations and most especially the urban poor.

Urbanization is an all-encompassing process; that is both the good news and the bad news. It is good news because it embodies the need for comprehensive solutions that recognize that the manifestations of the problem in an area such as housing are not solvable without considering the ways in which urban health is impacted, and vice versa. This realization compels us to abandon sector-by-sector thinking about urbanization and instead evolve solutions that address the underlying systemic causes of these problems. It is only by adopting such a mind-set that it is possible to devise effective and scalable approaches to the urban transformation challenge. At the same time, understanding that the challenge is all-encompassing has the potential to become not just bad news, but very bad news. If everything depends on everything else, we run the risk of attempting to embrace such a totalizing view that we become cynical about individual efforts and lapse into an overwhelming immobility. But we believe there is a way around this dilemma. By concentrating on a few strategic areas that are key components of the larger issue, we believe that it is possible to begin to get at the more comprehensive systems approach that is needed and thus build the capacity to embrace the larger complexity even as we address the specific manifestations of the challenges of this late-stage urbanization.

The strategic way forward

The origins of this volume are rooted in a series of four weeklong 'Urban Summits' (i.e. conferences) that we (Sclar and Volavka-Close of the Center for Sustainable Urban Development at the Earth Institute, Columbia University) organized for the Rockefeller Foundation in the summer of 2007 with the invaluable input of our colleague, Gabriella Y. Carolini. It became clear from these successive 'Urban Summit' meetings that the way forward on the challenge of the urban transformation required a strategic and selective approach if a proactive and effective strategy for ensuring that the urbanization benefits would be widespread and the costs minimized was to take root. In preparation of this volume, we turned to some of the authors among the several whom we invited to prepare working papers for those meetings and asked if they would revise and update them for this effort. Specifically, we asked authors who had written on health, shelter, water and sanitation to update their working papers and prepare them for this volume. We then reached out to colleagues in the Earth Institute, Columbia University, who are doing some of the outstanding and cutting-edge thinking on climate change and cities, and asked them to contribute their expertise to this effort. The chapters that follow are the result.

The areas chosen were selected because we see them as the most powerful and obvious places in which to begin a quest for scalable and comprehensive improvements in the global urban condition. Issues of health, shelter, water and sanitation, and climate change and natural hazard impacts must be made central to broader local, regional and national social development agendas. These matters are too strongly linked to one another to be considered in isolation and, as the populations of cities expand, so does the complexity of the interactions among them. This complexity must be well understood when designing specific interventions or plans for sustainable urban development.

Successful interventions also hinge on the quality of communication between and among different actor groups such as CBOs, local governments, financial institutions, international agencies and organizations, and urban professionals. While urban-related professions and urban-related scholarly studies have become narrowly focused over time, the complexity of today's problems requires solutions that are integrated and take into account the populations that are most at risk. The question as to how this might be done is one that the editors and contributors explore throughout this volume. In each case we have sought to learn more about what works and what does not work. What innovations have the potential of going to scale and which ones are limited in impact?

Population health and the urban transformation

Typically the term 'urban health' is used to mean either the health status of the urban population or the quantity and quality of health care services available in urban settings. For our purposes it is the former usage that is the more important, though the medical and other health care service delivery is also of concern. From the point of view of public policy, urban population health can be viewed as an input into creating a productive urban economy via its contribution to labor force productivity, or it can be viewed as the output of a productive, vibrant and socially equitable urban economy. When viewed as population health, urban health issues intersect a broad range of social determinants of health, including decent shelter, safe drinking water, adequate nutrition, good education, as well as the quantity and quality of available health care services. Further complicating matters, environmental factors such as air quality and climatic conditions also bear directly on population health.

The contributors to this section of the volume all reflect on this complexity in their various offerings.

Gordon McGranahan's chapter (Chapter 2) cuts across the different sections of this collection as he uses a health lens to look at the issues of housing, water and sanitation as well as climate change. He points out that cities that have effectively addressed the household-level environmental health risks of their most vulnerable populations are in a better position to cope with the effects of climate change. He makes clear that collective action – on the part of local governments and institutions as well as the poor communities themselves – is needed to address these interconnected challenges.

He specifically takes on the dualism of health as a measure of social well-being and income as a reflection of social well-being. He makes a strong case for considering human well-being from a health perspective, rather than or in addition to an economic perspective. Health indicators, even if narrowly conceived, can reflect the true level of social equity as made manifest in the level of urban environmental burdens at household (e.g. poor water, sanitation and hygiene) and community levels (e.g. outdoor air pollution), and somewhat less directly at the global level (e.g. climate change). They can also reveal where a population stands in terms of the epidemiological transition, or the shift of the disease burden from communicable to non-communicable diseases, which in turn is a reflection of how well cities are managed.

The successful urban transition in the Global North resulted in large part from the reduction of environmental health risks through late-nineteenth- and early-twentieth- century urban health and planning interventions, such as the introduction of piped safe drinking water and sanitation systems. Similarly, urban populations in the Global South are presently experiencing these problems plus other overlapping, multiple burdens that become manifest in the form of bad health outcomes, particularly among the urban poor. An urgent challenge of the twenty-first century, says McGranahan, is to address the inequalities of urban environmental risk without adding to the global environmental burden of climate change.

Trudy Harpham, in Chapter 3, delves deeply into the linkage between 'downstream' health outcomes and 'upstream' social determinants in the context of contemporary urbanization. She notes that, in the past, health research typically focused on multilevel individual characteristics (biological, demographic, psychological and behavioral) but there is now accumulating evidence that place – or community-level factors – have an independent effect on health. She and McGranahan agree on the need to see the issue of poverty in a multidimensional light. Harpham calls attention to the concept of the heterogeneity of poverty and believes that income-based metrics fail to capture the full extent of the urban health challenge. She explains that more useful measures are ones that incorporate social conditions, such as measures of people's vulnerability to the various physical, medical and social risks that affect health.

She provides examples of successful small-scale initiatives that have the potential to succeed at a large scalable level. In that regard she cites an intervention in Cali, Colombia, where enhancement of social capital (both bridging and bonding) led to a decrease in violence-related injuries. She identifies the multidimensional ways in which improving urban health must proceed.

The financial, political, social and educational factors she identifies also ring true for the challenge of slum housing upgrading, provision of infrastructure and mitigating as well as adapting to climate change.

David Vlahov and Waleska Caiaffa, cited earlier, bring the discussion of population health into sharper focus by highlighting examples of urban population health best practices that have emerged from the city of Belo Horizonte, Brazil. Belo Horizonte is an especially compelling example because it is among the multitudes of mid-sized cities that are expected to absorb most of the urban population growth in this century. These cities are growing faster in percentage terms than the mega cities (cities with populations of more than 10 million). It is a city that is quite typical of the challenge in the Global South, with a high percentage of its population residing in slums, or 'favelas' as they are called in Brazil. Vlahov and Caiaffa's linkage of a fiscal effort, participatory budgeting, to two more obviously health-related endeavors serves to point to the need for comprehensiveness in addressing any of the specific manifestations of the challenge of the urban transformation. The two health examples are the development of 'family health centers' and 'physical academies.' Participatory budgeting, the practice of permitting meaningful and widespread popular input into the annual municipal process of deciding spending priorities, is by now a well-ingrained exercise in Brazil. Vlahov and Caiaffa address the overlapping range of activities that must successfully interact if an effective and cohesive approach to urban health is to emerge. The Belo Horizonte experience provides an informative case study of what can happen in a city that takes a proactive approach to public health.

Dr. Susan Mercado and her associates provide evidence of the further complex interconnection between urban population health and economic development through their examination of the health vulnerabilities of the urban poor in what they term the 'new urban settings' of Asia. The context for this is the rapid economic transformation that many cities in Asia have undergone in the last four decades. Despite the prosperous transformation of these places, Mercado *et al.* observe in Chapter 5 that 'the existing public infrastructure, the urban environment and the traditional social fabric have all deteriorated' (p82). It is to this seeming contradiction that these contributors turn their attention. In response to this, they call for the need to reconsider the ways in which we look at the question of urban health vulnerability. As with all the other contributors to this volume, they too see the challenge as rooted in the exclusion of the urban poor from the prosperity that is growing up around them. Once more, as with Harpham, there is agreement that the social determinants of health, or the causes behind the causes, are the crucial issue. Simply put, maintaining the health of urban residents requires the sustainability of an urban environment that contributes to staying healthy rather than one that makes them ill and requires the repeated or continual delivery of medical care.

The Mercado team identifies five interrelated conditions that make the current urban context in Asia different from the past. These are 1) unprecedented rapid urban growth, 2) the emergence of primate cities (cities that are four to ten times larger than the second largest city) as the engines of this rapid urban growth, 3) the concentration of marginalized and socially excluded ethnic, cultural or religious groups in these cities, 4) the strengthening of networked cities and 5) the rapid transmission of biological, social, political and environmental tensions and risks along these networks. What is important about this identification is that it points to the need to think about the urban population health challenge as a comprehensive one. Put slightly differently, health is embedded in geography, sociology and economics.

Yet despite the complexity that this creates, there are remarkable examples of projects with characteristics that are scalable in addressing the problems. The review ends with lessons for how this scalability is achievable and transportable to other situations. Two conclusions emerge: engage with key players in existing social movements, and support global networks to exchange information on what works and how it works.

Financing shelter, water and sanitation as the key to the urban transformation

It is the physical nature of proximity that creates urban value. Therefore, it is the quality of the actual physical investments in shelter and infrastructure that make this urban proximity work better or worse. Simply put, the quality of urban life is directly linked to the quality of urban density and the efficiency qualities of the activity co-location it produces. Quality is the key, and comes down to resource investment or finance. The section on shelter, water and sanitation (Chapters 6–8) specifically addresses this crucial concern. How do we devise innovative finance mechanisms that ensure the allocation of resources to the shelter and infrastructure needs of the urban poor?

Diana Mitlin, one of the foremost scholars in the field of shelter finance for the urban poor takes on the all-important question of housing in two chapters in this volume. Her first chapter, 'The Need for Shelter Finance Improvements,' describes the limitations in current financing modalities for the urban poor and demonstrates the ways in which these are linked to the specific nature of the housing problem that the people face. In the second chapter, 'Innovations in Shelter Finance,' she provides us with a review of the alternatives ways forward and their potential for achieving scale. The strength of this work is her recognition of the need to build capacity on both the supply and demand sides of the housing market. On the demand side, she describes the need for financial instruments that can work with the limited resource capacity of the urban poor, but which meet the needs of those living in slum conditions to improve their lot through a combination of their own efforts with a supporting role from government. This approach could thus be termed 'post modern' to the extent that it does not require heroic assumptions about the competence of the State to supply needed housing services. Instead, she argues that a demand-side approach permits leveraging the energy and resources of the slum dwellers themselves to transform the conditions of urban shelter. As her examples demonstrate, it is indeed a credible way to achieve scale with these innovations.

Mitlin notes that there is a significant difference between the meaning of shelter in the Global North and the Global South. In the Global North, shelter is a package of services that always comes bundled together regardless of whether the tenure form is owner-occupied or rental housing. Each dwelling unit includes a clearly stipulated set of rules for attaining and maintaining locational tenure, and a connection to all of the relevant urban services that make density and co-location work. These services are water, sanitation, police and fire protection, access to transport when necessary, schools, etc. This is not the usual case in the Global South, where the package is incremental at best. She observes that 'providing basic services and infrastructure to the site and creating land-tenure security entail collective social and political processes as much as they do financial transactions.' Hence, she roots the challenge of finance in a larger social context. In her two chapters, she continually balances actions that are feasible on the demand side of the finance market with a clear description of the actions needed on the supply side. For her, the supply side of the market is not just comprised of the micro and macro lenders of the private market. It also includes government and the creation and institutionalization of the needed capacity within government to accomplish a well-orchestrated meshing of private supply and demand with a well-functioning city.

Sophie Trémolet, Rachel Cardone and Catarina Fonseca, in their chapter 'Investing in Urban Water and Sanitation Systems', follow a similar pattern of describing the unique characteristics of these problems in the Global South and then linking them to the finance challenges. Trémolet *et al.* view the issue of expansive water and sanitation systems (WSS) as an element of infrastructure combined with the complex need to balance capital costs and operating costs in a system that permits effective cost recovery by suppliers. The economic imperative in WSS is rooted in the dualistic nature of the good. Safe drinking water is obviously both a private good because it is individually consumed, and a public one because it is a population health necessity. Sanitation is similar, though its public health benefits tend to make its 'public good' aspects more obvious. In light of these dualistic economic characteristics, the authors explain that there are three sources of funding: user charges, government funding and international aid.

The ideal form of this service would be a system of water and sanitation supply fully funded by charges paid by system users. In the cities of the Global North where water and sanitation are universal, relying almost completely on user charges provides a feasible system of finance. It matters little whether the system is directly supplied as a public system or provided via some form of public–private partnership. However, in the rapidly urbanizing low-income cities of the Global South these factors become far more critical to consider, especially because such systems are not universal and a major challenge is the extension of them to accommodate the rapidly expanding urban populations.

Trémolet *et al.* explain the challenges of filling this gap in coverage and the associated difficulties of creating viable models of financing that can ensure both the adequacy of the capital budgets and the adequacy of the needed maintenance. For these authors, as with Mitlin, the good news is that there are ranges of ways to combine demand-side incentives with supply capacity to create effective and innovative financing systems – systems that are capable of establishing WSS that meet people's needs, are sustainable, accessible and affordable to all urban residents.

Climate change and the urban transformation

Climate change is a ticking time bomb. Over the next several decades it is going to badly disrupt the lives of hundreds of millions of urban residents. These impacts will take many forms, such as droughts, floods, heat waves and more frequent weather-related migrations of people from lands made less habitable to more suitable human habitats. These migrations can lead to conflicts and civil instability. The lack of infrastructure and associated health impacts discussed in this volume will all be further exacerbated by this climate change.

Even if it were possible to cause all greenhouse gas emissions to cease and desist immediately, the cumulative effects of the already existing carbon accumulations in the stratosphere would still cause these unwanted climatic impacts. John Mutter takes on that uncomfortable reality in his chapter 'Perceiving the Social and Economic Consequences of Natural Disaster Shocks or Getting Ready for Climate Change'. He points out that, although when natural disasters strike we often think we know exactly what happened, too often we are filtering the information about the actual event and its aftermath through lenses that permit us to see some relevant facts and not others. The result is that we respond in ways that are not as effective as they might otherwise be. More importantly, because mistakes will always be made, Mutter finds that we typically respond in ways that are systematically biased against the poorest urban residents.

If we are to respond effectively to climate events, as well as to future natural shocks, it is useful to glean important lessons from the ways in which we responded to past natural disaster shocks. Climate change will not involve earthquakes, for example, but the social response to disruptions such as these can tell us a great deal about how we are likely to respond in social and economic terms to future natural disaster shocks, including ones linked to climate change. Mutter makes clear to us just how powerfully the narratives we construct about these events are not the product of the actual impacts of the events but of the social and economic biases that color the ways in which we choose to interpret the information that we are receiving.

The paper by Solecki *et al.* 'Urbanization of Climate Change: Responding to a New Global Challenge' (Chapter 10) discusses the linkages between cities and climate within the context of urban vulnerability. These authors provide us with background on global trends in climate change impacts on cities across a set of sectors. Their analysis comes from their leadership of the Urban Climate Change Research Network, their related research and their editing of an extensive set of contributions to the *First Assessment Report on Climate Change and Cities* from over 100 lead and contributing authors from cities around the world representing a wide range of disciplines. Based on this work, they have concluded that cities are increasingly the first responders to climate change risk. As a result, it is important to build the capacity of cities to integrate climate change adaptation into the processes of building and rebuilding that are the ongoing challenges of global urban life. An important conclusion derived from both the Mutter chapter and the Solecki *et al.* one is that the all-important pro-poor adaptation strategies needed will not change the course of development unless we build the capacity within local governments to work in a positive and active way with the urban poor. As Mutter points out, there is a distinct danger that if this is not done we will end up viewing the poor, along with their homes, their neighborhoods and their businesses, as the problems rather than the victims of forces well beyond their control.

Conclusions

We view this volume as the beginning of a new and more well-grounded conversation on the all-important questions brought on by the twenty-first-century urban transformation. We hope that, by assembling a collection of papers that together demonstrate the global and interdependent nature of the challenge and at the same time focus on core strategic approaches to addressing it, a comprehensive and effective approach to realizing the promise of the urban transformation materializes. This is particularly urgent given the sheer magnitude of the transformation now underway and projected to continue for at least the next 40 years. Our authors demonstrate that there are successful innovations and interventions that have significantly improved the quality of life of the urban poor and that have achieved success at various scale levels. The challenge and the critical 'how' questions we hope that the discussions in this book will engender are sufficiently broad and sufficiently global to allow all the people of the world to share the benefits that this urbanization can make possible.

References

Rosenzweig, C., Solecki, W., Hammer, S.A. and Mehrotra S. (eds) (2011a) *Climate Change and Cities: First Assessment Report of the Urban Climate Change Research Network*, Cambridge University Press: New York.

UN-HABITAT (United Nations Human Settlements Program) (2003) *The Challenge of Slums: Global Report on Human Settlements 2003*, Earthscan: London.

United Nations, Department of Economic and Social Affairs, Population Division (2010) *World Urbanization Prospects. The 2009 Revision: Highlights,* UN: New York.

Chapter 2

Evolving urban health risks

Housing, water and sanitation, and climate change

Gordon McGranahan

Modern economic growth is centred in cities, and the environmental agendas of economically successful cities have changed radically in recent centuries. London, where I work, was dangerously unsanitary for much of the nineteenth century. The tipping point came with the 'Great Stink' of 1858, when parliament had to close down because of smells many feared were directly responsible for diseases such as cholera. Following that iconic event the city became a centre for sanitary reform, and by the end of the century sanitary conditions had improved considerably. Air pollution, however, had also deteriorated during the industrialization of the nineteenth century and continued to worsen well into the twentieth. The iconic environmental event of the twentieth century was the 'Great Smoke' of December 1952, a concentration of smog that reportedly caused 6,000 deaths. Ambient air and water pollution has now abated considerably, and London's biggest challenges today are to align its affluent consumption with the goals of maintaining global sustainability and slowing climate change. One hopes it won't take a 'Great Sink' – say, the flooding of parliament by storms and rising sea levels in the 2050s – to galvanize action this time.

Many urban dwellers, particularly in very low-income countries, still face health-threatening inadequacies of sanitation. Others, particularly in heavily industrialized and motorized middle-income countries, still face severe air-pollution problems. Problems such as climate change are not so readily localized, however. Although climate change is driven mostly by activity in affluent cities, the health burdens are likely to fall most heavily on the poorest cities.

I begin this chapter by explaining how and why health indicators can serve as a counterbalance to the more usual economic indicators in appraising the impact of urban environmental burdens. I then examine the health and urban transitions associated with modern economic growth; these, I argue, reflect the systematic tendency of growing urban affluence to spread environmental burdens across both space and time: spatially, from being highly localized in and around the home, to broader city and regional impact, and finally to genuinely global effects; temporally, from immediate and short-lived hardships to slowly growing but long-lasting burdens that will fall on future generations. Because transitions are not instantaneous, however, more traditional, localized environmental burdens overlap with the more generalized burdens imposed by the modern economy. Thus the burdens imposed by climate change are likely to exacerbate local environmental burdens such as sanitation, making it all the more urgent that the former be addressed. Finally, I note that inclusive urban politics, or what might now be described as good urban governance, was crucial to the historical improvements in sanitation and pollution; similar urban-planning efforts must now help to drive improvements in today's even more complex and multifaceted world.

Health as an alternative or complement to the economic lens for examining urban well-being

> If you have health, you probably will be happy, and if you have health and happiness, you have all the wealth you need, even if it is not all you want.
> – Elbert Hubbard

Human well-being is often viewed through a rather narrow economic lens. The market values of goods produced and consumed are routinely used to rank people, countries and indeed the world as a whole as it changes over time. These economic valuations were not designed to measure well-being, but they are often used for that purpose, particularly in the popular press. Income figures are readily available and have a certain popular and bureaucratic appeal, expressed as they are in the same units that measure personal and government budgets – money. As indicators of human well-being, however, they also have widely acknowledged flaws, including their failure to take account of important assets and transactions that have no market value, and their failure to account for distributional issues. To illustrate just one such failure related to distribution, few people would seriously claim that the fourth Rolex watch in a highflier's bedroom drawer is really contributing as much to human well-being as a five-year food supply for a struggling farmer, even if the market values are the same.

Health indicators are harder to come by and have their own problems. However often health is defined as complete physical, mental and social well-being (as it is in the World Health Organization [WHO] 1978 Alma-Ata Declaration)[1], health indicators tend to focus on disease, infirmity and death. The most comprehensive health measure available globally, the burden of disease estimates, cannot claim to reflect more than one dimension of human well-being – albeit an important one. Moreover, it does not consider the future, and so it omits long-term environmental and concomitant health impacts. More readily available health indicators, such as life expectancies, are even more problematic.

Health indicators and the challenge of moving beyond curative health care

In spite of its limitations, however, even a narrow conception of health can provide more egalitarian indicators of well-being than most income- or consumption-based indicators. Thus, for example, a disease burden is weighted equally no matter who experiences it, and regardless of what the patient may be able and willing to pay to avoid or treat it.

Furthermore, the health benefits a poor household can attain with additional income are likely to be greater than the health benefits an affluent household can gain with that same added income. The same effect holds at the national level: a given investment can typically yield far greater health improvements if it is targeted at poor countries than at the rich. If national income per capita is plotted against life expectancy, for instance, the health improvement associated with an increase of, say, $100 a year at the bottom end of the scale is far greater that the health improvement associated with an increase of $100 at the top end. Similar differentials, though perhaps less extreme, are likely to be evident with other health indicators. Thus measures designed to reduce urban vulnerability to disasters are more likely to favour the poor if the measures focus on reducing risks to health rather than to economic assets.

To the extent that health indicators do reflect important aspects of well-being, they are not always best addressed through curative, or even preventive, health care, conventionally defined. Indeed, there is a permanent tension in the health sector. On the one hand, the institutional and bureaucratic base for most health ministries and departments lies in the health care provided by doctors, nurses, pharmacists and others on the front line of medicine, along with the services and cures they dispense. On the other hand, urban health depends on many factors that have little to do with health care: water quality, sanitation, housing, transport, and national levels of economic production and distribution. In dealing with these factors, the health sector may have an advisory or regulatory position, but it is unlikely to have much authority. Moreover, rather than being asked to advise on how policies and practices could be changed to improve health or health equity, health officials are more typically asked to advise on highly specific topics, often related to standards and regulations.

The tension within the health sector between a broad mandate to improve health and a narrow focus on health care extends to health care workers themselves. Nancy Scheper-Hughes, in her account of the 'violence of everyday life' for poverty-stricken families in a Brazilian favela, describes a number of these tensions. Perhaps her most disturbing example is the doctor who treats a starving child with appetite stimulants, unwilling to face the inconvenient truth that the child has lost its appetite through not being fed (Scheper-Hughes, 1993). Although such perversity may seem shocking, it is only an extreme manifestation of a structural contradiction inherent in attempting to address health inequities generated by the socio-economic circumstances while staying within the health sector.

When health differences are more revealing than economic differences

Even economists recognize that health can provide a useful corrective to economic indicators. The Nobel prize-winning economist Robert Fogel observes that, though real wages in the US were increasing between 1820 and 1860, heights and life expectancy were falling. He conjectures that the same internal migration and urbanization that were responsible for about half the income growth were also principal factors in the spread of the major killer diseases of the time, including cholera, typhoid and dysentery. Those health statistics, Fogel argues, which also show the health of wealthier and poorer groups diverging, provide a better indication of changes in economic equality than do the conventional economic measures (Fogel, 2004b, pp34–35 and note 26).

When the health historian Simon Szreter encounters similar discrepancies, his inclination is to treat income as distinct from well-being, and, indeed, as inherently less revealing of well-being than health. For example, he notes, during roughly those same early decades of the nineteenth century in England, urban mortality rates increased as the economy grew, buttressing his argument that industrialization and economic growth brought disruption, deprivation, disease and death (Szreter, 2004). Thus despite their fundamental differences in historical interpretation, both Fogel and Szreter reject conventional income estimates as the basis for monitoring changes in human well-being. Instead, they gain a more sophisticated understanding of historical transitions in well-being by analyzing measures of health.

Health and urban transitions

> The 20th century will be remembered as when the goals of health for all became a realistic objective.
>
> – Arnold Toynbee

The concept of 'historical transition' has become a key element in the understanding of economic and demographic change – serving both as a convenient summary of the complex processes driving national trends and in some cases as a predictor of a country's future development trajectory. Industrializing and urbanizing countries are often described as going through a set of interrelated transitions. Thus the economic transition associated with industrialization refers to the shift from an economy dominated by agriculture to one dominated by industrial production. The urban transition, as its name implies, represents a shift in a nation's population from predominantly rural to predominantly urban.

Developing countries also undergo a shift from traditional to modern environmental health risks: from the risks posed, say, by smoky cooking fuels, polluted drinking water or the unsanitary disposal of human waste to the risks attributable to air pollution from vehicles, carcinogens from processed foods, and the indirect effects of global warming (McGranahan *et al.*, 2001; Smith and Ezzati, 2005).This environmental-risk transition is linked to its effects on the predominant manifestations of ill health – the so-called epidemiologic transition. Thus infectious diseases such as diarrhoea, malaria and acute respiratory infections are superseded as primary killers by non-infectious and chronic diseases such as cancer and heart disease. Such an epidemiologic transition is accompanied, in turn, by falling mortality, particularly among infants and children. Finally, falling mortality gives rise to the well-known demographic transition: from a society with the high fertility needed to keep pace with high mortality to a society whose low mortality leads to a commensurate drop in fertility.

The relations underlying these transitions are socially and politically con-tingent, rather than necessary stages in development. Not only do they vary over time and space, but they also depend on how people respond to the diverse challenges the transitions bring about, many of which threaten public health and well-being. Central to this response is how development is man-aged in cities.

After all, most of the enhanced productivity driving economic growth takes place in urban areas. Furthermore, long-term economic growth depends on making effective use of the economies of agglomeration that urban concentrations can provide, as well as the trade that urban centres enable. Thus, the environmental-risk and epidemiologic transitions depend on such urban health measures as sanitary reform, and those measures will be put in place only if citizens have sufficient political and economic power to demand improvement and local governments have enough capacity to implement the needed reforms. In particular, to achieve a decline in mortal-ity, public-health measures must substantially reduce local environmental risks: household-level risks associated with drinking water, waste disposal and housing. And to achieve the subsequent decline in fertility, health poli-cies, particularly in urban areas, may need to promote family-planning mea-sures that put fertility control into the hands of prospective mothers.

For the epidemiologic transition, it is also important to recognize that the shift from infectious to non-communicable diseases is relative. People in poor countries do indeed get non-communicable and chronic diseases, typically at higher rates for their age group than their counterparts in more affluent countries. But they also continue to get more infectious diseases and they continue to die from infectious diseases at an early age – which of course pre-empts non-communicable diseases as a cause of death. More-over, the chronic conditions and diseases suffered by the urban poor are often untreated and then are left out of health statistics, because the formal health system only records the complications or outcomes that require its intervention. Thus hypertension is often not recorded, but an eventual stroke or heart failure is; mental illness is often not recorded, but a suicide, homicide or other violent event is; diabetes is not recorded, but kidney failure is; early-stage tuberculosis is not recorded, but late stage is (for a more complete listing, see Riley *et al.*, 2007, Table 1, p5).

The urban environmental transition

Focusing on the environmental-risk transition in urban areas not only emphasizes the key role of public-health measures in making the demographic transition. It also provides a useful framework for considering how cities can best respond to the entire cluster of health risks their inhabitants face. Perhaps what is most striking about the urban environmental-risk transition is its shift from local environmental burdens, which pose direct health risks, to global burdens, which pose indirect health risks through their effects on life-support systems. Several dimensions of the transition are summarized in somewhat stylized terms in Figure 2.1 (see below).

The diagram was originally conceived as a stylized summary of available empirical statistics showing how (mostly urban) environmental burdens vary with per-capita national income (McGranahan *et al.*, 2001). The main household-level burdens, including urban access to potable water and sanitation, as well as the burden of indoor air pollution – all fall monotonically as national per-capita income rises (see the 'local' curve in Figure 2.1). The main global burdens – those imposed on a global scale by a nation's economic activities – including greenhouse-gas emissions as well as composite measures such as ecological footprints – tend to rise with income (see the

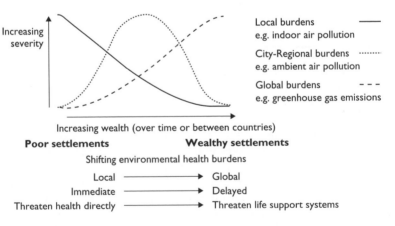

Figure 2.1 Stylized curves representing the urban environmental risk transition
Source: adapted from McGranahan *et al.* 2001.

'global' curve in Figure 2.1). Many of the burdens, particularly urban air pollution, that a nation's economic activities impose at the city or regional level lead to an inverted U-shape when plotted against per-capita income.

The diagram can also be viewed as representing change with time. For countries that industrialized in the nineteenth century, the declining 'local' curve can be taken to represent the revolution in sanitation of the late-nineteenth and early-twentieth centuries. Similarly, the declining part of the city-regional curve can be taken to represent the revolution in pollution abatement and control of the mid- to late-twentieth century. The hope that the 'global' curve for the industrialized nations will turn downward as well is implicit in contemporary aspirations for a revolution in sustainability.

Of course, no matter what these curves are taken to represent, they must be understood as idealizations, greatly oversimplified for clarity. They share no common units for measuring the severity of the various environmental burdens, and they mask considerable international diversity. Furthermore, their positioning and overlap vary as well, and, in rapidly developing countries, the transitions they portray, compared with the historical development of Europe and North America, are 'telescoped' in time (Marcotullio, 2007).

Historically, the 'local' aspect of this transition has often been accomplished by the physical displacement of environmental burdens (McGranahan et al., 2001). Sewers collect faecal material and release it beyond urban boundaries. High smokestacks displace air pollution from its source. Water and other resources are brought to urban centres from ever-longer distances, as local sources run out. More generally, spatial shifting enables people to avoid the environmental consequences of increasing production and consumption, at least locally.

An important element has been omitted from this discussion so far: the spatial dimension of environmental burdens, or, in other words, how the local-scale, regional-scale and global-scale burdens imposed by a nation's economic development vary from place to place. Adding such a spatial dimension certainly complicates any account of an environmental-risk transition, but, crucially, it also makes explicit the interdependence of various national development trajectories.

A prime example is the differential impact of the rise in greenhouse-gas emissions per capita as per-capita income rises. Existing estimates suggest that the health burden of the climate change resulting from such emissions is highest in low-income countries and lowest in the same affluent countries that are responsible for the burden. Smith and Ezzati (2005, p323) found that the ratio of climate-change risks imposed to those experienced varied by a factor of 7,000 across WHO-defined development regions: from 0.08 in part of Africa to 560 in North America. These numbers starkly reflect the environmental injustice of climate change.

The environmental health risks posed by a nation's economic development also vary from place to place within urban areas (Utzinger and Keiser, 2006).

Household-level burdens related to bad water, poor sanitation and indoor air pollution are all likely to be higher (i.e. worse) in very poor neighbourhoods than in wealthier ones, and are likely to be especially high in informal settlements where public services are not made available. City-regional burdens are also likely to fall more heavily on poor neighbourhoods, which are often downwind of ambient air polluters and downstream of water polluters. Even climate-change burdens are more likely to fall on poor and informal settlements, and for similar reasons. Groups of the poor are most likely to settle on urban flood plains, and so they are most at risk from rising sea levels and flooding (McGranahan *et al.*, 2007a). If climate change also leads to extended droughts that affect urban water supplies, groups of the poor are, once again, the most likely to suffer, just as they already do from seasonal droughts.

Thus the urban poor often face multiple burdens, which can be described in the framework of the urban environmental-risk transition as both temporally and spatially overlapping (Smith and Ezzati, 2005). In other words, the poor get the worst of both worlds, not only across the various phases of the environmental-risk transition, but also compared with neighbouring groups at any particular phase of the transition. Most people would agree that such environmental health inequalities are unacceptable. Yet at the same time, given the cumulative global environmental pressures already created by the affluent minority, the environmental-risk transition itself is hardly an acceptable way for poor and middle-income nations to follow on the road to economic development. Addressing the inequalities of urban environmental risk without adding to global environmental burdens is one of the most urgent challenges of the twenty-first century.

Housing, water, sanitation and health – the persistent environmental health challenge of urban poverty?

> The River Rhine, it is well known
> Doth wash your city of Cologne;
> But tell me, nymphs! what power divine
> Shall henceforth wash the river Rhine?
>
> – Samuel Taylor Coleridge

The environmental contribution to the current global burden of diseases is closely linked to conditions in and around people's homes and workplaces; in other words, to adopt the language of the preceding section, to environmental risks at the household level and at the city-regional level. When the WHO focused its World Health Report on risks to health, the only two environmental risks that figured in the top ten risks overall were unsafe water, sanitation and hygiene, and indoor air pollution (WHO, 2002). Their importance was reconfirmed in the 2006 update on the global burden of disease, which estimated that unsafe water, sanitation and disease accounted for 3.7 percent of the overall disease burden in low- and middle-income countries, and that indoor air pollution accounted for 3.0 percent (Lopez *et al.*, 2006). Most of this burden is linked to diarrhoea, in the case of unsafe water, sanitation and hygiene, and to lower-respiratory infection, in the case of indoor air pollution; in both cases, moreover, the burden falls most heavily on infants and young children.

Faecal-oral disease transmission in deprived urban settlements

In affluent urban settlements a number of barriers have been created, making it difficult for the infectious organisms that cause diarrhoea (be they viruses, bacteria, protozoa or helminths) to find their way from the faeces of one individual to the mouth of another. The conditions in most crowded, unserviced urban settlements are quite different. Barriers are less present and more permeable:

- Water is often collected from local wells, contaminated by local pit latrines.
- If the toilets are distant or have long queues, some people will defecate in the open or dispose of faeces by wrapping them in paper or in plastic bags. (The method is known as 'wrap-and-throw' – and the bags, sometimes literally thrown away, become 'flying toilets'.)
- Children are especially unlikely to use distant, crowded or costly toilets, and their faeces are especially hazardous.
- Household solid waste remains unbagged and uncollected, providing a breeding ground for flies and other pests.
- Children without safe places to play are likely to encounter faecal material in the neighbourhood environment. Those with diarrhoeal or respiratory infections are a particular hazard both to their playmates and to their families.
- Food preparation is often done outside or in unscreened kitchens where flies are present.
- Hand washing is often inconvenient. By one estimate, following the recommendation to wash one's hands after defecating or handling children's faeces and before handling food would require, on average, 32 hand washes a day and consume 20 litres of water (Keusch *et al.*, 2006, p377). For those who fetch water from far away, or pay vendors to do so, such standards are unrealistic.
- Shared toilets, and particularly public toilets, are hard to keep clean and hazardous when they are unclean.

Measures to interrupt faecal-oral disease transmission

The level of risk for diarrhoeal disease is influenced by a large set of factors, many of which are public and outside of any individual's control. The complexity of the problem follows from the enormous diversity of faecal-oral routes (person-to-person, waterborne, food, flies and so forth), local conditions (with variabilities in poverty, climate, crowding, service deficiencies and hygiene behaviours) and faecal-oral pathogens (with their different infective doses, latencies and abilities to persist and reproduce in the environment). Unfortunately, there is a tendency in the policy circles to focus on interventions that address single, well-defined risks and that result (ostensibly) in easy-to-monitor improvements.

The tendency to first focus narrowly on the provision of clean drinking water is a case in point. In the Millennium Declaration of the United Nations General Assembly, from which the Millennium Development Goals are derived, the original water target was 'to halve, by the year 2015, the proportion of the world's people who are unable to reach or to afford safe drinking water'. Since clean drinking water (mostly) affects the health risks of individuals, such a focus would seem to invert the emphasis on public risks and benefits in favour of individual ones. In any event, making clean drinking water the number-one priority, in effect, presupposes that how to reduce exposure to faecal pathogens is already settled – which it decidedly is not. (The number of rigorous epidemiological studies of the effectiveness remains small (Fewtrell *et al.*, 2005).

The emphasis on clean water has been reinforced by the term 'waterborne diseases'. What is misleading is that diseases classified as 'waterborne' need not be spread by water; indeed, virtually any waterborne disease can also be spread directly from person to person and, in unsanitary conditions, by a number of other routes as well. Other diseases also have complex links with water supplies, though not to drinking water quality per se. Malaria is spread by mosquitoes that breed in unpolluted freshwater. Dengue is spread by mosquitoes that can also breed in water, typically in the small household water containers that are particularly common where water supplies are intermittent or distant. Schistosomiasis is spread by worms often contracted by people fetching water from open sources.

Thus the near-universal focus on clean drinking water sets an agenda for action that cannot be justified on health grounds. Indeed, environmental health specialists have long expressed concern that, among the possible interventions for improving health, water provision gets undue emphasis over enhanced sanitation and improved hygiene behaviour, and that water quality gets undue emphasis over the quantity of wash water available to households. The excessive focus on water quality is further bolstered by the interests of more affluent households – typically with greater political access – who already have adequate sanitation and a piped water supply.

Table 2.1 summarizes the reductions in the risk of diarrhoea estimated for various interventions. The sharp difference between interventions at the public water source versus interventions that target house connections is based on direct empirical findings, backed up by the fact that households

Table 2.1 Estimated reduction in diarrhoea attributable to water supply, sanitation and hygiene promotion

Intervention	Reduction in diarrhoea (percent)
Water supply	
Public source	17
House connection (additional reduction)	63
Excreta disposal	36
Hygiene promotion	48

Source: Cairncross and Valdmanis (2006).

tend to use far less water if they must go beyond their residences or plots to fetch it. The comparatively high reduction estimated for hygiene promotion reflects growing evidence that behaviour is central to the prevalence of diarrhoea (Cairncross and Valdmanis, 2006). Promoting specific measures such as hand washing, for instance, have been surprisingly effective. A 2003 review found that washing hands with soap can reduce the risk of diarrhoeal diseases by between 42 and 47 percent – which implies that interventions to promote hand washing could save a million lives a year (Curtis and Cairncross, 2003). Even measures to improve sanitary conditions or water supply depend on changes in hygiene behaviour. Thus new sanitation facilities are far less likely to reduce the prevalence of diarrhoea if children do not use them.

All this is not to say that improving water quality in the home makes little difference to health. On the contrary, several recent studies and reviews suggest the difference is appreciable, but that in most circumstances other improvements are probably more important, as well as more cost effective (Cairncross *et al.*, 2010). In any case, even important and low-cost improvements are not much use unless they can be achieved, preferably on a large scale.

Implications for action

Preventing excessive transmission of faecal-oral diseases in urban neighbourhoods typically requires coordinated action on the part of government authorities, utilities and the residents themselves. In relatively affluent settings, a combination of taxes and tariffs can fund services convenient enough that they encourage people to live hygienically, whether or not there are social pressures to do so. Once such services are in place, people have little to gain by engaging in such practices as open defecation, open dumping, drinking from unsafe water sources or releasing human waste into open waterways.

But in low-income settings – particularly in informal settlements or in communities whose legality is questioned – governments, utilities and residents all face far greater challenges. Governments are often loath to allow, let alone enforce, the provision of infrastructure in informal, illegal or substandard settlements; officials and their constituents outside the settlements may fear that the very act of providing infrastructure will encourage the expansion of the settlements. As for utilities, they are often so underfunded that they try to avoid expanding subsidized services to deprived neighbourhoods. And the residents of low-income settlements are often so poorly organized and ill-informed that they can neither address their own environmental health issues nor negotiate effectively with governments and utilities that could (and should) help them resolve them.

In essence, two kinds of change are needed. First, water, drainage, sewerage and other networks and/or environmental services need to be provided or extended. Second, residents need to change their behaviours.

Extending water and sanitation networks

Efforts to extend such networks to all residents of cities in low- and middle-income countries have had only limited success. UNICEF and WHO (WHO/UNICEF, 2010) estimate that as of 2008 some 790 million people in urban areas still lack access to 'improved' sanitation, and 140 million urban dwellers have no 'improved' source of water. These numbers, moreover have been rising.[2] Limited funding has been part of the problem, but only part (UN-Habitat, 2003). Public utilities were once held to be the best model for extending affordable water and sanitation to urban populations, but in many low- and middle-income countries they ended up in financial trouble. Low-cost services reached only limited parts of the populations.

During the 1990s, private-sector participation was promoted on the grounds that commercial efficiency would replace public bureaucracy and political patronage, and that private partners could bring in private capital. After a flurry of concession contracts, however, privatization began to falter. Private capital showed little interest in extending water and sanitation to deprived households. It proved difficult even to design and regulate contracts that would give private operators the incentive to provide quality services efficiently and equitably. And governments that had not been able to manage public utilities turned out to be no better at managing contracts with private operators. In any case, many of the obstacles to providing water and sanitation in the informal settlements, where most of the urban poor live, could not be overcome simply by changing the operation of utilities (Budds and McGranahan, 2003). Thus perhaps it should not be surprising that there is little evidence that private-sector involvement has had much influence on the efficiency or extent of service delivery (Clarke *et al.*, 2004; Kirkpatrick *et al.*, 2006).

Although extending the water and sanitation networks remains important, it is also important, especially from a health perspective, to improve conditions in areas the networked system is unlikely to reach in the foreseeable future. This principle applies especially to sanitation and conventional high-cost sewer systems.

Organizing to improve sanitary conditions in deprived settlements

Whatever the mix of public and private collaboration in the latest round of efforts, it seems likely that many of the most deprived urban residents will continue to do without centrally organized water and sanitation services. Hence alternate ways of providing those services must be considered. And without good water and sanitation facilities, improving hygiene behaviour becomes especially critical.

People do not change their hygiene behaviour for reasons of health alone. They are far more likely to respond to reasons that appeal to convenience, status or cleanliness. Yet the perception of health benefits can certainly reinforce certain behaviours. Health benefits undoubtedly have helped tea-drinking to spread, for example. Furthermore, tea offers physical reassurance that the water has been boiled, even to those who did not engage in its making. Heat is the obvious indicator, but colour and taste are also important, and still apply in countries like Indonesia where cold tea has been very popular. Such complex embedding of hygiene improvements in cultural practices can be highly effective, though it can be problematic to rely solely on such criteria to protect large, migrating populations or groups undergoing rapidly changing environmental conditions.

One possible conclusion, then, is that governments need to determine which key services and hygiene behaviours are most important to promote – and then promote them, not on grounds of health, but on whatever grounds are most appealing. Programmes such as the public–private partnerships between soap companies, governments and agencies such as the World Bank fit this mould.[3]

One problem with this conclusion is that market-responsive enterprises expand or contract along with the profits they make, not the health benefits they provide. Sellers often try to induce people to buy products they do not inherently want. But when advertising succeeds, product sales not only signal demand for more, but they also finance the expansion needed to ramp up supplies. By contrast, successfully promoting good hygiene does not necessarily furnish a basis for expansion. In attempts to link hygiene behaviour to commercial products, there is the danger that the advertising will favour the product over the behaviour – the consumption of soap over the washing of hands. And if advertising is not linked to a commercial product, it will not have the same self-financing characteristics as it does in the private sector – that is, its increasing costs will not be offset by the increasing sales of a product.

Advertising raises other problematic issues as well. Some health promoters may feel it would undermine the trust necessary for evidence-based health education, on the grounds that advertising is inherently manipulative. Perhaps just as important, because of the continuing uncertainty about which measures are likely to be most effective in reducing faecal-oral disease, the wrong measures could be promoted. If the promotions draw on local residents' scarce income, the net health effects could well be negative.

These considerations lead to a second possible approach to improving the environmental health of poor communities: recognize the importance of local knowledge, and provide support to advocates and organizations for the urban poor in improving local health conditions. If one takes this approach, it is important to re-emphasize that health is rarely the main reason people want to improve their water supplies, sanitary facilities or hygiene behaviour. People do want better health for themselves, their families and their communities. But a WHO report calculated that, whereas the benefits of improvements in water and sanitation typically exceeded the costs, the time savings made a larger contribution to the benefits than health improvement did (Hutton and Haller, 2004).

The potential for time savings can be astonishing. In one urban settlement in the Philippines it takes three to four hours to collect water, largely because of waiting times, despite the presence of public taps within 100 meters (Aiga and Umenai, 2002). This example illustrates the danger of making recommendations on the basis of health considerations, narrowly conceived (or even on the basis of the cost-effectiveness of various measures to improve health). Particularly in conditions of poverty, a narrow pursuit of health may lead to recommendations that go against the interests of local residents. Non-health concerns can be important, and not just as a means of convincing people to take action to improve their health. As a quantifiable measure of progress in the struggle against poverty, public health may be more equitable than some predefined level of gross domestic product, but it does have its dangers.

It is inherently difficult, and at times contradictory, to pursue acceptable health standards for the unacceptably poor. Such difficulties and contradictions are amplified when resident-government relations are bad. The colonial government in Accra (Ghana), for example, enforced sanitary regulations so vigorously that in some years thousands of women were prosecuted for having standing water or filth in their compounds, and the routine 'he' used to designate the accused in the District Court was reportedly changed to a routine 'she' (Robertson, 1984, p34). In the post-colonial period, few governments have relied so heavily on the courts to enforce sanitary regulations, but unrealistically high standards have taken their toll in a variety of other ways.

One of the most successful efforts to expand sanitation in low-income settings has been that of the Orangi Pilot Project-Research and Training Institute

(OPP-RTI) of Karachi, Pakistan (see also the brief description in Chapter 5 by Susan Mercado *et al.*, p91). There are two features of the OPP approach that illustrate the advantages of interventions that are not restricted narrowly to the health sector, even when pursuing health improvements:

• OPP activists are intimately familiar with local conditions and living arrangements, and standards are designed to provide affordable, desirable, safe and effective sanitation.
• The first step of a new project is to hold meetings and to mobilize people, creating the basis for collective action.

Many of the other successful attempts to engage local residents in improving local water and sanitation provision have similar features. In fact, some of the most promising initiatives are not situated either within the health sector or the water and sanitation sector. Rather, they are part of more broad-based attempts to help the urban poor to improve their living conditions. Three additional features that most of these initiatives have in common with OPP are (McGranahan *et al.*, 2007b):

• They promote local ownership.
• They encourage incremental improvements.
• They support alternate forms of community organizations within low-income settlements.

Addressing other local environmental hazards

Though there is insufficient space in this chapter to give them proper attention, there are numerous other environment and health problems linked to the quality of people's homes, workplaces and neighbourhoods. They often pose similar challenges. As indicated earlier, for example, acute respiratory infection is often linked to indoor air pollution in somewhat the same way that diarrhoeal diseases are linked to contaminated water and poor sanitation. Reducing indoor air pollution, like improving water and sanitation, is often presented as a question of improving service delivery (and providing clean fuels rather than clean water). Yet particularly in conditions of extreme poverty, considering effective interventions also raises behavioural issues, as well as the need to adopt affordable, second-best solutions. And, as with the risks of faecal-oral disease transmission, gender and childcare issues arise: women and young children, for example, are more exposed to smoke than men are because of the solid fuels used for cooking.

While there is a tendency to try to address these local problems in a top-down fashion, the motivation needed to drive improvements already exists within the deprived communities. The challenge is to create the political, legal, economic and social basis for that motivation to become the basis for positive change. As I have shown, this requires support from 'above', and in some cases may require centralized solutions. But the challenges posed by such problems are quite different from the challenges posed by the city-regional and global burdens associated with industrialization, motorization and affluent consumption. Indeed, there is a real sense in which just as the resolution of the local problems needs to be driven by local collective action, so the institutional resolution of the global problems needs to be driven by global collective action. After all, unlike reductions in faecal pollution or indoor air pollution, reductions in local greenhouse-gas emissions provide no real local benefits, unless there are institutions delivering these benefits (e.g. carbon credits). At the same time, when it comes to adapting to climate change, local incentives re-emerge as paramount, and indeed overlap with some of the same environmental hazards (e.g. sanitation problems caused by flooding that is associated with climate change).

Global climate change, urban development and health – a growing environmental challenge of urban affluence?

> Climate change is the biggest global health threat of the 21st century... [T]he impacts will be felt all around the world – and not just in some distant future but in our lifetimes and those of our children.
> – *The Lancet*, 2009.

As I noted earlier, the deprived urban populations who suffer the most from household and local environmental risks, such as inferior housing, polluted water and inadequate sanitation, are also the most vulnerable to the global risk of climate change. Indeed, without immediate mitigation efforts, climate change is likely to amplify and exacerbate the existing local problems. Even if the environmental-risk transitions were to eliminate the household and local risks to health in deprived urban communities (a big 'if'), the global risks of climate change would still fall most heavily on the urban poor.

The similarity in the incidence of those local and global risks – the outsize burdens that each kind of risk imposes on the environmental health of poor neighbourhoods – does suggest a common tactic: local measures taken on the basis of locally determined priorities that can address both kinds of risk may be the best way to improve health in such neighbourhoods. Thus, even in low- and middle-income countries, urban settlements that have managed to address their local environmental challenges efficiently and equitably are probably in a better position to adapt to the challenges of global environmental change. Settlements that have already addressed the water and sanitation challenges of their most vulnerable populations are likely to be in the best position to cope with increasing water scarcity efficiently and equitably. Similarly, urban settlements that have already addressed the land

and housing challenges of their most vulnerable populations are likely to be in the best position to cope with increasing flood risks efficiently and equitably.

Unfortunately, the reverse is true as well. In settlements where challenges to health have not been managed well, or where institutional weaknesses have undermined improvements in sanitation, water and housing, adaptation to climate change is likely to be equally ineffectual.

Climate change and its effects

What are the most likely environmental consequences of global warming? The science of climate change and its impacts is highly uncertain, though this does not distinguish it from the science of water and sanitation. The Intergovernmental Panel on Climate Change (IPCC) has assembled several of the most sophisticated computational models of climate change, developed by several independent scientific groups, in an attempt to identify the most significant climate changes that can be expected by 2100. The models of the IPCC's Fourth Assessment Report project temperature increases of between roughly 1 and 6 Celsius degrees (IPCC, 2007).[4] For the same period the models project sea-level rises of between 20 and 60 centimetres. Because the IPCC could not reach consensus on the contributions of melting ice sheets in Greenland and Antarctica to sea-level rise, that factor was omitted from the projections. Thus, the projections almost certainly underestimate the future rise in sea level: with the rapid and ongoing changes in ice flow, the actual rise could be much higher.

The amount of warming is expected to be greater, on average, over land than over water, and to be particularly acute at high northern latitudes. Heat waves and periods of exceptionally high precipitation are likely to become more common. Tropical cyclones (typhoons and hurricanes) will probably become more intense. The models strongly suggest increases in overall precipitation at high latitudes and decreases in most subtropical land areas. We should also expect to have to cope with surprises – climate changes are both poorly understood and known to involve thresholds and sudden shifts.

Health risks of climate change

The potential health impacts of climate change range from quite direct (e.g. ill health – 'thermal stress' – from heat exposure) to extremely indirect (e.g. changes in the transmission and evolution of infectious diseases, declining food supplies, malnutrition resulting from an economic depression that climate change may help create). The health consequences of global environmental burdens such as climate change are typically more indirect than those caused by local burdens, and global burdens are also more likely than local ones to affect health by undermining life-support systems. Thus climate change is likely to have major impacts on ecosystems, which will in turn influence such critical factors as the supply of food and the spread of diseases.

Not all the impacts of climate change on health will be negative, but the net effect almost certainly will be, particularly if few adaptive measures are taken. The main problem is that large-scale change, and particularly rapid change, is disruptive and damaging to any human culture and its life-support systems. Furthermore, even if steps are taken immediately to mitigate climate change, some global warming and other related changes are already inevitable: they are 'in the pipeline'.

Table 2.2 lists a range of examples of how climate change can create direct health risks.

Rising temperatures, heat waves and thermal stress

Thermal stress from higher temperatures is perhaps the most obvious health risk associated with climate change (Harlan and Ruddell, 2011). The European heat wave of August 2003, which caused some 15,000 deaths in France alone, clearly showed how severe the impact can be for an unprepared population, even a relatively affluent one. Elderly people, as the French experiences have shown, are at special risk.

One would also expect greater vulnerability to heat waves among low-income populations, and in low-income countries, than in their higher-income counterparts. Affluence and preparedness clearly can reduce vulnerability. For example, one study concluded that the 2003 heat wave in Shanghai led to far fewer deaths than a similar heat wave there in 1998. The lifesaving changes in that five-year period included more air conditioning, larger living areas, increased urban green space, higher levels of heat awareness and the implementation of a heat-warning system (Tan et al., 2007).

But as Table 2.2 makes clear, thermal stress is not the only health risk associated with higher temperatures. Other risks, including an increased risk of food-contracted diarrhoea, are likely to rise along with temperature in impoverished conditions. Shakoor Hajat and his colleagues recently compared mortality increases on very hot days in Delhi, Sao Paulo and London (Hajat et al., 2005). The increases varied inversely with affluence: they were highest in Delhi and lowest in London, with Sao Paulo intermediate. In London, moreover, the increased mortality was offset within a few days of lower temperatures by decreased mortality, whereas in Delhi the increase continued for weeks. The authors concluded that 'those most susceptible to heat are likely to remain susceptible if there is not due attention paid to infectious disease, diarrheal illness and other major causes of early mortality in these poor populations' (Hajat et al., 2005).

Table 2.2 Examples of direct (urban) health risks of climate change

	Rising temperatures and heat waves	Floods and storm surges	Droughts and wildfires
Temperature stress	Thermal stress, enhanced by urban heat island effects	Loss of housing leading to exposure to ambient temperature extremes	Lack of water exacerbating effects of thermal stress
Faecal-oral diseases	Higher temperatures increasing risk of food poisoning (e.g. salmonellosis)	Exposure to faecally contaminated flood waters; damaged water and sanitation systems	Declining water resources leading to water supply interruptions and hygiene problems
Vector-borne diseases	Altered distribution of mosquitoes and other vectors change, increasing disease transmission	Altered breeding conditions for mosquitoes and other vectors, and loss of protective shields (e.g. windows, screens)	Altered breeding conditions for mosquitoes and other vectors
Respiratory diseases	Secondary chemical reactions within the urban atmosphere, elevating levels of pollutants such as ozone	Dampness and mould in the home environment, increasing susceptibility to respiratory diseases	Inhalation of smoke from wildfires, increasing susceptibility to respiratory diseases and allergies
Injury	Work-related injuries as a consequence of overheating	Collapse of shelter; contact with submerged objects; vehicle incidents	Burning injuries from wildfires in peri-urban zones
Malnutrition	Loss of traditional crop production, leading to food shortages	Crop damage and lower food supplies; loss of livelihoods and income-based access to food	Reduced agricultural productivity and food supplies
Mental health	Psychosocial responses to discomfort	Psychosocial responses to danger, disruption, illness, displacement and losses	Psychosocial responses to danger, disruption, illness, displacement and losses

Sources: Draws heavily on and replicates parts of Table 1 in Few, R. (2007) 'Health and climatic hazards: framing social research on vulnerability, response and adaptation', *Global Environmental Change*, vol 17, no 2, pp281–295. Also includes examples from McMichael, A.J., Woodruff, R.E. and Hales, S. (2006) 'Climate change and human health: present and future risks', *The Lancet*, vol 367, no 9513, pp859–869.

Floods and storm surges

Urban disasters and environmental hot spots are already concentrated in coastal areas. People have long been drawn to the coast. The coastal area within ten meters above sea level, referred to as the Low Elevation Coastal

Zone (LECZ), covers just 2 percent of the world's land but is home to 10 percent of the world's population (McGranahan *et al.*, 2007b). Climate change will add increased flood risks to the perils of coastal living, both because of sea-level rise and more severe storms.

Although the risk to small island states is (rightly) publicized, large low- or middle-income countries with heavily populated delta regions make up the bulk of countries with large populations in the LECZ. Indeed, about half the world's population in the LECZ is in five Asian countries: China (144 million), India (63 million), Bangladesh (62 million), Vietnam (43 million) and Indonesia (42 million). For Vietnam this represents 55 percent of the national population, for Bangladesh 46 percent, making them especially vulnerable.

The LECZ is more urban than other areas, particularly in low-income countries, where more than 40 percent of the national urban population lives in the zone. (For comparison, less than 30 percent of the urban populations of other countries inhabit the LECZ (see Figure 2.2). In some countries, notably China, urbanization is driving people toward the coast. Even in Africa, where only 7 percent of the total population lives in the LECZ, 12 percent of the urban population does. Larger urban areas are also more likely to extend into the LECZ, and almost two-thirds of urban settlements – over 5 million in population – fall at least partly in the zone.

Floods, of course, can have a broad range of adverse impacts: the drownings and bodily injuries that can result from physical contact with the floodwaters, as well as such secondary health effects as exposure to sewage, disruption of water supplies, loss of housing and the resulting stresses on mental health (Ahern and Kovats, 2006). In low-income urban settings – and especially where emergency responses are slow – those secondary health effects are likely to be particularly significant. The risk of

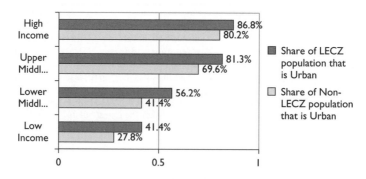

Figure 2.2 Urbanization within and without the Lower Elevation Coastal Zone (LECZ)
Source: McGranahan, Balk and Anderson, 2007a.

diarrhoeal diseases, which seems low after flooding in affluent countries, is a serious but hard-to-measure consequence of flooding in lower income countries (Ahern *et al.*, 2005). In their description of the health impacts of the Mozambique floods of 2000, Sandy Cairncross and Manuel Alvarinho (2006) note that there were both increases in diarrhoea and outbreaks of cholera when the floods caused thousands of urban septic tanks to overflow, contaminating piped-water supplies in eight small towns. Flooding in Dhaka, Bangladesh, has also been linked to large increases in diarrhoea (Alam and Rabbani, 2007). Other infectious diseases have also been documented in the wake of floods and storms (Ahern *et al.*, 2005; Shultz *et al.*, 2005).

The numerous smaller floods of the past several years may already be causing more sickness and injury than major disasters in the same period, and the smaller floods will likely increase with rises in sea level and more severe storms. Such floods are not well documented, and their health effects are hard to estimate. Again, however, low-income urban populations are almost certainly more vulnerable to them than wealthier groups are. A recently published article portrays the lack of preparedness in six African cities (Douglas *et al.*, 2008), but the problems are more general. Drainage systems are often rudimentary and quickly clogged with waste. Sanitation systems are prone to overflowing. Faecal material can easily find its way into floodwaters. Planners and architects seldom take account of how impermeable urban surfaces can spread gushing floodwaters across large areas. Many urban dwellers still depend on open wells – readily contaminated by floodwaters. Perhaps most important, as I noted earlier, is that land in the floodplains of coastal urban settlements is often inexpensive, in part because formal development there is not allowed. Hence those areas attract low-income residents.

The number of people living in informal settlements who are vulnerable to coastal flooding is rarely documented locally, let alone internationally. As sea levels rise, though, living in such settlements will become increasingly dangerous to health. The obvious solution, especially where protection against flooding is too costly, is to negotiate resettlement. Unfortunately, relations between settlers and government authorities are typically poor, particularly in cities where the residents' struggle to obtain land has historically led to conflicts, illegal settlement and evictions. And a range of factors inhibits efforts to improve conditions: the residents' lack of economic resources, the weakness of local governments and their unwillingness to provide (or in some cases even allow) public support for these settlements, and the similar unwillingness of international agencies to provide assistance.

As these considerations make clear, the primary challenges that climate change poses for the urban poor are the same challenges the poor have faced throughout the environmental-risk transition – and, indeed, before it began. Addressing the problems of sanitation, water and housing calls for collective action, not only on the part of local governments and institutions with access to substantial resources, but also on the part of the poor communities themselves. After all, the poor are in the best position to determine their own priorities and self-interests. Yet governments and local elites have at best an ambiguous attitude toward informal urban settlements. These powerful groups have generally been opposed to well-organized settlements capable of pursuing their own collective interests – which of course are not all environmental. They are no more likely to welcome the voices of poor communities in addressing global warming than they have been in dealing with local environmental issues.

Droughts and water scarcity

The IPCC's Fourth Assessment Report projects that average river runoff and water availability will decrease by between 10 and 30 percent in some dry mid- and low-latitude regions (Adger *et al.*, 2007). For example, the report estimates that in Africa between 75 and 250 million people will experience greater water stress due to climate change (Adger *et al.*, 2007). Superficially, those data might seem to imply a fairly direct connection between climate-change-induced drought and the health of the urban poor.

On closer inspection, however, the impacts of climate change on health will depend, once again, as much on governmental and institutional responses as they do on physical declines in a vital resource. What is essential to keep in mind is that deprived urban groups, economically impoverished, politically weak and socially fragmented as they are, face difficulties getting adequate water (and sanitation) regardless of the water resources available in the surrounding region. Water scarcity may drive up the price of water, but that effect is swamped by price variations from place to place within a city that depend on whether the water is distributed through a piped system or by itinerant vendors who carry the water door-to-door (UN-Habitat, 2003).

The risk that drought and declining agricultural production will increase malnutrition in urban areas raises similar issues. As Amartya Sen has famously argued, famine is rarely the result of absolute food scarcities (Sen, 1982). Rather, it is better conceived of as a crisis in entitlements, which may be set off by declining food production but can also have other roots. The most dangerous effect of an agricultural crisis for the urban poor is that it can raise food prices, because such groups are particularly vulnerable to high food prices.

An agricultural crisis could also have a severe impact on certain groups of the rural population, driving increased migration from farm to city. Urban authorities are likely to blame the migrants for the increasing demand on urban services, including water and sanitation. Such demands can become yet another excuse for not addressing service deficiencies in the informal settlements of the urban poor. Better services, after all, could encourage still more migration (McGranahan *et al.*, 2007b; Tacoli *et al.*, 2007). This example shows how difficult it is to predict how crises will unfold, and predicting the full spectrum of health effects from climate change is no exception.

Implications for adaptation

In building urban resilience to climate change, David Satterthwaite and his colleagues (Satterthwaite *et al.*, 2007) have argued that it is important to do so in a way that:

- builds on existing experience with urban disasters;
- assembles a strong knowledge base within the threatened localities recognizes the importance of:
- competent and accountable local governments having good working relations with all residents, including those living in informal settlements and working in the informal economy;
- well-organized civil-society groups, particularly those representing the urban poor;
- national governments and international agencies that are willing to support local governments and foster better relations between local government and groups of the urban poor;
- a private sector that responds efficiently to market demands that contribute to urban resilience and is willing to engage publicly on the basis of its collective interest in adapting to climate change.

Climate change has been created by a process of environmental displacement driven by economic growth. Those who have benefited from this economic growth have a responsibility not only to mitigate climate change, but also to help vulnerable groups adapt. In adapting to climate change, however, it is important to adjust the environmental agenda to reflect the scale of burdens imposed and borne. In low-income settings, local priorities about local burdens can guide the appropriate action. In affluent settings, by contrast, local burdens should not necessarily guide the choice of action, but the priority must still be to reduce greenhouse-gas emissions that are responsible for climate change. No one agenda, rich or poor, should be allowed to dominate the various responses.

The poorest are also the most vulnerable to almost every calamity, and there is a tendency for advocates of every environmental improvement, from biodiversity protection to climate-change mitigation, to point this out. But these same low-income populations are also vulnerable to policies, even ones promulgated in their name. And even if they are more vulnerable than the affluent to climate change, they are still more vulnerable to bad water and sanitation. To make climate change the number-one priority in the name of the poor would be disingenuous. Rather, in taking health as a measure of well-being and applying transition analysis, one is led to a new perspective on the priorities for responding to climate change. The point is to bring some balance to the discussion, recognizing the importance of all kinds of burdens, but allowing people at all economic levels to set reasoned priorities.

Notes

1   Declaration of Alma-Ata, International Conference on Primary Health Care, Alma-Ata, USSR, 6–12 September, 1978, http://www.who.int/hpr/NPH/docs/declaration_almaata.pdf
2   These figures are far less than the number of urban dwellers without safe or adequate water and sanitation; 'improved' is not intended to imply safe or adequate, and using the same definitions in rural and urban areas neglects the particular problems of unserved urban areas (Satterthwaite and McGranahan, 2006).
3   http://www.globalhandwashing.org
4   The comparisons refer to 2090–99 relative to 1980–99.

References

Adger, N., Aggarwal, P., Agrawala, S., Alcamo, J., Allali, A., Anisimov, O., Arnell, N., Boko, M., Canziani, O., Carter, T., Casassa, G., Confalonieri, U., Cruz, R.V., de Alba Alcaraz, E., Easterling, W., Field, C., Fischlin, A., Fitzharris, B.B., García, C.G., Hanson, C., Harasawa, H., Hennessy, K., Huq, S., Jones, R., Bogataj, L.K., Karoly, D., Klein, R., Kundzewicz, Z., Lal, M., Lasco, R., Love, G., Lu, X., Magrøn, G., Mata, L.J., McLean, R., Menne, B., Midgley, G., Mimura, N., Mirza, M.Q., Moreno, J., Mortsch, L., Niang-Diop, I., Nicholls, R., Nováky, B., Nurse, L., Nyong, A., Oppenheimer, M., Palutikof, J., Parry, M., Patwardhan, A., Romero Lankao, P., Rosenzweig, C., Schneider, S., Semenov, S., Smith, J., Stone, J., van Ypersele, J-P., Vaughan, D., Vogel, C., Wilbanks, T., Wong, P., Wu, S. and Yohe, G. (2007) *Summary for Policymakers: Contribution of Working Group II to the Fourth Assessment Report*, Intergovernmental Panel on Climate Change, Geneva
Ahern, M., Kovats, R.S., Wilkinson, P., Few, R. and Matthies, F. (2005) 'Global health impacts of floods: epidemiologic evidence', *Epidemiologic Reviews*, vol 27, no 1, pp36–46
Ahern, M. and Kovats, R.S. (2006) 'The health impact of floods', in R. Few and F. Matthies (eds) *Flood Hazards and Health: Responding to Present and Future Risks*, Earthscan, London, pp28–53
Aiga, H. and Umenai, T. (2002) 'Impact of improvement of water supply on household economy in a squatter area of Manila', *Social Science and Medicine*, vol 55, no 4, pp627–641
Alam, M. and Rabbani, M.D.G. (2007) 'Vulnerabilities and responses to climate change for Dhaka', *Environment and Urbanization*, vol 19, no 1, pp81–97

Budds, J. and McGranahan, G. (2003) 'Are the debates on water privatization missing the point? Experiences from Africa, Asia and Latin America', *Environment and Urbanization*, vol 15, no 2, pp87–113

Cairncross, S. and Alvarinho, M. (2006) 'The Mozambique floods of 2000: Health impact and response', in R. Few and F. Matthies (eds) *Flood Hazards and Health: Responding to Present and Future Risks*, Earthscan, London, pp111–127

Cairncross, S. and Valdmanis, V. (2006) 'Chapter 41: Water supply, sanitation, and hygiene promotion', in D.T. Jamison, J.G. Breman, A.R. Measham, G. Alleyne, M. Claeson, D.B. Evans, P. Jha, A. Mills and P. Musgrove (eds) *Disease Control Priorities in Developing Countries*, World Bank and Oxford University Press, Washington, DC, pp771–792

Cairncross, S., Hunt, C., Boisson, S., Bostoen, K., Curtis, V., Fung, I.C.H. and Schmidt, W.P. (2010) 'Water, sanitation and hygiene for the prevention of diarrhoea', *International Journal of Epidemiology*, vol 39, ppi193–i205

Clarke, G.R.G., Kosec, K. and Wallsten, S. (2004) 'Has private participation in water and sanitation improved coverage? Empirical evidence from Latin America', Policy Research Working Paper 3445, World Bank, Washington, DC

Costello, A., Abbas, M., Allen, A., Ball, S., Bell, S., Bellamy, R., Friel, S., Groce, N., Johnson, A., Kett, M., Lee, M., Levy, C., Maslin, M., McCoy, D., McGuire, B., Montgomery, H., Napier, D., Pagel, C., Patel, J., Puppim de Oliveira, J.A., Redclift, N., Rees, H., Rogger, D., Scott, J., Stephenson, J., Twigg, J., Wolff, J. and Patterson, C. (2009) 'Managing the health effects of climate change', *The Lancet*, vol 373, no 1976, pp1693–1733

Curtis, V. and Cairncross, S. (2003) 'Effect of washing hands with soap on diarrhoea risk in the community: a systematic review', *Lancet Infectious Diseases*, vol 3, no 5, pp275–281

Douglas, I., Alam, K., Maghenda, M., McDonnell, Y., McLean, L. and Campbell, J. (2008) 'Unjust waters: climate change, flooding and the urban poor in Africa', *Environment and Urbanization*, vol 20, no 1, pp187–205

Fewtrell, L., Kaufmann, R.B., Kay, D., Enanoria, W., Haller, L. and Colford, J.M. Jr (2005) 'Water, sanitation, and hygiene interventions to reduce diarrhoea in less developed countries: a systematic review and meta-analysis', *The Lancet Infectious Diseases*, vol 5, no 1, pp42–52

Fogel, R.W. (2004b) *The Escape from Hunger and Premature Death, 1700–2100: Europe, America, and the Third World*, Cambridge University Press, Cambridge

Hajat, S., Armstrong, B.G., Gouveia, N. and Wilkinson, P. (2005) 'Mortality displacement of heat-related deaths: a comparison of Delhi, Sao Paulo, and London', *Epidemiology*, vol 16, pp613–620

Harlan, S.L. and Ruddell, D.M. (2011) 'Climate change and health in cities: impacts of heat and air pollution and potential co-benefits from mitigation and adaptation', *Current Opinion in Environmental Sustainability*, vol 3, no 3, pp126–134

Hutton, G. and Haller, L. (2004) *Evaluation of the Costs and Benefits of Water and Sanitation Improvements at the Global Level*, World Health Organization, Geneva

IPCC (2007) 'Climate Change 2007: Working Group I: The Physical Science Basis, Section 10.5.4.2, Perturbed Physics Ensembles', http://www.ipcc.ch/publications_and_data/ar4/wg1/en/ch10s10-5-4-2.html, accessed March 30, 2012

Keusch, G.T., Fontaine, O., Bhargava, A., Boschi-Pinto, C., Bhutta, Z.A., Gotuzzo, E., Rivera, J., Chow, J., Shahid-Salles, S.A. and Laxminarayan, R. (2006) 'Chapter 19: Diarrheal Diseases', in D.T. Jamison, J.G. Breman, A.R. Measham, G. Alleyne, M. Claeson, D.B. Evans, P. Jha, A. Mills and P. Musgrove (eds) *Disease Control Priorities in Developing Countries*, World Bank and Oxford University Press, Washington, DC, pp371–387

Kirkpatrick, C., Parker, D. and Zhang, Y-F. (2006) 'An empirical analysis of state and private-sector provision of water services in Africa', *The World Bank Economic Review*, vol 20, no 1, pp143–163

Lopez, A.D., Mathers, C.D., Ezzati, M., Jamison, D.T. and Murray, C.J.L. (2006) 'Global and regional burden of disease and risk factors, 2001: systematic analysis of population health data', *The Lancet*, vol 367, no 9524, pp1747–1757

Marcotullio, P.J. (2007) 'Variations of urban environmental transitions: The experiences of rapidly developing Asia-Pacific cities', in P.J. Marcotullio and G. McGranahan (eds) *Scaling Urban Environmental Challenges: From Local to Global and Back*, Earthscan, London, pp45–68

McGranahan, G., Balk, D. and Anderson, B. (2007a) 'The rising tide: assessing the risks of climate change and human settlements in low elevation coastal zones', *Environment and Urbanisation*, vol 19, no 1, pp17–37

McGranahan, G., Mitlin, D. and Satterthwaite, D. (2007b) 'Land and services for the urban poor in rapidly urbanizing countries', background paper for the UNFPA's State of the World Population 2007, International Institute for Environment and Development, London

McGranahan, G., Jacobi, P., Songsore, J., Surjadi, C. and Kjellén, M. (2001) *The Citizens at Risk: From Urban Sanitation to Sustainable Cities*, Earthscan, London

Riley, L., Ko, A., Unger, A. and Reis, M. (2007) 'Slum health: diseases of neglected populations', *BMC International Health and Human Rights*, vol 7, no 2

Robertson, C.C. (1984) *Sharing the Same Bowl: A Socioeconomic History of Women and Class in Accra, Ghana*, University of Michigan Press, Ann Arbor, MI

Satterthwaite, D. and McGranahan, G. (2006) 'Providing clean water and sanitation', in M. O'Meara Sheehan and L. Starke (eds) *State of the world 2007: Our Urban Future*, Earthscan, London, pp26–45

Satterthwaite, D., Huq, S., Reid, H., Pelling, M. and Romero-Lankao, P. (2007) 'Adapting to climate change in urban areas: the possibilities and constraints in low and middle income nations', Working Paper, IIED

Scheper-Hughes, N. (1993) *Death Without Weeping: The Violence of Everyday Life in Brazil*, University of California Press, Berkeley

Sen, A. (1982) *Poverty and Famines: An Essay on Entitlement and Deprivation*, Clarendon Press, Oxford

Shultz, J.M., Russell, J. and Espinel, Z. (2005) 'Epidemiology of tropical cyclones: The dynamics of disaster, disease, and development', *Epidemiologic Reviews*, vol 27, no 1, pp21–35

Smith, K.R. and Ezzati, M. (2005) 'How environmental health risks change with development: the epidemiologic and environmental risk transitions revisited', *Annual Review of Environment and Resources*, vol 30, pp291–333

Szreter, S. (2004) 'Industrialization and health', *British Medical Bulletin*, vol 69, pp75–86

Tacoli, C., McGranahan, G. and Satterthwaite, D. (2007) 'Urbanization, poverty and inequity: is rural-urban migration a poverty problem, or part of the solution?', background paper for the UNFPA's State of the World Population 2007, International Institute for Environment and Development, London

Tan, J.G., Zheng, Y.F., Song, G.X., Kalkstein, L.S., Kalkstein, A.J. and Tang, X. (2007) 'Heat wave impacts on mortality in Shanghai, 1998 and 2003', *International Journal of Biometeorology*, vol 51, no 3, pp193–200

UN-Habitat (2003) *Water and Sanitation in the World's Cities: Local Action for Global Goals*, Earthscan, London

Utzinger, J. and Keiser, J. (2006) 'Urbanization and tropical health – then and now', *Annals of Tropical Medicine and Parasitology*, vol 100, no 5–6, pp517–533

WHO (World Health Organization) (2002) *The World Health Report 2002: Reducing Risks, Promoting Healthy Life*, WHO, Geneva

WHO/UNICEF (2010) *Progress on Sanitation and Drinking-Water: 2010 Update*, WHO/UNICEF Joint Monitoring Programme for Water Supply and Sanitation, WHO/UNICEF, Geneva

Chapter 3

Urban health systems[1]

Trudy Harpham

Introduction

The urban health system can be defined as the determinants and outcomes of urban health and the activities that link them. Because the range of environmental, social and service factors that can determine health in cities is so complex, it is useful to think about determinants in dimensions that span both multiple sectors (education, energy, industry, tourism, transportation, sanitation, water supplies, health and the like) and multiple levels (family dwellings, neighbourhoods, cities, regions and the like). Health systems often used to be thought of as being limited to health services or health care, and the broader ways of thinking are still quite new for the health field in general – though they are reflected in recent trends such as the rise in interest in and research on the social determinants of health (e.g. CSDH, 2008). Indeed, urban planners are arguably more familiar than health professionals are in dealing with multiple sectors and levels.

Determinants

Multisectoral determinants

In the 1970s, evidence emerged from the Global South that providing health services alone is not enough to improve health. Although this evidence did not come solely from urban areas, the 'field laboratories' for most of the research were situated predominantly in urban settings. That evidence drove the push for primary health care that was set forth in the 1978 'Alma Ata Declaration on Primary Health Care.'[2] The Declaration presented a truly comprehensive vision of primary health care, with multisectoral action at its heart. Yet what emerged in practice was selective primary health care that retreated to providing health services alone (and often focusing on only a few diseases): the individualistic, 'people-based' approach of traditional medicine.

So the need to expand planning and action from health services to a much more inclusive understanding of public health is very much with us today. In fact, there is a need to go one step further: evidence increasingly shows that even interventions that encompass public health as a whole – but do not go beyond it – are not enough. In India, for instance, investigators demonstrated that, although piped water reduced the frequency of child diarrhoea, that benefit bypassed households in which the mother was poorly educated (Jalan and Ravallion, 2001). Thus education – particularly maternal education – must be part of the health system.

Multisectoral action requires 'joined-up government,' a government in which the various departments communicate and coordinate their activities with one another in a complementary way. City governments in both the North and the South generally fall far short of that ideal. The leading initiative that takes an explicitly multisectoral approach to urban health is the beleaguered Healthy City Project (HCP), promoted by the World Health Organization (WHO). The HCP's main thrust is to induce all sectors at the city level (transport, industry, tourism and so forth) to consider the impact of their activities on health. It is essentially a comprehensive, 'place-based' strategy (the emphasis is intended to contrast with the traditional people-based, or even illness-based, approaches); and, indeed, many cities focus on such particular places as schools, markets and the like.

The HCP's objectives are as follows (WHO, 1995, p11):

1   Mobilize political action and community participation in preparing and implementing a municipal health plan.
2   Increase the awareness of health issues in urban development efforts by municipal and national authorities, including non-health ministries and agencies.
3   Enhance the capacity of municipal governments to manage urban problems and to form partnerships with communities and community based organizations (CBOs) in order to improve living conditions in poor communities.
4   Create a network of cities for information exchange and technology transfer.

The 'healthy city' concept thus recognizes the importance of decentralization in urban health, both in stressing the importance of the power of the municipality vis à vis the central government, as well as in recognizing the key role of communities and other units of urban organization smaller than the city itself. Unfortunately, though, implementing the HCP concept has continued to be a struggle in the Global South. An evaluation (Harpham et al., 2001) of HCPs in countries as diverse as Bangladesh, Egypt, Pakistan and Tanzania found only limited development of municipal health plans – one of the main components of the healthy city strategy. (HCPs in Europe have similar shortcomings.) Harpham et al. also documented only limited political commitment to HCPs by local governments and little influence by the projects on municipal policies. The reason may stem from the lack of 'buy-in' at the very start: most of the projects were instigated by donors instead of being requested by the municipalities.

Multilevel determinants

Health research used to focus on individual characteristics (biological, demographic, psychological and behavioural). But there is increasing evidence that place, or, in other words, community-level factors, has an independent effect on health. For example, a neighbourhood made up of high-density, low-quality dwellings built on former wetlands might well have adverse effects on the health of its residents, no matter what the mix of individual characteristics in that neighbourhood. Research in this realm also tackles factors such as social relationships and the role of institutions and services (whether or not they are related to health care), in addition to the physical and environmental factors I mentioned earlier.

This multilevel focus complements the multisectoral perspective by adding 'geography' to health, a concept that makes a good fit with conceptual frameworks already used by urban health researchers since the mid-1980s. The emphasis on place is also helpful in prompting planners to consider health as an 'added value' to projects that otherwise have no explicitly planned health benefits: the location of schools, food outlets, recreation facilities and the like. Neighbourhood studies that investigate such place-specific features as the physical environment of the neighbourhood, its services and social networks, its crime, its reputation and so forth garner much more attention and credibility than studies that merely aggregate individual characteristics to study the effects of place.

Just as community or neighbourhood determinants of health have become part of the health-research agenda in the past decade, the importance of communities *not* defined by neighbourhood has more recently come to the fore. In this research the emphasis is on communities defined by religion, race, age, sex, type of work and so forth – or, in other words, on people who have strong social ties but are not necessarily living in close proximity. This line of research, still in its earliest stages in the Global South, also examines the enduring linkages between rural and urban populations – a factor of great potential importance for understanding urban health. After all, each population seems likely to influence the health-related attitudes and behaviour of the other, and people are likely to travel from rural to urban regions (and vice versa) to access health services.

Despite such extended research priorities, one group of workers continues to suffer from neglect: informal sector workers. The informal sector is defined as the self-employed, those working for firms of fewer than five employees, those with no registration, owners of a family business with fewer than five employees, and family members working in a family business without a specified wage. About 70 per cent of employment in West African cities is informal (Mabogunje, 2007), and many such workers are exposed to distinctive, and substantial, health hazards when scavenging, balancing on precarious scaffolding, recycling batteries, weaving in and out of traffic, squinting in poorly lit rooms, and the like. Yet perhaps unsurprisingly, there remains a dearth of systematic information about occupational safety for these diverse workers. As Edmundo Werna, one of the founders of the International Labour Organization's (ILO) urban group, has said: 'What seems to be missing is a whole approach to "occupational safety and health in urban areas" as such' (personal communication, 2007).

Both the most recent scholarship and experience on the ground suggest that any parsimonious conceptual framework hoping to identify the determinants of urban health must at least take into account the role of poverty, the social and the physical environment, and the quality, accessibility and affordability of health services. I consider them in turn below.

Poverty

In the past decade, analyses of urban poverty have become increasingly sophisticated and the understanding of the phenomenon has substantially deepened. Both developments have implications for health-related action. The key finding is the *heterogeneity* of poverty, both in space and in time. First, the idea that the urban poor reside in slums as a homogeneous mass is increasingly being questioned. Mark Montgomery and Paul C. Hewett (Montgomery and Hewett, 2005), for example, found in their analysis of urban data from 85 demographic and health surveys (DHSs) that 'poor' neighbourhoods were not uniformly poor. One in ten neighbours of a poor household was relatively affluent (i.e. in the upper quartile of city-wide living standards, as measured by consumer durables and housing quality).

The presence of poor households in mixed urban neighbourhoods has both pros and cons for health care. On the one hand, as Montgomery and Hewett point out, mixed neighbourhoods may have more resources (e.g. social capital) for, say, providing health care volunteers, disseminating messages about healthy living or lobbying for community services. On the other hand, richer residents may siphon resources (e.g. grants for housing improvements or other environmental upgrades) away from their poorer neighbours. Furthermore, municipal authorities must target mixed as well as 'poor' communities if they are to reach all poor households, creating a need for even more resources. Targeting households or individuals (instead of entire communities) through means-testing is one way to avoid the costs of neighbourhood-wide relief, but only by paying the high price of the testing. That trade-off has come into sharp focus recently in Johannesburg, where city authorities are considering whether to extend social protections such as child health benefits to entire (spatially defined) areas of the city. The more blanket approach may simply be cheaper than making individual determinations of need.

As for temporal heterogeneity, a long-standing analyst of African urban poverty, Akin Mabogunje, notes that 'the urban poor should not be considered ... a homogeneous group but as a social underclass undergoing continuous differentiation' (Mabogunje, 2007, p3). He classifies the urban poor as either new poor (recently retrenched); borderline poor (unskilled, employed, but below the poverty line); or chronic poor (those who have lived at least five years in poverty, often as a result of the transition from rural to urban living rather than because of urban conditions per se). In addition, urban poverty is volatile: people move in and out of poverty, often while remaining in the same geographical location. How does health differ among these groups in different cities? Only systematic, longitudinal research can answer such questions, and, to date, very little investment has been made in such studies.

What is specifically urban about urban poverty and what does it mean for health? Judy Baker and Nina Shuler (2004, p3) neatly summarize the characteristics that are most pronounced and require specific analysis. For clarity, I have added (in italics) some of the potential health implications of each characteristic on their list.

- Commoditization (reliance on a cash economy); *poorer nutritional levels than those of the rural poor who practice subsistence farming, reduced care of infants and children because of travel to distant workplaces.*
- Overcrowded living conditions (slums); *infectious diseases, accidents.*
- Environmental hazard (stemming from density, hazardous location of settlements and exposure to multiple pollutants); *respiratory diseases, diarrhoea.*
- Social fragmentation (lack of community and interhousehold mechanisms for social security, relative to those in rural areas); *poor mental health.*
- Crime and violence; *homicide, injuries, poor mental health.*
- Traffic accidents; *injuries and death.*
- Natural disasters; *injuries, communicable diseases and death.*

Several metrics that arguably gauge the foregoing characteristics of urban poverty are in common use, but it is important to ask, 'To what degree are they useful for describing and monitoring urban health? Any such measure must take account of how both multisectoral and multilevel factors can affect health. But the typical measures of urban poverty involving money (ratio of income to consumption, degree to which basic needs are unmet, presence or absence of various asset indicators and the like) fail to capture the multisectoral determinants of urban health. In contrast, the most useful multisectoral measures are ones that incorporate social conditions, such as measures of people's vulnerability to the various physical, medical and social risks that affect health – though they are hard to operationalize.

Understanding the effects of multilevel factors – how various factors affect health at each of several levels – requires a great deal of disaggregation of data. Of course, breaking measures down by individual, household and neighbourhood levels carries its own methodological challenges. But once data are disaggregated and sorted, say, geographically, the power of maps, often overlooked by urban analysts, can be brought into play. Maps can show politicians at a glance how public health is faring in parts of their own election districts, which is often a powerful prompt for action.

Social environment

The term 'social' is often defined too broadly to be either empirically or operationally useful in identifying the determinants of urban health. Definitions often include labour, services, religion, arts – anything that people do. In this context, however, it is limited to the interactions between people: social connections and what emerges from them. It includes negative social interactions such as violence (both intimate-partner violence and street violence), as well as feelings of insecurity.

Knowledge about the level and kinds of social interactions in the city and their associations with health has increased enormously in the last few years. The new knowledge has come largely from research on the links between social capital (an individual's social connections and the support they provide) and health (particularly mental health), along with the review work of the Commission on the Social Determinants of Health of the WHO. Although most of this work has been done in the Global North (particularly in the United States, by scholars such as Robert J. Sampson and Ichiro Kawachi), similar studies in the South are beginning to reveal commonalities and important implications for action.

In reviewing the empirical research on social capital and its relation to health, it is important to distinguish such factors as structural social capital (the behavioural networks among people – 'what people do') from cognitive social capital (trust, sense of belonging – 'what people feel'). For example, studies have found that high cognitive social capital is good for mental health, whereas high structural social capital (at least among low-income women) is sometimes bad for mental health. The reason for the latter finding may be that such women must play too many roles at once (productive, reproductive and community). As quasi-political figures, they may also have relatively strong (and justified) fears of negative social evaluation.

Given the plentiful evidence linking social capital and health, what do we do with the evidence? An obvious answer is that we need social capital interventions and we need to assess the impact of those interventions on health. One intervention study in a low-income urban setting in the Global South was done in Cali, Colombia, a city with one of the highest homicide rates in the world. In 2000 the Cali municipal health department declared that the medical model was not effective in tackling this public-health problem; a social model was needed instead. Intriguingly, this decision was made before burgeoning international research demonstrated the strong relation between social capital and health. The populations most at risk were youth from ages 15 through 25, and the municipality realized that any intervention it performed would not be trusted by the disaffected youth. Accordingly, the city approached a long-standing health non-governmental organization (NGO), which intervened with one community and left a control community alone. (I omit the name of the NGO here because the organization prefers anonymity.) The intervention essentially strengthened the 'bonding social capital' (the interrelations among the youth) and the 'bridging social capital' (the relations between the youth and various institutions, such as churches). An evaluation showed that, in the intervention community, levels of social capital remained intact over a three-year follow-up period, whereas they plummeted in the control community. And although the mental health of the youth in the intervention community stayed the same, some violence-related indicators improved. The importance of this study was its demonstration that outside intervention can strengthen social capital, even in a particularly insecure population; over time, moreover, it can affect some health-related indicators (Harpham et al., 2004; Snoxell et al., 2006).

Physical environment

Although the understanding of the role of social determinants in health is increasing, there remain very few programmes like the Cali intervention that explicitly tackle social characteristics to improve health. Many efforts remain grounded in proven, traditional areas such as environmental health.

It is now well accepted that environmental health factors (water, sanitation and hygiene) cause roughly 90 per cent of all child diarrhoea and between 4 and 8 per cent of the overall burden of disease (WHO, 2002). There is no need for further research to demonstrate either the extent of environmental health hazards or the health impact they have in low-income urban areas. There is a need, however, for more research into *behavioural* factors related to environmental health: the feasibility of reducing exposure to pollutants from cooking fires, for instance. This behavioural research goes hand in hand with the need for more evaluations of the cost-effectiveness of interventions that aim at reducing environmental contamination.

For some physical phenomena such as housing, however, the health impacts are more difficult to measure, and so the evidence for a direct link between such phenomena and health is more patchy. Nevertheless, the evidence demonstrates that poor-quality housing conditions (cold, hot or damp housing, mould, pest infestation, lead paint and overcrowding) are associated with health problems such as respiratory infections, asthma, lead poisoning, tuberculosis and other infectious diseases and injuries in children. Access to affordable housing can also affect health, because paying a large proportion of one's income for housing can lead to increased stress (and poor mental health), as well as to less cash for other requisites to good health (such as the food needed for decent nutrition) (Flournoy and Yen, 2004).

Health services

Although I have emphasized that the health system is more than health services alone, the latter remain important in urban health planning. Health services vary in availability, ease of access (measured in part by distance from the population served and the convenience of opening times), appropriateness to the population served (How skilled are they? How effective? Are they culturally sensitive to the patient pool?) and affordability. Although by such measures urban populations generally fare better than their rural counterparts, the urban poor still often face appalling choices. For example, they can choose to rely on brusque and inadequately trained personnel at inadequately supplied public-sector facilities, or spend a high proportion of their income on private-sector care that may be no higher in quality on some of these dimensions. Moreover, a prevalent health-seeking behaviour in low-income urban areas is self-medicating with 'over-the-counter' drugs bought at retail outlets, and so those outlets, too, need to be viewed as part of urban 'health services'.

In 2007 Jishnu Das and Jeffrey Hammer studied the quality of care provided by private and public medical practitioners across seven rich and poor neighbourhoods in Delhi, India. Their findings included the following:

> The concentration of more competent providers in richer neighborhoods, combined with the low use of public hospitals[,] impl[ies] that the poor in the city are particularly underserved for several reasons:
>
> 1   Competence among the private-sector providers they visit is low.
> 2   They receive worse medical care both due to the direct effects of lower competence and the indirect effects of lower effort.
> 3   Lower effort in the public sector offsets the benefits of somewhat higher competence.
>
> The poor receive low-quality care from the private sector because doctors do not know much and low-quality care from the public sector because doctors do not do much. [That said,] in poor neighborhoods, despite the lower competence of providers in the private sector[,] the quality of advice that patients receive compares favorably to [what they receive from providers in] the public sector: Households in

poor areas are better off visiting less-qualified private providers than more-qualified public doctors.

Das and Hammer, 2007, p4

Das and Hammer concluded that it would be a waste of money to add yet more training to public-sector providers (where competence is often higher than it is in the private sector, but practice and effort are worse). Instead, they urged awareness campaigns to create better-informed users, in the hopes that such users would then demand higher quality care and become more resistant to 'providers' who offered inappropriate antibiotics, injections and the like. Of course, a 'health awareness campaign' is no magic bullet: any such campaign must cover a long list of topics, and mounting a successful campaign whose goal is to enable unempowered people to contradict and make demands from doctors traditionally perceived to be in positions of power would be particularly challenging.

Outcomes

The 'double burden'

One particularly useful concept for studying the health of the urban poor is the epidemiological, or health, transition: a shift seen in cities of the Global North in the past two centuries in which communicable or infectious diseases (malaria, TB, AIDS) have been replaced by non-communicable diseases (cancer, heart disease) as the main killer diseases. Unfortunately, in many cities of the Global South, the fight against communicable diseases is stalling because of persistent poverty and contaminating environments. Yet chronic health problems such as mental ill health, diabetes and heart disease are increasing. The result, particularly for the urban poor, is a 'double burden' of disabling or lethal diseases, both communicable and non-communicable (Montgomery et al., 2004, p287). Evidently, then, any development programme that aims to improve the health of the urban poor must take particular account of the double burden of infectious and chronic diseases.

The concept of a double burden can sometimes be applied even to a particular factor affecting health. Take nutrition. In some South African cities there is emerging evidence of malnutrition in children and, in the same household, obesity in adults (particularly in mothers). The coexistence of two patterns of ill health, which have traditionally been separated, is a particular challenge for any actions aimed at improving the health of the urban poor.

The 'urban penalty'

In the 1980s and early 1990s, much of the literature comparing health from region to region pointed out that, on average, health in rural areas was worse than it was in cities (Fotso, 2006, 2007). Most of this research focused on mortality rates among infants (less than a year old) and children (as old as 5), or on child nutritional status (malnutrition tends to be a good predictor of mortality). This research suggested that city dwellers have an 'urban advantage' in health, but more recently expert consensus has shifted to the discussion of an 'urban penalty'.

The term 'urban penalty' (*'le handicap urbain'*) was prompted by an analysis of mortality data in Europe during the Industrial Revolution. In that period, urban mortality rates, particularly from tuberculosis, were starkly higher than rural rates. In 1875, for instance, the infant mortality rate (IMR) in rural Prussia was 190 (per thousand), compared with 240 (per thousand) in urban areas (Vögele, 2000). Public-health measures, such as supplying clean water and sanitation, along with socio-economic changes, led to a decline in urban IMRs beginning around 1893. By 1905 or so, rural and urban IMRs were similar (Vögele, 2000, p170). In Britain, the politics of the public-health movement – constitutional change and political organization – was the critical factor behind similar changes.

What about an urban penalty in developing countries? W.T.S. Gould (Gould, 1998), analyzing DHS data from sub-Saharan Africa, stated that:

> Without urgent and substantial commitment to urban improvement – in the public domain and in the domestic domain, and by international donors and agencies as well as by national governments – there really might then be a serious threat of an 'urban penalty' emerging in Africa within the next decade, and particularly for the rapidly growing mass of the urban poor.
>
> Gould, 1998, p179

Does the evidence back up Gould's claim? Although there is little good data about trends, some evidence does suggest that the health of the urban poor in Africa may be deteriorating. Lawrence Haddad and his colleagues (Haddad *et al.*, 1999) have shown that both the number of underweight preschoolers and the proportion of urban preschoolers among all underweight children in Africa have been increasing in the past 15 years. Gould and Jean-Christophe Fotso (Fotso, 2007) also argue that the rural-urban gap has narrowed in the past few decades because urban health has declined. By contrast, however, another comparative analysis of DHS data (Montgomery *et al.*, 2004) found that urban children are taller and heavier than rural children, thereby showing that an urban advantage survives, at least in those measures of child health.

What is one to make of such apparently conflicting evidence? In recent years more refined analyses have been exploring how various health indicators may reflect urbanization in quite different ways. Consider the two indicators I mentioned earlier, child mortality and child malnutrition. In general, mortality can be closely related to the availability of health services, whereas malnutrition is directly linked to poverty (and the food shortages related to poverty) and to a poor physical environment. Marianne Fay and her colleagues (Fay *et al.*, 2005), using DHS data from 39 developing countries, found that the incidence of stunted growth (a measure of chronic child malnutrition) declines with urbanization (measured by the percentage of a nation's urban population), but that child mortality increases, even though there is better access to health care and its infrastructure in urban settings. The authors speculate that the public-health effects of crowding and pollution account for the latter finding, or it might be associated with more severe environmental risks and higher HIV/AIDS in urban areas (Dyson, 2003).

Unfortunately, the DHS data underlying such comparisons are aggregated data, and investigators have realized at least since the 1990s that the 'average' picture painted by such aggregated data can make only a crude comparison between urban and rural. What is needed instead is a more refined, disaggregated comparative picture – which could, for example, help call attention to the need to commit programs and funding to urban population health. Many of the samples in the available population-based data sets, however, are too small to be further disaggregated (for example, by socio-economic status within urban areas). Yet some recent studies have been able to control for wealth, and there the gross urban-rural differences can disappear. Globally speaking, the urban poor sometimes have both greater malnutrition and higher mortality rates than their rural counterparts (Montgomery *et al.*, 2004). Analyses within specific countries in Latin America (Brazil, Colombia, the Dominican Republic and Paraguay) find a similar pattern: infant and child mortality are higher there among the urban poor than they are among the rural poor. Furthermore, the percentage of chronic child malnutrition is higher among the urban poor than the rural poor in Colombia, Nicaragua and Paraguay (Bitran *et al.*, 2005). In the end, however, the evidence relevant to this debate is still contradictory; from that evidence, plus case studies suggesting deteriorating health conditions among slum dwellers, Montgomery and his colleagues conclude that 'we cannot draw strong conclusions about trends in urban health advantage' (Montgomery *et al.*, 2004, p282).

What about mental health? Do the poor enjoy an urban advantage or suffer an urban penalty, compared with their rural counterparts? Very few good, direct comparisons exist, partly because the only samples available to many studies are self-selected users of health services. One exception is a recent study in South Africa, which managed to investigate random samples from an entire population. The study showed that common mental disorders (depression and anxiety) were significantly more prevalent in peri-urban (edge of city) populations (35 per cent) than they were in a rural poor population (27 per cent). The risk factors also differed. In the peri-urban populations, being female, unemployed or a substance abuser were key risks, whereas in the rural population the main risk factors were poverty and lack of education (unpublished data from the University of Cape Town).

Urban-rural migrants

Migration is a central fact of life in many developing countries, particularly from rural to urban environments – though the importance of migration within or between cities should not be underestimated. And one might expect migration to have major effects on health – though whether the net effect is positive or negative depends on a complex interaction of several possible factors. According to the selectivity hypothesis, movers are different from the people they leave behind – indeed, they may have less in common with the people they leave, in terms of attitudes and behaviours that affect health, than with their new urban neighbours. To the extent that this effect is dominant, perhaps the health of movers should improve, because their new social connections would be stronger, and because the traditional pressures from kin back home would be weaker than they would be for people who were, say, uprooted against their will.

In contrast, the disruption hypothesis focuses on the move itself, the possible ruptures in the mover's social connections, the (perhaps temporary) consequences of being unfamiliar with the new health care system and the many extra stresses and discontinuities of major shifts in one's living environment. If these issues are primary, the health of movers would probably deteriorate. Finally, the adaptation hypothesis focuses on how people may change their behaviours and attitudes after they move, to fit in to their new community. There is plenty of empirical evidence that demonstrates that such change is common (Brockerhoff, 1995; Montgomery et al., 2004). So if adaptation is the central aspect of the mover's experience, its effect on health should depend on whether the new community already enjoys an urban advantage or suffers an urban penalty. In other words, movers should be subject to the same health determinants as their new neighbours are.

What about the effects of rural-urban migration on mental health? One might guess that the stresses of moving and rupturing long-time social networks would be more likely to affect mental than physical health. One study examined the demographics of a northern suburb of Bangkok, Thailand, whose population is growing at the exceptionally high rate of 5 per cent per year. In a survey of 1,000 people aged 16 to 24, the investigators found that nearly half of them were migrants from rural areas. Disorders related to alcohol were 30 per cent more prevalent among the migrants than among non-migrants, but the only migrants who differed from non-migrants in substance-abuse rates were the oldest cohort of men (Jirapramukpitak et al., 2007). The study did not determine the reason for the male-female discrepancy in drug use, but perhaps men generally have less effective strategies than women do for coping with stress (one coping strategy that would clearly be 'less effective' is the use of drugs). Or perhaps the men were less willing (or less able) than the women were to take advantage of resources that might have helped them cope – though in the study there were no gender differences between the migrants and the non-migrants in the level of social support they received from their closest friend or confidant.

By the same token, the study did not determine why the female migrants seem to have been protected from drug use. The authors of the study speculate that the Thai female migrants were more dutiful than their male counterparts; women come to Bangkok with a responsibility to send money that can support their parents and children back home. But, as with all cross-sectional studies, reverse causality cannot be excluded: the oldest male migrants may have used drugs before they migrated, and their drug use may have contributed to their migration. More research is urgently needed to determine the effects of rural-urban migration on mental health, particularly longitudinal research that can rule out reverse causality.

Inequalities in the city

Although migration can be a risk factor for health, particularly mental health, studies that have controlled for wealth show that poverty as a risk factor trumps migration. In other words, it is being a *poor* migrant in the city that is particularly risky to health.

Cities of the Global South have some of the most striking inequalities in the world: slums that are cheek by jowl with areas of affluence. Some evidence indicates that such wealth inequalities themselves are bad for health. Richard Wilkinson's work (Wilkinson, 1992), based on data sets from the Global North, suggests that inequalities and the associated *relative* deprivation can sometimes be a better predictor of a country's health than *absolute* wealth levels. Although Wilkinson's analysis is still being debated (see, for instance, Mackenbach, 2002), it has usefully drawn attention to issues of equity, resentment, the practice of 'kicking down' (in which poor groups 'punish' others who are even poorer) and psychological health in Northern cities. For example, intriguing research is emerging on the link between perceived inequalities, lack of respect and violence among youth in US cities. In one study that demonstrates some of these links (Leary *et al.*, 2005), the authors find the results compelling enough to call for interventions that can help youths handle disrespect without resorting to violence. Much of the debate about youth violence in Southern cities links it to absolute poverty. Yet the role of relative poverty in Southern cities, which exhibit the greatest inequalities, has been virtually ignored.

Health inequalities in cities have been demonstrated by measures such as infant-mortality rates, which can be as much as four times higher among the urban poor than they are among the rest of the urban population. The biggest health differentials in the world occur in Latin America, and within Latin America those differentials are consistently greatest in Brazil and Peru (Bitran *et al.*, 2005). Thus even if there is no urban penalty for the poor, the health differentials alone make a persuasive reason for prioritizing action for the urban poor.

Conclusions

A shift in urban health and current challenges

In recent decades much has been learned about the complexities of urban health in the Global South, and a new model with shifts in emphasis and in intervention tactics has emerged. These shifts are summarized in Table 3.1; they include changes in disciplinary interest, in focus populations and in kinds of programmes.

To expand on just a few of these points, the scientific studies of the past few decades have simply changed the terms of the debate about urban health. Experts have gradually recognized that the urban poor can be as vulnerable to health risks as their rural counterparts – though the pattern of health determinants and illness outcomes differs from group to group. Fewer gross, undifferentiated comparisons are made between rural and urban populations. Health inequalities within cities are highlighted. There is a consensus that establishing and maintaining a health system encompasses much more than merely providing health services. In summary, the current picture of urban health is more sophisticated and more evidence-based, with specific implications for appropriate actions.

These actions must address an array of challenges along multiple dimensions:

Financial

A typical impoverished African country spends less than US$5 per person per year on public-sector health (Sachs, 2004). Such deprivation makes it imperative to ruthlessly prioritize expenditures and, at the same time, to lobby for the health system to get a greater allocation of the national budget. The financial input of other sectors – education, energy, housing, social welfare and the like – must be harnessed to improve health. Although providers apart from the public sector, such as private organizations and NGOs, are there to fill the gap, advocates must recognize that they have their own agendas, and their contributions are not always either the most appropriate to the situation or even of the highest quality. Equally important to remember

Table 3.1 Old and new models of urban health

	Old	New
Causation/ determinants	Proximate determinants (e.g. exposure to infections), physical environment	Distal and proximate determinants, multiple causation, social and economic determinants
Range of problems	Infectious diseases, malnutrition	Acute and chronic (particularly mental health) 're-emerging' problems (e.g. tuberculosis, malaria), violence, 'lifestyle' diseases
Population group emphasis	The 'urban poor', 'rural-urban comparisons', 'vulnerable groups'	Rural-urban interactions. City as a whole and intra-urban differentials, within- and between-household differences
Provider group emphasis	Public-sector focus, role of hospital, referral system	Pluralism of providers including government, municipal, district, private, traditional, retail sector, self-treatment
Disciplinary emphasis	Epidemiology, public health	Geography of health, epidemiology, public health, social sciences
Common concepts	Urban poor as 'reservoir of infection' and suffering 'worst of both worlds'	Inequity, social capital, burden of disease, sustainable livelihoods
Management approach	Through Ministries of Health	Decentralization, health sector reform, governance
Intervention examples	Vertical (e.g. urban expanded programme on immunization slum improvement projects)	Healthy City Projects, multisectoral approaches, urban district health team strengthening, contracting out services to array of providers

Source: Harpham and Molyneux, 2001.

in budget debates is that comparing the percentage of the government health budget going to urban areas with the percentage going to rural areas can be highly misleading. Indeed, the former is almost always higher than the latter, but the numbers are skewed because tertiary level (specialized care available in hospitals as opposed to primary health clinics) expenditures, as opposed to primary care, still dominate many country health budgets, and hospitals are almost always located in urban areas. Primary health care in cities could well be starved for funding, even though the overall urban health care budget, compared with the budget for rural health care, looked robust.

What about financial constraints at the individual level? Are there practical ways for the poor to help themselves. One obvious answer is insurance, which in theory spreads the cost of individual misfortune among the community. But the costs of health insurance and social insurance also remain out of reach for most of the urban poor. Even in Latin America, where the development of health insurance is relatively advanced, less than 20 per cent of the urban poor have access to some kind of insurance (Fay, 2005). There are increasingly sophisticated health insurance and social insurance schemes, but they need to become pro-poor if this vulnerable group is to be protected. For example, insurance coverage for the most vulnerable and their health problems must be provided at an affordable cost.

Political

A key political challenge to urban health development is the general weakness of municipal structures in the Global South. Administrative responsibility for health in a city often falls outside the purview of local government and rests instead with provincial- or federal-(state-)level government. For example, as I suggested earlier, services such as hospitals often come under central authority as opposed to local authority. In some countries, such as Brazil, when a political party gains power in a province, it often loses power in the province's leading city. And each time a new party comes to power it wants to sweep away the programmes and policies of the preceding one. Thus an entire political context can change with every election, with the result that HCPs in Brazil have frequently suffered discontinuities in focus and shifts in their objectives.

Another particular problem for HCPs is the lack of any administrative body powerful enough to coordinate health-related activities across sectors. Although the mayor's office in many countries officially serves as the main office of an HCP, responsibility for its activities is usually delegated to the health services department of the local government – rarely a player strong enough to mobilize other sectors.

Social

Getting key people in the health world to recognize the importance of the 'social' in public health is a top priority. Another challenge, as I noted earlier, is to convince the leaders of other kinds of (non-health) social interventions that their projects can incorporate the 'added value' of a positive health impact for virtually no extra cost. Unfortunately, the potential benefits of such an effort are not yet widely recognized in the Global South.

As for the challenges of social mobilization, small-scale lobbying and advocacy action have been successful for decades – by health-related urban CBOs and NGOs (particularly in Asia and Latin America). But there are few examples of such enterprises being successfully scaled up.

Scientific

Improving urban health doesn't require much high-tech science. The priorities are to roll out such basic technologies as electricity (particularly for domestic fuel use), hygienic sanitation, insecticide-treated bed nets and an adequate supply of essential drugs at primary health facilities. Extending such 'simple' technologies to previously excluded populations (e.g. squatter settlements) would reduce the burden of such common killers as diarrhoea and malaria. But effecting such changes among the poor demands political will, a health budget allocation and education campaigns to help ensure that new 'technology' is incorporated in daily behaviours (for example, see Gordon McGranahan's discussions of hand washing in Chapter 2).

Methodological

Health research on low-income urban populations is fraught with potential difficulties: lack of sampling lists (prompting the need to map each dwelling – a laborious and expensive task); high rates of residential mobility (making longitudinal studies a nightmare); the reluctance of subjects to talk to 'authorities' (unregistered rural-urban or urban-urban migrants in China and Vietnam, for instance, are highly suspicious of anyone with a clipboard); the dependence of subjects on a cash economy and their consequent expectation of cash incentives for participating in research; the need for field researchers to visit dwellings during non-working hours, and to tolerate a degree of physical insecurity; the difficulty of defining a 'community' (see later); and the high numbers of respondents with no fixed abode (pavement dwellers, street children, informal traders). All these potential factors must be taken into account when designing population health research in low-income urban areas.

Need for multilevel research

The exciting research that is being done mainly in US cities needs replicating in the Global South. Two leading authorities, Rebecca Flournoy and Irene Yen, succinctly list some of the benefits and difficulties of investigating how neighbourhoods affect health.

> More recently, researchers have used multilevel methods to look at the health of neighborhoods after controlling for the health and other characteristics of individuals. Researchers can investigate the effects of place on health through compositional factors (the characteristics of people in particular places), contextual factors (opportunity structures in the local environment such as access to food and transportation resources) and collective factors (socio-cultural and historical features of neighborhoods). Methodological challenges for researchers wishing to study the effects of place on health include accurately

defining neighborhood boundaries; determining the most appropriate level of geography; determining which characteristics of the social
and physical environment are most relevant for health; measuring
neighborhood characteristics; and determining the relative influence
of neighborhood and individual characteristics.

Flournoy and Yen, 2004, p70

The definition of community is particularly challenging in low-income
urban settings. It is a prominent issue, for instance, in research on social
capital, where the term must be defined in a standardized way that is also
meaningful to the respondents. Most studies settle on a geographical area of
reference, even though the area might be vaguely stated (e.g. 'around here').
But there is also a growing interest in the social capital of non-spatial communities, such as work, school, and religious and family groups. The definition of these communities is less problematic, since questions can be phrased
about 'the people you work with', 'people you go to school with' and the like.

When studying a spatial community the main decision is whether to use an
officially recognized area, such as an electoral ward or a post code area, or
to explore respondents' constructions of their community qualitatively, then
apply the most meaningful definition in the quantitative survey. Here, the practice of geographers in the 1970s might be usefully resurrected: residents are
asked to draw a map of their 'community' and mark its salient points on the
map. Although the resulting 'mental maps' will inevitably vary from person to
person, they may also feature commonalities that enable investigators to study
an area more meaningful to the residents than some official designation.

The problem of defining community varies by context. For example, the
word 'community' is almost never used by elderly respondents in the UK
(Blaxter and Poland, 2002). In Vietnam, however, where the 'commune' is
a resilient and highly meaningful geographical construct, no such problems
were encountered (Tuan *et al.*, 2005).

Need for intervention research

Although the number of studies describing 'the problem' is growing, there is
a dearth of 'before and after' studies that yield data about the effectiveness
of interventions designed to improve or protect the health of the urban poor.
One of the main constraints is that projects or programmes rarely collect
appropriate (if any) baseline data before the intervention begins.

Need for longitudinal research

Linked to the need for intervention research is the need for longitudinal
research on the causal relations between risk factors in the urban environment and health outcomes. Such prospective, time-series research is expensive. The knowledge base would improve dramatically, however, if funding

agencies declined to support yet more short-term cross-sectional studies and allocated their funds instead to a few, robust, large longitudinal studies. Such studies could be enormously beneficial because they could track both quantitative and qualitative elements.

Moving from vulnerability to resilience

In the past decades, studies of urban health have begun with the concept of ill health. (This negative condition is often called vulnerability, but this term should not be used interchangeably with 'ill health'. After all, vulnerability is a potentiality, whereas ill health is a current condition. Of course, there is a relation: ill health clearly makes one vulnerable to other problems.) That approach has led to a much better understanding of the health problems of the urban poor, as well as how economic, social, environmental and health service conditions affect their health.

But focusing solely on problems or weaknesses gives only a limited set of guidelines for taking positive action. To take an entirely different perspective on urban health, why are some individuals, households or groups better able to cope with their conditions, and, consequently, to enjoy better health? *What* can we strengthen among low-income urban populations to protect and promote their health, and *how* can we strengthen it? Answering those questions requires information about resilience – adaptive capacity – not vulnerability: the positive rather than the negative. Is resilience merely the reciprocal of vulnerability: that is, the resilient have high scores in the same variables for which the vulnerable have low scores? Or does it differ from vulnerability in several other significant ways? (Again, addressing this question requires carefully defining vulnerability and identifying its elements.) Perhaps the investigative resources spent in exploring this paradigm shift will be more than repaid in improvements to the health of the urban poor in the next decades.

Notes

1   An earlier version of this paper appeared in the journal *Health and Place* (Harpham, 2008).
2   Declaration of Alma-Ata, International Conference on Primary Health Care, Alma-Ata, USSR, 6–12 September, 1978, http://www.who.int/hpr/NPH/docs/declaration_almaata.pdf

References

Baker, J. and Schuler, N. (2004) 'Analyzing urban poverty: a summary of methods and approaches', Policy Research Working Paper 3399, World Bank, Washington, DC.

Bitran, R., Giedion, U., Valenzuela, R. and Monkkonen, P. (2005) 'Keeping health in an urban environment: public health challenges for the urban poor', in M. Fay (ed.) *The Urban Poor in Latin America*, World Bank, Washington, DC, pp179–195

Blaxter, M. and Poland, F. (2002) 'Moving beyond the survey in exploring social capital', in C. Swann and A. Morgan (eds) *Social Capital for Health: Insights from Qualitative Research*, Health Development Agency, London

Brockerhoff, M. (1995) 'Child survival in big cities: the disadvantages of migrants', *Social Science & Medicine*, vol 40, pp1371–1383

CSDH (Commission on Social Determinants of Health) (2008) *Closing the Gap in a Generation: Health Equity through Action on the Social Determinants of Health*. Final Report of the Commission on Social Determinants of Health, World Health Organization, Geneva

Das, J. and Hammer, J. (2007) 'Money for nothing: the dire straits of medical practice in Delhi, India', *Journal of Development Economics*, vol 83, pp1–36

Dyson, T. (2003) 'HIV/AIDS and urbanization', *Population and Development Review*, vol 29, pp427–442

Fay, M. (ed.) (2005) *The Urban Poor in Latin America*, World Bank, Washington, DC

Fay, M., Leipziger, D., Wodon, Q. and Yepes, T. (2005) 'Achieving child health related Millennium Development Goals: the role of infrastructure', *World Development*, vol 33, pp1267–1284

Flournoy, R. and Yen, I. (2004) *The Influence of Community Factors on Health*, Policy Link, Oakland, CA

Fotso, J.C. (2006) 'Child health inequities in developing countries: differences across urban and rural areas', *International Journal for Equity in Health*, vol 5, p9

Fotso, J.C. (2007) 'Urban-rural differentials in child malnutrition: trends and socio-economic correlates in sub-Saharan Africa', *Health and Place*, vol 13, pp205–223.

Gould, W.T. (1998) 'African mortality and the new "urban penalty"', *Health and Place*, vol 4, no 2, pp171–81

Haddad, L., Ruel, M. and Garrett, J. (1999) 'Are urban poverty and under-nutrition growing?', *World Development*, vol 27, no 11, pp1891–1904

Harpham, T. (2008) 'Urban health in developing countries: what do we know and where do we go? *Health and Place*, vol 15, pp107–116

Harpham, T. and Molyneux, C. (2001) 'Urban health in developing countries: A review', *Progress in Development Studies*, vol 1, no 2, pp113–137

Harpham, T., Burton, S. and Blue, I. (2001) 'Healthy city projects in developing countries: the first evaluation', *Health Promotion International*, vol 16, no 2, pp111–125

Harpham, T., Grant, E. and Rodriguez, C. (2004) 'Mental health and social capital in Cali, Colombia', *Social Science and Medicine*, vol 58, no 11, pp2267–2278

Jalan, J. and Ravallion, M. (2001) 'Does piped water reduce diarrhea for children in rural India?', Policy Research Working Paper No. 2664, World Bank, Washington, DC

Jirapramukpitak, T., Prince, M. and Harpham, T. (2007) 'Rural-urban migration and substance use in the young Thai population', unpublished manuscript

Leary, J.D., Brennan, E.M. and Briggs, H.E. (2005) 'The African American adolescent respect scale: a measure of a pro-social attitude', *Research on Social Work Practice*, vol 15, no 6, pp462–469

Mabogunje, A. (2007) 'Global urban poverty research agenda: the African case', *Woodrow Wilson Comparative Urban Studies Project*, vol 10, pp1–19

Mackenbach, J. (2002) 'Evidence favouring a negative correlation between income inequality and life expectancy has disappeared', *British Medical Journal*, vol 324, pp1–2

Montgomery, M. and Hewett, P. (2005) 'Urban poverty and health in developing countries: household and neighborhood effects', *Demography*, vol 42, no 3, pp397–425

Montgomery, M., Stren, R., Cohen, B. and Reed, H. (eds) (2004) *Cities Transformed: Demographic Change and Its Implications in the Developing World*, National Academies Press, Washington, DC

Sachs, J. (2004) 'Health in the developing world', *World Health Organisation Bulletin*, vol 82, pp947–952

Snoxell, S., Harpham, T., Grant, E. and Rodriguez, C. (2006) 'Social capital interventions: a case study from Cali, Colombia', *Canadian Journal of Development Studies*, vol 27, no 1, pp65–81

Tuan, T., Harpham, T., Huong, N.T., DeSilva, M., Huong, V.T.T., Long, T.T., Van Ha, N.T. and Dewitt, D. (2005) 'Validity of a social capital measurement tool in Vietnam', *Asian Journal of Social Science*, vol 33, no 2, pp208–222

Vögele, J. (2000) 'Urbanization and the urban mortality change in Imperial Germany', *Health and Place*, vol 6, no 1, pp41–55

WHO (World Health Organization) (1995) *Building a Healthy City: A Practitioner's Guide*, WHO, Geneva

WHO (2002) *The World Health Report 2002 – Reducing Risks, Promoting Healthy Life*, WHO, Geneva

Wilkinson, R. (1992) 'Income distribution and life expectancy', *British Medical Journal*, vol 304, pp165–168

Chapter 4

Healthy urban governance and population health

Participatory budgeting in Belo Horizonte, Brazil

David Vlahov and Waleska T. Caiaffa

Introduction

In 2007, for the first time in history, more than half of the world's people were living in urban areas (United Nations, 2005). Projections suggest that the urban proportion of the global population will continue to increase, becoming nearly two-thirds by 2030. Most of this growth will occur in the less wealthy nations, and much of that will be concentrated in areas of urban poverty: in slums (USAID, 2004). Currently a billion of the earth's people live in slums, and that number is expected to double by 2030 and reach three billion by 2050 if current trends continue (United Nations Human Settlements Programme, 2003).

A substantial literature documents the relatively poor health associated with areas of concentrated disadvantage, compared with health in other areas within the same urban settings or within broader regions of the same country. Such health inequity is the result of differences in the physical environment (water quality, water-delivery systems, sanitation systems, housing, land tenure, provision of electricity and the like), as well as social factors (social exclusion or discrimination, poverty, income inequality and gender roles, among other factors, but also access to participatory government, education and employment opportunities) (Vlahov *et al.*, 2007; Ompad *et al.*, 2007). Place of residence can also affect health: living near natural or man-made disasters or close to other local environmental threats – in housing built on landfills, for instance – can obviously have negative health effects. Social capital, including levels of trust and the density and strength of social networks, plays another important role in determining health (Kawachi, 1999).

With so many factors imposing health inequity on the poor, few would disagree that improving health in urban areas – and particularly health in urban slums – is one of the greatest challenges of the twenty-first century. Indeed, a number of United Nations Millennium Development Goals (MDGs) address many of these factors directly: among the MDGs are reducing poverty and hunger, empowering women, ensuring environmental sustainability and developing basic and technologically advanced utilities. By so committing its resources, the UN has set the agenda for actions and interventions aimed at improving the lives of millions of slum dwellers (UN-Habitat, 2010a).

Increasingly, the development community has also recognized that a critical factor in public health is governance: government's ability both to assume its responsibilities as a steward of public goods and to work collaboratively with other sectors of society. Good governance is essential to formulating policies and implementing programmes that make it possible for a country's people to be as healthy as they can be.

Throughout the world the strategy and design for effecting better governance has varied widely. In some countries, broad, structural interventions have been put in place, which aim to decentralize power and resources so as to improve capabilities at the municipal level, and in some cases the community level. In other countries, more targeted efforts are attempting to improve systems or outcomes in a certain neighborhood or sector: increasing people's access to water and sanitation services, say, or controlling the spread of communicable diseases. These interventions in governance may come from within or without: grassroots activists or other actors within the country or municipality (such as local or central governments) can play the leadership role, or actors such as a non-governmental organization (NGO) or the UN may become a major agent of change. But whatever their origins, the efforts of single actors seldom scale up; instead, they are generally limited to their area of influence.

As the complexity and interrelated nature of the problems and barriers faced by the poor in the developing world have become better recognized, the development community has increasingly embraced and implemented interventions that cut across many sectors at once: education, water distribution, food, sanitation and so forth. In addition, it has become clear that slum dwellers and other vulnerable groups must take part both in designing and implementing programmes if they are to be sustainable. Thus participatory frameworks and community-driven development have become strong trends both in Latin America and beyond.

But given multisectoral involvement and community-driven development, which programmes are likely to be most effective in improving the plight of the poor? One good place to begin answering this question is to identify existing programmes that not only exemplify 'best practices', but that are also – unlike most interventions – able to 'scale,' at least in the sense that they can serve as models for development in other cities and regions. To catalogue best practices, the Together Foundation and UN-Habitat have been collecting solutions to urban problems that various communities around the world have developed and reported on since mid-1995. The information is now available in an online database that is searchable by region, country, ecosystem, area of impact (solid-waste disposal, provision of housing, policies toward energy, poverty reduction and the like), potential partners and keywords.[1] This wealth of information makes it possible for decision-makers at the local level, who know what works best in their own communities, to consider the options.

One item missing from the database, however, is a category titled 'urban health.' That limitation is unfortunate because it has allowed several projects that have made significant contributions to the quality of life in cities to go largely unreported, at least beyond their regions of immediate impact. Thus, without duplicating the impressive work of the Together Foundation and UN-Habitat, we want to expand the scope of that work by highlighting two intriguing examples of best practices for improving urban health that have emerged from the city of Belo Horizonte, Brazil. They are, first, the use of 'participatory budgeting' and, second, the development of localized 'family health centers' and 'physical academies'.

Part of the reason for taking such a close look at one city is to explore how the two programmes built upon one another, became interconnected and addressed an overlapping range of activities that interact to create a cohesive approach to urban health. Furthermore, the experiences in Belo Horizonte make an informative case study of what can happen in a city that takes a proactive approach to public health. Finally, the programmes in Belo Horizonte deal with urban features that, though not unique to Latin American cities, typify the challenges to improving urban health on the continent.

One of the main challenges in Latin America is the growth of mid-size cities such as Belo Horizonte; El Alto, Bolivia; Manaus, Brazil; Temuco, Chile; and on and on. Such cities are often growing even faster than megacities are, and the former also have fewer resources to cope with their growing pains. Providing clean water, sanitation, adequate housing and accessible health care to existing residents as well as to new migrants poses a substantial challenge to municipal and public health officials (Linden, 1996). A second and related problem in Latin America is the growth of peri-urban settlements known as 'favelas' in Brazil, 'pueblos jovenes' in Peru or 'ranchos' in Venezuela. In Mexico City almost half the population lives in such spontaneous settlements, where sanitation, education, employment, health services and links to the formal urban economy are often precarious (Tabibzadeh and Liisberg, 1997).

Belo Horizonte, Latin America and best practices for urban health

Brazil's 'City of Beautiful Horizon' is situated in the southeastern part of the country, in the state of Minas Gerais, and the population of the metropolitan area has grown from 4.1 million people in 2002 to more than 5 million in the metropolitan area and 2.4 million in the city today. The city extends across some 330 square kilometres, giving it a population density of nearly

7,300 per square kilometre. On the Human Development Index (HDI) Belo Horizonte scores 0.839, placing it higher than the average for Brazil overall (0.80). GDP per capita is US$6,050, but what that average figure does not reveal is that Belo Horizonte has the second worst income inequality among Brazil's 12 largest cities and ranks second in the number of favelas within the city (another clear indicator of urban poverty) (Caiaffa *et al.*, 2005). The economy is divided mainly between commerce and services (about 80 percent) and industry (20 percent) (Caiaffa *et al.*, 2005). As its population has grown, the city's age profile has also changed: between 1970 and 2000 the proportion of the population 15 years old or older increased by nearly a quarter, from 61.6 percent to 75.7 percent. This increase in the proportion of young people mandates renewed focus on family planning, education and jobs, as well as on crime prevention.

Belo Horizonte's two innovative public health programmes were spurred in part by the city's income inequality, as well as by these changing demographics. The first programme, participatory budgeting, is one part of an even more comprehensive participatory master plan for a city. The first attempt to implement such a master plan started more than 20 years ago, in Porto Alegre, Brazil, and by now some 250 participatory master plan programmes are in place throughout the world (though primarily in Latin America and particularly in Brazil) (Cabannes, 2004). Although the description of participatory budgeting has said little about the detailed benefits it can bring to public health, adopting it to effect urban health reform has theoretical advantages at several levels. Perhaps its most important advantage is that it makes it natural to deal with social determinants as well as physical factors – which studies have shown, as we noted earlier, are clearly linked to health (Vlahov *et al.*, 2007).

Belo Horizonte's second programme aims to incorporate both family health centers and physical academies within each of the discrete areas known as planning units of the city. This approach is not unique to Belo Horizonte. But a field description of how it has worked and, more specifically, how it has interacted with the participatory-budgeting process, provides a concrete example of what can be accomplished by a programme specifically designed to address the health needs of the most disadvantaged portion of the urban population.

Participatory budgeting

Participatory budgeting can be defined as any kind of political system that allows citizens direct or indirect knowledge of and influence over the annual budget priorities of their own municipality. Although there is no identified 'ideal' model of participatory budgeting, the vanguard status of the Porto Alegre version of the process (started in 1989) and its apparent success have contributed to its role as the international standard. Of course, the Porto

Alegre process itself has continued to evolve into what is now considered a model of participatory governance.

Participatory budgeting in Belo Horizonte began in 1993 as a municipal initiative by the then newly elected social democratic government. A first Directive Plan for the city was published in 1996; the plan to develop a governance structure and system was put together through municipal offices. This plan established procedural guidelines that, among other things, specify procedures for identifying and implementing interventions and projects deemed both necessary and feasible. An elected set of citizen delegates to a committee known as the COMFORÇA, intended to give citizens a voice at the municipal level in the process, assists in monitoring plan activities periodically. At the overall municipal level a management board made up of representatives from all city departments and agencies that are affected by participatory budgeting coordinates municipal activities that are related to the participatory-budgeting process. Belo Horizonte is divided into nine administrative regions of about 250,000 people each, 41 subregions, 81 planning units and 465 discrete neighborhoods and vilas.[2] The planning units set priorities according to a process coordinated by the administrative region to which they belong, and citizens apply for funds for specific projects that fit the criteria set by their administrative region.

The planning process starts with the meeting of an intersectoral, municipal government committee, which creates and updates the master plan for the city (the so-called *Plano Plurianual de Ação Governamental*, or PPAG). Representatives from five sectors – urban policy, urban planning, office for disadvantaged populations (social exclusion), environment and sanitation – meet to discuss and develop the overall city blueprint and establish citywide criteria for new projects (for example, a road in one participatory-budget district must connect with roads outside the district). Yet, though that intersectoral committee establishes the municipal master plan, the participatory-budgeting process sets funding priorities for projects. The procedures for the participatory-budgeting process leading to a successfully funded project are described in Box 4.1.

Funds allocated to the total participatory budget are divided among the nine administrative regions according to an established formula. Fifty percent of the total is simply divided equally among the nine regions. This ensures that some less-populated regions with higher-than-average incomes, but also with slums, receive at least some project funding. The other 50 percent of the participatory budget is allocated according to a score developed by the municipal government, based on the population and the so-called Urban Quality Life Index (UQLI) of each of the 81 planning units in Belo Horizonte (a planning unit is made up of a series of homogenous contiguous neighborhoods). The UQLI combines measures of several variables (levels of access to clean water and effective sanitation, use of social assistance, sporting and cultural opportunities, infant mortality, premature birth rate,

Box 4.1 Participatory budgeting: How a proposal becomes a funded project in Belo Horizonte

The life of a new project begins with a petition signed by at least 10 people. Once petitioned, a proposal for the project is reviewed at the overall municipal level for consistency with the PPAG that was previously approved by an intersectoral, municipal-government committee. A proposal inconsistent with the PPAG is rejected, but a proposal that survives PPAG review proceeds to an assembly organized within one of the 41 subregions of Belo Horizonte relevant to the project.

Any citizen of the subregion can participate in the assembly. Those who attend the assembly vote to 'pre-select' as many as 15 projects for consideration by a central planning council. Thus as many as 41 times 15, or more that 600 projects, can be pre-selected for the citywide council to consider. Most of them involve construction of roads, schools, housing, health centers and so forth.

The assembly also chooses between 100 and 200 citizens (depending on the number in attendance) as delegates to the next step of the process. Those delegates then select 20 percent of their number (that is, between 20 and 40 citizen delegates) to become members of the COMFORÇA. Citizen representatives thereby take part in the selection and review of each proposed project, the auditing of each step in the selection process and the tracking of its progress.

Out of all the preselected projects within each of the nine administrative regions of the city (on average about one-ninth of 600, or 67, of them), 14 survive the next round of cuts. Delegates from the COMFORÇA then make site visits to the proposed site of each of the 14 times 9, or 126, finalist projects (a process known as the 'priority caravan'). The finalists are discussed once again in the regional assemblies, with crucial input from neighborhood coalitions, which can play a critical role in getting projects successfully through the process. Finally, the entire list of possible projects is put to a vote in a general election.

Votes for projects are weighted in favor of delegates from the more vulnerable subregions of Belo Horizonte. For example, in the Barreiro administrative region slum-dwellers account for 9.9 percent of the population, whereas in Centro-Sul they make up 14.9 percent. The vote-weighting gives each delegate from Barreiro 1.3 votes, whereas each delegate from Centro-Sul gets 1.4 votes. This weighting advantage can swing (and has swung) decisions in favor of Centro-Sul, but only if voter turnout there is high enough to overcome the turnout in Barreiro or another competing administrative region.

access to health care and the like) into a simple, overall indicator of community vulnerability. The (population plus UQLI) scores of each planning unit within an administrative region are finally combined into a total score for each region.

The participatory-budgeting process is weighted not only in the voting by the COMFORÇA for specific projects (see Box 4.1) and among the various administrative regions by population and UQLI scores, but also, more generally, toward projects that set up services and establish infrastructure for the most vulnerable populations. In practice, that has meant that about 60 percent of the funded projects are focused solely on those vulnerable populations. At the same time, to ensure middle- and upper-class involvement, at least 30 percent of the budget is reserved for projects that benefit all citizens (including vulnerable populations). In practice, about 40 percent of the funded projects fit the latter category.

The impact of participatory budgeting has been both deep and wide. In 2006, 90 percent of the population lived within 1,000 meters of a project funded through participatory budgeting. Since its inception, the process has accounted for $300 million committed to various projects, some 3 percent of the annual municipal budget. (The figure, however, is somewhat misleading: it covers only the material costs of the projects – e.g. bricks and mortar – not such expenses as municipal staffing (about 100 city staffers are assigned to the projects) and expert consultation (engineers, health officials), which are allocated to other parts of the municipal budget. Furthermore, the participatory budget covers only the cost of the first year of a project (more recently, the first two years) only. In other words, the participatory funding from the community are intended to demonstrate enough serious intent to initiate a project, while the initial year or two of operations demonstrate its viability. At that stage funding from the World Bank and other NGOs is expected to complete the projects. In spite of all these hurdles, more than 1,000 construction projects have been completed in the past 14 years.[3]

Outcomes and health indicators of participatory budgeting

Programme evaluation is always essential, but determining just what improvements in public health can be attributed to participatory budgeting is perhaps more art than science. Still, the circumstantial evidence for its benefits is striking. In Porto Alegre, where participatory budgeting began, infant mortality rates declined to 12 deaths per 1,000 live births in 2005, down from 18 per 1,000 in 1999 (Goldani *et al.*, 2002). The city now enjoys both the highest standard of living and the longest life expectancy (76 years) of all Brazilian cities (WHO Commission on Social Determinants of Health, 2010; Menegat, 1998). In Belo Horizonte the mortality rate for children under five had declined to roughly 25 per 1,000 in 2005, down from a whopping 80 per 1,000 in 1994 (UN-Habitat, 2010b).

Porto Alegre, Belo Horizonte and other cities have also taken advantage of participatory budgeting to put programmes in place that have positive effects on the social determinants of health (though this is not necessarily their articulated purpose). Such programmes include efforts such as upgraded housing, extended utilities to underserved areas and allocated space for cultural or recreational activities. Between 1989 and 1996 the number of households in Porto Alegre with access to water services rose to 98 percent, up from 80 percent; and the population served by the municipal sewage system rose to 85 percent, up from 46 percent (Minos, 2007; Wagle and Shah, 2010). Between 1988 and 1999 the government had built nearly 12,000 units of public housing, garbage collection had doubled, roughly 25,000 light posts had been installed and nearly 6 million square meters of pavement had been added to the city (Minos, 2007).

In Belo Horizonte, the part of the population whose income was less than a dollar a day declined to 5.6 percent in 2000, down from 7 percent in 1991 (UN-Habitat, 2010b). With investment priorities set through the participatory-budgeting process, 38 health centers have been constructed, 33 public schools have been extended and 3,059 units of housing have been approved (UN-Habitat, 2010c). In other cases, health-specific resources such as the family health centers we will now describe have been created.

Family health centers and physical academies

Family health centers

In 2005 Belo Horizonte established its second innovative programme for urban health: a network of 140 family health centers (FHCs) throughout the city. The FHCs deliver health care to some 450,000 families living in areas of medium to high vulnerability. (The city also has 14 major medical centers for emergencies and 18 referral centers for specialty care.) Although neighborhood primary care had existed before 2005, the FHC network brought with it a remarkable change. Each family was assigned to a unique referral team from the local FHC, made up of a physician, a nurse, two physician's assistants and three outreach workers. The outreach workers were required to be residents of the neighborhood to which their FHC team was assigned.

To get a feel for how a center operates 'on the ground,' we took a close look at the FHC in the neighborhood of Tirol (pronounced 'CHEE-rohl'), on the south side of Belo Horizonte. That FHC has five referral teams, each team responsible for 4,000 people. The three outreach workers from each team, all garbed in blue smocks prominently marked with the letters 'BH' (for Belo Horizonte), routinely visit each house in their assigned neighborhood at least once a year. At each house they collect a wide range of health-related data, give a brief orientation on preventing adverse health effects, and monitor the health of the residents. The information they gather includes data on immunization, nutritional status, prenatal care, breastfeeding and family health planning; asthma and other respiratory diseases; data relevant to cancer screening and prevention; the incidence of hypertension, diabetes and other non-transmissible diseases among adults; infectious diseases such as tuberculosis, leprosy and dengue; drug use among children and adolescents; domestic violence; and violence, abandonment and neglect toward the elderly.

Although about four-fifths of all FHC medical staffers are permanent, the other 20 percent is mainly a temporary workforce – making physician turnover an ongoing problem for the city's health department. In Tirol, for instance, many of the doctors are new graduates (with undergraduate degrees) who stay at the center for just a year before moving on to better jobs. The nurses also usually leave after a year. Initially, doctors also resisted taking positions with any of the FHCs because the jobs called for eight hours a day (earlier clinic positions required only four hours a day, leaving the rest of the doctor's time for more lucrative private practices). Yet an FHC salary is competitive – similar to that of an associate professor at the Belo Horizonte medical school – and so many young doctors take FHC positions to save the startup money for a private practice.

The neighborhood outreach workers are likely to remain on the job at an FHC much longer than members of the medical staff. What turnover there is among outreach workers is brought about chiefly by the stress of the work itself: neighborhood residents seeking advice can call on them at all hours of the day or night.

The Tirol FHC is a product of community mobilization and action through participatory budgeting. Those funds paid for the construction of the building housing the clinic just a few years ago. It is situated in a compound with high walls, gates that close at night and bars on its windows – all primarily to protect the somewhat antiquated equipment inside when the complex is closed at night. Most of the time, though – 16 hours a day – the center is open, and a pharmacist is on duty throughout that period, with limited stocks of common medications on hand. Some specialists, such as a dentist, a psychologist and a gynecologist, are on the premises 20 hours a week. Anyone, including people who live outside the district, can use the FHC, though its outreach workers do not go beyond their assigned area.

The Tirol FHC staff participate in two of the FHC's advisory boards, each of which meets once a month. Their highly local outlook nicely complements the work of the citywide health department in formulating health priorities. One of the boards brings outreach and clinician teams together to discuss how to deal with the latest health issues facing the neighborhood. For example, in response to outbreaks of dengue, this advisory board organized teams of workers to go door to door, educating households about the risks of breeding dengue-carrying mosquitoes in standing water. The board meeting is always open to all community outreach workers, who bring their well-informed observations and perspectives to the table, as well as to ordinary members of the community, who can voice their own opinions.

The second advisory board is made up of representatives from various agencies, including church and civic organizations. They meet to coordinate actions addressing health problems and to mobilize for political action – in fact, they continue the same discussions that prompted the building of the Tirol FHC in the first place. At the top of the current agenda are diseases such as obesity and diabetes; immunizations; prenatal and pediatric care; and broader health issues such as unsafe roads and pedestrian injuries. In response to those last issues, for instance, this advisory board successfully lobbied for stop signs. The board also recognizes violence, especially domestic violence, as a major problem – though board members are well aware that women are often unwilling to report domestic violence, particularly when it comes to involving the police.[4]

Physical academies

FHCs, as we noted earlier, are a reorganized version of an earlier system of neighborhood health clinics, rather than an altogether new programme. But another programme recently initiated by the city health department is a genuine innovation, with no prior counterpart. That programme has developed what are called 'physical academies,' community centers intended primarily for exercise but also for educating the local citizenry about nutrition. Physical academies are generally sited near FHCs. The first one in Belo Horizonte opened in the neighborhood of Mariano de Abreu, in the Eastern Sanitary Health District.

The Mariano de Abreu neighborhood literally came into being on January 5, 1985, when 11 families were moved there as squatters from their former homes (also as squatters) near an open sewage area. Since the move, which sparked an angry political response, the city has installed basic utilities (e.g. water and electricity) in Mariano de Abreu, and a local FHC has been established that operates as a social center as well as health center with a heavy patient load. Two factions or parties (the '05 Janeiro 1985' Communist Party and the Esperançia Workers Party) have dominated the politics of the community ever since the squatters arrived. Although relations between the two can become strained at times, both cooperate in the participatory-budgeting process, taking turns in alternate years to propose a project that the other agrees to support. Through this coalition and working within the participatory-budgeting process, the community petitioned to clean up a small, abandoned, open-strip iron mine that had become a dumping ground for the bodies of victims of violence, which were brazenly tossed off the cliff above the mine. Sewage runoff from houses above the cliff also collected around the old mine.

Originally, the project was simply to grade the area and make it into a football (soccer) field. But as the budgeting process went forward, the health department joined the discussions and cut a deal not only to create the football field, but also to build a physical academy on the site. Today a paved access road leads to the new field; the play area is fenced and a new brick building stands alongside, with toilets and showers for children's use after sports. Also to the side of the field is a second new, but larger, brick structure, which serves as a community center. Two-thirds of the space inside functions as a common room, where exercise classes are held, and the rest of the space is allocated to a computer room and to 'evaluation rooms,' where the baseline fitness and exercise progress of participants can be tracked. Residents using the community center can access, among other things, Internet-based, participatory-budgeting voting ballots.

To join the exercise classes each resident must be examined by a trained physical-education instructor, who takes the resident's height, weight, blood pressure, medical history, measures of strength and flexibility, quality of life and client satisfaction with the center. The programme offers moderate exercise and stretching – to minimize injuries – plus light calisthenics, power walking and the like. With limited budgeting, the instructor has worked creatively within the center's means: dumbbells, for instance, have been fashioned out of broom sticks and soda bottles filled with sand. The programme is also staffed by student interns, training in physical education or nutrition, under the supervision of the manager and a professional nutritionist.

The physical academies are reportedly popular among the poor, in part because – as the city health department has noted – it offers what the FHCs, with their emphasis on health care, cannot provide: a place to socialize for those who are well, particularly the poor. That has the secondary benefit of placing less strain on the FHCs, which can then more efficiently care for those most in need of their services. At the Mariano de Abreu football field even the body-dumping has stopped, though the sewage runoff remains a problem.

The physical academies in Belo Horizonte are now incorporated as part of the municipal health programme. By next year some 48 new ones should be in place in the most vulnerable areas of the city. Public health researchers from the Urban Health Observatory at the Federal University of Minas Gerais are evaluating the physical academies, comparing the effectiveness of the early sites with that of the ones more recently built.[5]

Limitations of evaluation approach and potential contribution of evaluation

In spite of such evaluation efforts, a lack of adequate data sources seriously limits the ability to chart – much less to understand – how urban health interventions that follow best practices affect specific health outcomes over time. One difficulty with the available data is that proponents of governance innovations and development interventions do not always articulate their project visions in terms of effects on public health. More often, such projects are justified as benefits to human rights or social justice. Yet health outcomes are a strong indicator of quality of life (for a fuller discussion of this point see the opening sections of 'Evolving Urban Health Risks: Housing, Water and Sanitation, and Climate Change,' by Gordon McGranahan, Chapter 2 of this volume). Further, healthy citizens are in general more able than the sick and the infirm to contribute to the needs of the community, the city or the continuing development of shared resources. For some cities, data are available to plot changes in life expectancy or infant mortality with time, but it is not always clear how these changes relate to specific interventions or programmes. Data on services delivered or infrastructure created may also be too limited, contradictory or incomplete to assess the impacts of such initiatives on health.

How, for instance, is the development community to give an unbiased evaluation of participatory budgeting? The extensive spread of participatory budgeting across Latin America and Europe, as well as the anecdotal evidence of positive benefits in Belo Horizonte and other cities, has given strong currency to the idea that citizens can be active participants in the development and maintenance of their cities. Yet rigorous, health-specific quantitative data for measuring the effectiveness of the diverse models and applications of participatory budgeting are generally lacking. Those data that are available are typically qualitative rather than quantitative, or concern outcomes that have only indirect effects on health: percentage of budget allocated to certain sectors or projects, for instance, service provision or infrastructure generated (such as number of households with access to water and sanitation services, or number of health centers built) and the like. In the case of Belo Horizonte, we and our colleagues, in partnership with UN-Habitat, developed the evaluation process for participatory budgeting (UN-Habitat, 2010a), based on various indicators that are relatively easy to measure and update: sanitation, housing, education, social health, and cultural and physical activity, among others.

Those data can clearly help guide decision-making and ensure accountability of funding decisions, and it is imperative to improve the collection and reporting of such data. But quantitative data on specific heath outcomes can also be highly informative for allocating funds. A case in point: in Belo Horizonte no specific health indicators are currently being tracked. Some observers have suggested deriving proxy indicators from public records (homicides, drug-overdose admissions to emergency rooms and the like) and conducting periodic health surveys. As we noted earlier on pp67–68, in the UQLI some public health data from the decennial census are factored in. But the census data have been collected only once since the participatory-budgeting process began, so, though they are useful for taking a snapshot of health vulnerability, they are of little use for evaluating programme changes over time.

The resolution scale of aggregate data – in essence, the denominator used in reporting percentages – has been another topic of considerable discussion in designing evaluations. Such 'natural' aggregates as neighborhood populations and 'planning units' are too small to yield statistically significant comparisons. The city is generating hydrographic maps of its 256 watersheds (enough to provide a statistically adequate number of areas for comparison), but compiling health data that match the watershed boundaries remains a challenge. Indeed, the municipal offices for participatory budgeting acknowledge that key questions about how one part of the city compares with another have not been addressed: How do direct health indicators such as morbidity and mortality correlate with various health programmes and the degree of programme implementation? What, if any, is the relation between new programmes and such indirect indicators of programme success as level of participation, satisfaction of the participants, enhancement of the community's social capital and so forth)?

The work needed to answer these questions is ongoing. And most observers would agree that systematically collecting and analyzing health data both over time and across a city could make the city's efforts to offer primary health care to its citizens substantially more efficient. But there are several barriers to implementing such data-driven interventions: lack of financial resources within a community, lack of infrastructure, technical training or time available, not to mention how to justify making data collection and analysis a priority when so many other needs seem more pressing. External funders interested in identifying, broadening and strengthening the information base on best practices for urban health and development should offer substantial financial and technical assistance to encourage and support evaluation efforts. Providing such assistance at the municipal level, which would enable the systematic collection of data across a number of cities, could help enormously in designing interventions with the best chances of success.

Disseminating and applying best practices

We believe that the experience with participatory budgeting in Belo Horizonte, as well as with the development of FHCs and physical academies there, can both serve as models of 'best practices' for urban health. Each programme illustrates a process of intense engagement between citizens and various levels of government that cities across the globe might do well to consider. As always, however, translation to other areas requires a thoughtful approach. Differences in history and culture; in physical, financial and technical resources; in extant infrastructure, governance, social capital or other important contextual factors not only call 'best practice' models into question, but also the very idea that building model programmes intended to be applied in new circumstances is the best way to address those circumstances.

Participatory budgeting, for instance, has not proven as successful in other cities as it has in Porto Alegre and Belo Horizonte. In Costa Rica the central government tried to introduce a 'Triangle of Solidarity' into the budgeting process, which was intended to facilitate communication flow among the central government, local government and community organizations.

But the 'Triangle of Solidarity' broke down in high-need urban areas. In two neighborhoods, Rincon Grande de Pavas and San Felipe, the process became bogged down in land titling and negotiations. Many of the projects slated for those neighborhoods had to be scrapped (Smith, 2004).

In Peru the municipal government of Villa El Salvador set up participatory budgeting in 2000, committing 35 percent of its budget to the process. Citizens were supposed to take part in the meetings that established projects, as well as to provide the labor for them. But after initial success, participatory budgeting was scaled back once a new mayor was elected. Difficulties arose in coordinating and organizing the influence of the various stakeholders in civil society. Many municipal officials thwarted what they saw as a threat to their power. And neighborhood leaders, in turn, responded by confronting the municipal officials instead of trying to work with them.

What those failures underscore is that participatory budgeting demands a high level of civic action and responsibility. Perhaps the social capital in a municipality or neighborhood must reach some threshold level before participatory budgeting can lead to successful outcomes. Some communities, for instance, may lack the internal (bonding) social capital needed to organize themselves. In communities with high levels of distrust in government or other external bodies, or with severe social disorganization and violence, participatory budgeting is unlikely to work at all. (Technical assistance from professional groups and NGOs can sometimes enhance social capital and foster community cohesion, but the process can take many years (Schusterman and Hardoy, 1997; Snoxell *et al.* 2006).

Participatory budgeting also depends on the amount of support from the municipal government, as well as on the financial and professional assistance it makes available. And in some countries the central government, not the municipal government, controls many of the available resources (Cabannes, 2004).

Yet it would be a mistake of undue caution not to adopt the Belo Horizonte programmes as models for interventions elsewhere. Though lacking in rigorous data on health outcomes, both of the 'best practices' we have described have strong theoretical underpinnings in the current understanding of the social determinants of health – and thus in the understanding of how to modify those determinants to improve health, either directly or indirectly. Initiating (and evaluating) more programmes will supply a more nuanced understanding of how to improve urban public health. But even at current levels of understanding it seems that, though large differences in social capital may affect health outcomes, small differences may not matter. Within Belo Horizonte and Porto Alegre the levels of social capital and the social determinants of health vary from neighborhood to neighborhood, yet both participatory budgeting and the development of FHCs and physical academies have remained viable in both cities (Baiocchi, 2005). Although there are no guaranteed rates of success for these programmes in other cities, the evidence is compelling that they can improve the lives of many people from a variety of backgrounds.

We take four general lessons away from these model urban health programmes and the supporting literature:

1   Citizens can and should be called upon to engage actively in urban planning and improvements.
2   Public health is determined by many factors; thus, efforts to improve it should take account of all relevant sectors and be targeted at macro, or structural, determinants as well as individual ones.
3   Intervention efforts should be long term as well as iterative. They should also seize the moment, or, in other words, capitalize on the mobilization of human energy and capital typically spurred by the completion of a successful project.
4   Routine monitoring and analysis are key elements in assessing and enhancing programmes aimed at improving best practices for urban health.

Conclusion

We have described two initiatives in Belo Horizonte in order to contribute to the growing supply of case studies of programmes that exemplify 'best practices' for improving urban health. The goal in building up such a supply of proven, model programmes is to encourage others to demand their transfer to new settings. Several points are worth noting in compiling such a list.

Content of case studies

What issues should urban health programmes address? According to one conceptual framework, the answer is: living conditions – not only because they affect both individual and population health, but also because they are remediable. They encompass both the physical and the social environment, as well as the availability of health and social services (Freudenberg *et al.*, 2006). The UN-Habitat list of best practices, for instance, lists various factors of the physical and social environment as important elements of urban health.

We suggest this list can and should be broadened. Best practices ought to include effective outreach that provides both preventative health measures and social services for urban populations. Best practices should also incorporate effective approaches to the immediate and long-term control of infectious diseases. Describing best practices might take an even broader perspective, discussing how to determine what fundamentals (pre-existing conditions, leading figures, funding) are necessary to plan and implement a particular project.

Multiple case study approach

How can two or more programmes build on each other in a particular context? Most 'best practices' are reported as individual projects, yet in many cities or neighborhoods several projects are underway simultaneously. Describing how projects intersect concurrently, or reporting the temporal sequence of various projects or conditions, might provide key information about necessary pre-conditions or simultaneous requirements. Consumers of case studies that include such information are more likely to be able to evaluate the information and translate it to their own contexts. Furthermore, when case studies describe the context of a programme (at least when they go beyond the immediate problem and setting), the descriptions are often inconsistent. We are acutely aware of this issue, since we ourselves are describing how multiple projects have interacted in one city. We welcome suggestions from our readers and colleagues about ways in which multiple-project case studies of other specific areas can be improved and strengthened.

Mixed methods of evaluating case studies and 'natural experiments'

What can be done to improve programme evaluations? To date, descriptions and evaluations of best practices in urban health programmes have been primarily qualitative. We ourselves were forced to take that approach in reviewing the programmes for this report, because of the paucity of quantitative information on the possible health impacts of the programmes. Evaluations in the literature typically refer to case reports that describe a problem, the actors, obstacles and the process. Some of these reports quantify the results of a programme in terms of products delivered (e.g. number of new construction projects started or completed; number of participants in the programme; number of people served). But including multiple, quantitative indicators would provide a much stronger and more useful report of a programme and a much more realistic expectation of what it can achieve.

Likewise, few case studies compare community health before and after the rollout of a programme, or the health of a community affected by a programme with that of a control group. For example, in programmes that focus on clean water sources, sanitation or poverty reduction, few case reports directly examine whether the programmes led to changes in the health (reflected, say, in a reduction of disease rates) of those served.

We have already noted several reasons that case reports rarely include an analysis of quantitative data. Existing data are usually collected on large entities (entire cities, for instance) for purposes other than evaluation. Those data may be missing key indicators, or reported only as aggregates that cannot be further broken down into information about subgroups of the population. And of course original data are expensive to collect.

Perhaps a more fundamental reason for the dearth of quantitative data in evaluations is the assumption in some quarters that conditions in each setting are sufficiently unique that such data could only yield meaningless comparisons. For example, in major efforts to upgrade slums, the most informative evaluation designs are frequently not feasible or even desirable. Such efforts can include so many components and occur at so many levels that they may be hard or even impossible to replicate. Having a non-intervention (or control) group, moreover, might be ethically unthinkable.

Still, quantitative data can make a compelling case for agencies and funders to adopt or adapt a programme. Funding and other support may depend on feasible evaluation designs that provide quantitative information. One approach to the ethical dilemma of withholding a promising intervention in order to provide for a control group is the 'natural experiment'. After the intervention is planned, evaluators simply designate an area where it will not, in fact, be done as the control (or, in the case of multiple factors in the intervention, multiple areas, one as control for each factor). In that way there is no question of intentionally withholding an intervention for the purpose of future evaluation.

In some favorable circumstances, key quantitative indicators of health in an urban area may be available both before and after a project is begun. Frequently, though, one is not so fortunate: the areas of intervention do not lie within the areas where data have been collected, or are too small for data that are available to be meaningful. The available measures may be too crude. The best practice for evaluation may be to choose areas in which household surveys that assess needs and track various health indicators are already being done. A related tactic is to implement programmes in stages, so that some areas receive a programme earlier than others – as is the case of the physical academies in Belo Horizonte. This evaluation method is known as the 'step wedge' design. If measurements are made in multiple neighborhoods, evaluators can compare the results at each stage of the programme across early versus later sites of implementation. Thus they can make interim evaluations and suggest mid-course corrections, as well as preparing a final evaluation of a programme's effectiveness.

Understandably, extreme urban poverty and its consequences for human health foster a sense of urgency and an impatience to put remediation programmes into place. Without programme evaluations, however, the law of unintended consequences may well create 'cures' that are worse than the urban disease. For that reason, as well as many others, evaluation efforts must become ever more sophisticated: fast enough, cheap enough and accurate enough so as not to be omitted. Developing such evaluations should be the next major focus in building best practices for improving urban health.

Acknowledgement

The authors gratefully acknowledge the assistance of Fernando Proietti, Sara Putnam and Andrew Quinn in the preparation of this chapter.

Notes

1   http://www.bestpractices.org
2   In Belo Horizonte, 'favela' is a term that is considered stigmatized and considered interchangeable with 'vila'.
3   Information was collected including interviews with Ana Luiza Nabuco Palhano, Adjunct Secretariat in the Municipal Planning Department of Belo Horizonte, and Maria Auxiliadora Gomes and Marcos Ubirajara de Carvalho e Camargo, administrators of the participatory budgeting program at the Municipal Planning Department.
4   Interviews were conducted with Denise Vianna Amador, the administrator of the Tirol FHC, Raner Pacheco da Silva and Giovanni Fonseca.
5   Interviews took place with Maria Angelica de Salles Dias, Assistant Commissioner of Health, Maria de Fátima Pereira Batista, Health Manager of Eastern Sanitary District, Marisette of the 'January Five, 1985 Association' and Sandra of the 'Hope Association,' both community leaders in this neighborhood.

References

Baiocchi, G. (2005) *Militants and Citizens: The Politics of Participatory Democracy in Porto Alegre*, Stanford University Press, Stanford, CA
Cabannes, Y. (2004) 'Participatory budgeting: a significant contribution to participatory democracy', *Environment and Urbanization*, vol 16, no 1, pp27–46
Caiaffa, W., Almeida, M.C., Oliveira, C., Friche, A.A., Matos, S.G., Dias, M.A., Cunha, Mda. C., Pessanha, E. and Proietti F.A. (2005) 'The urban environment from the health perspective: The case of Belo Horizonte, Minas Gerais, Brazil', *Cad. Saúde Pública*, vol 21, no 3, pp958–67
Freudenberg, N., Galea, S. and Vlahov, D. (eds) (2006) *Cities and the Health of the Public*, Vanderbilt University Press, Nashville, TN
Goldani, M.Z., Benatti, R., da Silva, A.A., Bettiol, H., Correa, J.C., Tietzmann, M. and Barbieri, M.A. (2002) 'Narrowing inequalities in infant mortality in Southern Brazil', *Rev. Saúde Pública*, vol 36, no 4, pp478–83
Kawachi, I. (1999) 'Social capital and community effects on population and individual health', *Annals of the New York Academy of Sciences*, vol 896, pp120–30
Linden, E. (1996) 'The exploding cities of the developing world,' *Foreign Affairs*, vol 75, no 1, pp52–65
Menegat, R. (1998) *Atlas Ambiental de Porto Alegre*, Universidade Federal do Rio Grande do Sul/Prefeitura Municipal de Porto Alegre/Insituto de Pesquisas Espaciais Brazil, Brasilia
Minos, D. (2007) 'Porto Alegre, Brazil: a new, sustainable and replicable model of participatory and democratic governance?', Centre for Development and the

Environment, University of Oslo, http://www.tni.org/sites/www.tni.org/archives/archives/chavez/portoalegre.pdf, accessed March 25, 2012.

Ompad, D., Galea, S., Caiaffa, W. and Vlahov, D. (2007) 'Social determinants of the health of urban populations: methodologic considerations', *Journal of Urban Health*, May, vol 84 (3 Suppl), pp42–53

Schusterman, R. and Hardoy, A. (1997) 'Reconstructing social capital in a poor urban settlement: the Integral Improvement Programme in Barrio San Jorge', *Environment and Urbanization*, vol 9, no 91, pp120

Smith, H. (2004) 'Costa Rica's triangle of solidarity: can government-led spaces for negotiation enhance the involvement of civil society in governance?', *Environment and Urbanization*, vol 16, pp63–78

Snoxell, S., Harpham, T., Grant, E. and Rodriguez, C. (2006), 'Social capital interventions: a case study from Cali, Colombia', *Canadian Journal of Development Studies*, vol 97, no 1, pp65–81

Tabibzadeh, L. and Liisberg, E. (1997) 'Response of health systems to urbanization in developing countries', *World Health Forum*, vol 18, nos 3–4, pp287–93

UN-Habitat (2010a) 'Localising the Millenium Development Goals', http://www.unhabitat.org/content.asp?cid=4921&catid=312&typeid=13, accessed March 25, 2012.

UN-Habitat (2010b) 'Localizing the Millenium Development Goals in Belo Horizonte', http://www.politicassociales.gov.ar/odm/PDF/localizacion_odms_belo_horizonte.pdf, accessed March 25, 2012.

UN-Habitat (2010c) 'Citizen advancement and participatory budget in Belo Horizonte', http://www.unhabitat.org/bp/bp.list.details.aspx?bp_id=3177, accessed September 12, 2010

United Nations (2005) 'World urbanization prospects: the 2005 revision', http://www.un.org/esa/population/publications/WUP2005/2005wup.htm, accessed September 12, 2010

United Nations Human Settlements Programme (2003) *The Challenge of Slums: Global Report on Human Settlements 2003*, Earthscan, London

USAID (2004) *Improving the Health of the Urban Poor: Learning from USAID Experience*, USAID, Washington DC.

Vlahov, D., Freudenberg, N., Proietti, F., Ompad, D., Quinn, A., Nandi, V. and Galea, S. (2007) 'Urban as a determinant of health', *Journal of Urban Health*, May, vol 84 (3 Suppl), pp16–26

Wagle, S. and Shah, P. (2010) 'Case study 2 – Porto Alegre, Brazil: participatory approaches in budgeting and public expenditure management', http://siteresources.worldbank.org/INTPCENG/1143372-1116506093229/20511036/sdn71.pdf, accessed March 24, 2012

WHO Commission on Social Determinants of Health (2010) 'KNUS case studies', WHO Knowledge Network on Urban Settings, http://www.who.or.jp/publications/2008-2010/KNUS_final_report.pdf, accessed 4 April, 2012

Chapter 5

Addressing health vulnerabilities of the urban poor in the 'new urban settings' of Asia

Susan Mercado, Kirsten Havemann, Keiko Nakamura, Andrew Kiyu, Mojgan Sami, Ira Pedrasa, Divine Salvador, Jeerawat Na Thalang and Tran Le Thuy

Introduction

Asia is home to 60 per cent of the world's population. Demographers estimate that in the next few decades more than 60 per cent of the increase in the global urban population will be in Asia – mostly in China and India, but also in Pakistan, Bangladesh, the Philippines and Vietnam (Ling and Phua, 2006). Urban growth in Asia is the product of natural growth (the excess of births over deaths), net in-migration (the excess of inflow over outflow) and the growth that results from administrative changes or the redrawing of boundaries that reflect the reality of urban sprawl. In each country, these three sources of urban growth combine in unique ways, with unique implications for urban administration and national policy.

Unlike urban growth elsewhere, the growth of Asian cities and municipalities has usually been accompanied by economic prosperity. The Asian economic miracle was one of the most significant global developments of the twentieth century, and it has brought many benefits – higher incomes, better education, better health outcomes, declines in rates of infant mortality and longer life expectancies – not only to the East Asian 'tiger economies', but also to many other countries in South and Southeast Asia: the per-capita gross domestic product (GDP) of Asian cities is often higher than the per-capita national GDP, an economic pattern that well reflects the attraction of those cities for rural migrants seeking better economic opportunities. These benefits will continue to drive the rural-to-urban population shift for the foreseeable future, as well as the ongoing high levels of migration both within and between countries. These migrations play an important role in a nation's economic transformation, but they also demand a rethinking of how development policies may affect the health of urban populations.

Nevertheless, the economic picture in Asian cities is far from being uniformly positive. Where urbanization has been unplanned or has progressed at an unmanageable pace, the existing public infrastructure, the urban environment and the traditional social fabric have all deteriorated. Growth and wealth in such cities no longer confer their former 'urban advantage'. In those developing countries of Asia where the national and municipal authorities have not been able to cope with the speed of change, the net effect is failure of governance, increased and unabated inequity, and the urbanization of poverty. In developed countries, economic inequities have intensified throughout the population, in addition to such traditional determinants of wealth as ethnicity, gender and age.

Unplanned growth has led to similar inequities in population health. In rapidly urbanizing environments, groups that are well-off co-exist with economically vulnerable groups who face serious threats to their health, even though both 'live in the same city'. Unfortunately, those differences may not be easy to glean from routine health statistics. To unmask the differences and develop relevant interventions for combating health inequity, new ways of looking at and evaluating health vulnerability are needed. The priorities of public health may need to move beyond simply improving the access to and quality of health services, and toward creating fairer opportunities for good health across entire urban regions.

Among those whose health is most at risk are the people in low-income and informal settlements ('slums')[1] (WHO Centre for Health Development, 2005). By some estimates, 60 per cent of the world's informal settlers and slum dwellers live in Asian cities. In South Central Asia, slums and squatter settlements constitute 58 per cent of the total urban population; in Eastern Asia, the corresponding number is 36.4 per cent; and in South Eastern Asia, 28 per cent. In absolute terms, the population of urban slum dwellers in three regions totals more than 500 million (Ling and Phua, 2006).

The social determinants of health

A number of scholarly studies, including papers by Wratten (1995), Rakodi (1995), Satterthwaithe (1997), Sen (1999), Kawachi and Wamala (2007) and the Knowledge Network on Urban Settings of the WHO Commission on Social Determinants of Health (WHO Centre for Health Development 2007), have pointed out that poverty is not only a matter of limited financial or material resources. It is also characterized by a diverse set of restrictive social conditions that determine health risks and outcomes, including lack of:

- *opportunities* (for employment and access to productive resources)
- *capabilities* (access to education, health and other public services)
- *security* (vulnerability to economic risks and violence)
- *empowerment* (absence of voice, power and participation in governance)
- a health-supporting physical *living environment* (poor housing, unsafe working conditions, unnecessary exposure to biological, chemical and physical threats to health).

These characteristics of poverty apply in both rural and urban settings, but they tend to be severe in the urban living environment (WHO Centre for Health Development 2007).

The urban poor who live in deprived urban settings, informal settlements and slums constitute the single largest group of vulnerable populations in Asian cities today. Subgroups within this population include women, children, the disabled, minority groups of various ethnic origins or countries, street children, commercial sex workers, survivors of HIV/AIDS, 'dalits' (outcastes), indigenous peoples, sexual minorities, transient workers and hawkers, among others. The knowledge and means to provide services to such vulnerable groups and treat their diseases are available. But health vulnerability is closely related to living and working conditions, to social status, and to the systematic social and political exclusion that renders vulnerable groups 'invisible' and powerless. Thus, although health vulnerability is reversible in principle, overcoming the social and political barriers to equitable health opportunities is a formidable challenge.

It is therefore not enough to address health vulnerability merely by providing better access to health services or information. The social determinants – 'the causes behind the causes' – of ill-health in urban settings demand attention. For the urban poor in Asia this means that stopping the development of new slums in urban settings is of paramount importance (Garau et al., 2005). The logic behind this priority has been aptly summarized by Sir Michael Marmot, Chair of the WHO Commission on Social Determinants of Health: 'Why do we keep treating people, only to send them back to the conditions that made them ill in the first place?' (Marmot, 2006).

Urban governance and health inequity

It is widely believed that the urban poor should fend for themselves and that better job opportunities will erase social inequity in cities. Yet the data show otherwise: despite economic prosperity in many Asian cities, the growth of slums and informal settlements has escalated as well.

In Asia, as in other parts of the world, cities are 'engines of growth' that concentrate power and wealth, but they are also centres of opposition and dissent. Deep suspicions and polarizing disputes among various factions have given rise to conflicting policies and political stalemate in addressing the structural determinants of health for the urban poor. The reality is that uneven power structures, incomplete decentralization and weak local governmental capacity, coupled with cultural bias and social discrimination against the urban poor, remain deeply embedded both in health systems and in larger systems of governance. A framework for better urban governance is needed to change the urban socio-ecological phenomena that cause health inequity and unnecessary vulnerability. In other words, governance must be reformed if the half-billion people who live in Asian slums are to have better lives.

We take 'governance' to mean 'the management of the course of events within a social system' (Barten et al., 2007). It encompasses a wide range of actors in addition to those in positions of governmental authority. Looking at health from the perspective of governance can help identify nodes of power and influence that can enable the urban poor to gain greater control of their life circumstances and the determinants of their health (Barten *et al.*, 2007, Burris *et al.*, 2007). Such participation by the governed is one key feature of good governance, and so an emphasis on enabling participation underscores the importance of good governance in achieving better health for vulnerable groups. At the same time, the proliferation of informal settlements and the growth of slums reflect a 'failure of governance' – that is, current systems of governance have turned out to be inefficient, corrupt, unresponsive or irrelevant to the needs of the governed. Here, then, are some key principles of good governance:

1 Participation, the degree of ownership and involvement that stakeholders have in the political system.
2 Fairness, the degree to which rules are applied equally to everyone.
3 Decency, the degree to which rules are formed and implemented without humiliating or harming particular groups of people.
4 Accountability, the extent to which those with governing power are responsible and responsive to those who are affected by their actions.
5 Sustainability, the extent to which current needs are balanced with those of future generations.
6 Transparency, the extent to which decisions are made in a clear and open manner.
7 Political commitment to policies and procedures that implement the six principles above.
8 Equitable enforcement of laws.
9 Protection of human rights.

If one of the central goals of good governance is the creation of systems, institutions and processes that promote a higher level and fairer distribution of health in urban settings, we can list further principles of 'healthy urban governance' that are critical for improving population health in cities:

• Holding local governments accountable for health outcomes.
• Enabling and supporting the urban poor as they gain control over factors that determine their health and the quality of their lives.
• Putting health and development at the centre of urban planning, policies and action.
• Developing mechanisms that promote dialogue and cooperation among various groups in the private, public and civil society sectors, including national and local authorities.
• Winning and using resources – aid, investment, loans – to improve the living conditions of the urban poor.

Health in the 'new urban settings' of Asia

As early as 300 BC, the development of cities in Asia was linked to trade. Cities interconnected by the Silk Road flourished, as gold, silver, ivory, silk, precious stones and exotic animals and plants were traded between East and West. Asian cities engaged with the rest of the world through trade and commerce, and became strategic hubs for economic growth across the continents.

Recent proposals suggest how these historic trends will continue: land bridges are planned for connecting Europe through China (a route with stops in Tianjin, Beijing, Ulaanbaatar, Ulan and Irkutsk). A trans-Korean railway may one day join Japan with Eurasia through the Korean peninsula. In the near future, Bangladesh may become the transport hub of the entire Southeast Asian region, the gateway to the world for such countries as Bhutan, India, Myanmar and Nepal, via the Bangla Bandha land port and the Chittagong seaport. Malaysia has recently positioned itself to compete with Singapore as the key Southeast Asian shipping hub for the region. Its port city of Tanjung Pelepas, on the southern tip of the Malay Peninsula, faces the Strait of Malacca, one of the world's most important international shipping channels.

These lines of connectedness hold great potential for generating economic growth and prosperity. But as recent history has shown, extensive city-to-city connectedness also exposes every city in the trade network to serious risks: the spread of infectious diseases, harmful products such as tobacco and illicit drugs, and social tensions 'imported' from densely populated regions elsewhere in the world.

So what is different about Asian cities today?

Five interrelated conditions distinguish the current Asian urban context from that of any other historical period:

1   The unprecedented rate of urban growth and its effect on municipal governments.
2   Faster and continuing growth of market economies in 'primate cities' (a primate city is between four and ten times the size of a country's second largest city, which dominates urban life). Such growth is accompanied not only by marked improvement in quality of life and living conditions in some places, but also by an upsurge in poverty, slums, informal settlements and inequity in others.
3   Regrouping of marginalized and socially excluded groups along ethnic, cultural and religious lines within cities (the sub-communities of Nepalese refugees in the slums of New Delhi, for instance).
4   Sustained city-to-city interconnectedness through trade, commerce, industry and international travel.

5 New and emerging health vulnerabilities brought about by a confluence of biological, social, political and environmental tensions and risks.

Those cities, in which all five of these conditions hold, constitute what the WHO Centre for Health Development refers to as 'new urban settings'.

Given the practical and theoretical understanding described in the foregoing, we assessed a number of innovative programmes that aim to eliminate health inequities by addressing the social determinants of health and by improving urban governance. We identified examples of innovations from work by the WHO Healthy Cities project in the WHO Western Pacific Region and the Southeast Asian Region; by the Alliance for Healthy Cities; and by the Knowledge Network on Urban Settings of the WHO Commission on the Social Determinants of Health, of which the WHO Kobe Centre is the hub. (The lead author of this chapter, Mercado, as well as co-authors Havemann and Sami were all affiliated with the WHO Kobe Centre at the time this paper was written.) In all, we reviewed more than 500 case studies and reports. They included innovations that tackle upstream determinants of health (socio-ecological drivers) as well as downstream ones (access to quality health care, information, services and programmes). Where documentation was insufficient or outdated, we commissioned the writing of case reports through the Southeast Asian Press Alliance, an independent network of Asian journalists.

We considered a broad range of criteria in evaluating the programmes for rollout or adoption in other venues:

1 Their effectiveness in reducing the health vulnerability of the urban poor (we maintained that criterion even though we recognized that some programmes (e.g. providing low-cost public transport from urban to rural areas) do not target the urban poor per se, but the poor in general).
2 The attention they paid to overcoming social barriers to health, via interventions clearly consistent with principles of good governance.
3 The documentation they provided or that we were able to assemble through the efforts of the Southeast Asian Press Alliance. We wanted documentation at least to include lessons learned from implementing a programme, but we preferred reports that discussed tools, offered guidelines, and explained the methodology behind a successful programme, since those details would enable others to apply an innovative programme.

More specifically, we considered an improvement in disease morbidity and mortality to be only one of several sources of information relevant to judging the effectiveness of an innovation. For example, we looked at the indicators of good governance we listed earlier (participation, fairness, decency, accountability, sustainability, transparency, political commitment, enforcement of laws and protection of human rights). We also considered the principles of healthy urban governance (accountability for health, support of the urban poor in controlling their own health, making health central to urban planning, promoting dialogue and cooperation among groups and investing resources in the lives of the urban poor); health-systems indicators (efficiency, capacity- and institution-building, sources and uses of funds for health); environmental health indicators (quality of housing, quality of indoor air, amount of pollution); and political and community indicators (public perception of the programme, community participation in it, the degree to which the programme fostered or improved social cohesion, support for policy and adherence to public health policies such as quarantine measures).

Innovative approaches to reducing health vulnerabilities of the urban poor

After evaluating more than 500 programmes according to the criteria stated earlier, we found that the most effective innovations incorporate one or more of six general features:

1   They encourage the urban poor to become key drivers and decision-makers in the upgrading of their own communities.
2   They help local governments learn to improve urban health and thereby hold themselves accountable for healthy urban settings.
3   They take advantage of infectious disease outbreaks to promote healthy settings over the longer term.
4   They improve the efficiency of financing health promotion in cities.
5   They apply information technology to population health activities.
6   They seek to optimize the social determinants of health in urban settings.

Each of these six features deserves individual discussion.

Encouraging the urban poor to become key drivers and decision-makers in the upgrading of their own communities

What makes change happen? What, for instance, has been the driving force behind what is arguably the most important innovation in population health for Asia: the effort to link the right to health of the urban poor to the more general requisites of a decent life – secure housing, land rights and access to credit through microfinancing? The answer is not the actions of ministries of health or housing. Rather, the urban poor themselves have made this link into an issue of social justice. They have the desire, the political will, the capacity to negotiate, the willingness to promote dialogue and the time and energy to manage funds and projects for upgrading their own communities. The primary stakeholders of this movement for social justice in the face of health inequities are organized groups of urban poor, who negotiate for the requisites of a decent life and better health. These groups have discovered the power of their numbers, as well as the value of direct contact with other organized groups, international donors, partners and advocates for the poor throughout the world. They understand that these other groups, often outsiders, can act as 'nodes of governance' that help bring powerful gatekeepers and interests to the negotiating table.

The organizations and groups that have been most effective in facilitating this movement for health justice are the ones that have worked steadily to reshape common misperceptions about the role of the urban poor by others, as well as by the urban poor themselves. The poor have emerged from being 'targets' and 'beneficiaries' to being redefined as 'key drivers' and 'decision-makers'. Their incremental and hard-won gains in promoting the participation, decency, fairness and accountability of good local governance have led to meaningful changes in their day-to-day existence. Organizations and groups that have helped the poor to realize their powers have also documented the changes that resulted; such organizations include the Society for the Promotion of Area Resources Centres (SPARC), the Asian Coalition for Housing and Rights (ACHR), Slum Dwellers International and its member groups, the Women's Development Bank Federation, Nepalese National Squatters Federation, Philippines Homeless People's Federation, National Slum Dwellers Federation/Mahila Milan, and Homeless International.

Changing power relations

What the urban poor federations have done is to show that an effective housing policy for low-income groups is actually about changing the relationships of 'slum shack' and 'pavement' dwellers with official agencies – not about physical improvements. The physical improvements – in housing, housing tenure and basic services – come from these changing relationships.

Satterthwaite, 2005, p4

David Satterthwaite reached this conclusion as long as seven years ago, in a paper presented at a social policy conference in Arusha, Tanzania (Satterthwaite, 2005). He singled out six organizations, including the Community Organization Development Institute (CODI) in Thailand, that demonstrate how participatory and inclusive processes have brought good services, including health care, to slum and squatter settlers. CODI mobilized neighbourhood groups of slum dwellers, networks of sectors and networks of important stakeholders and leaders who were able to make a difference. The organization's tactic of forming 'networks of networks' has now been applied in 415 communities and 30,000 households in 140 Thai cities (Boonyabancha, 2005).

What accounts for its success? Somsook Boonyabancha, Director of CODI, explains that networking among organized groups creates new power bases (Boonyabancha, 2005). When communities of the urban poor can look at their city in its entirety, she notes, they no longer feel isolated within their individual settlements – they have allies and friends with similar difficulties, similar fates and similar ways of doing things. Their wider perspective can lead to political engagement, which can result in more direct access to power as well as greater influence over decision-making. The entire process can even lead to new 'nodes of governance' (Burris *et al.*, 2005) and power structures that are fairer, more responsive, more accountable and more transparent.

Confronting patronage politics and moving toward democratization

Municipalities – and municipal politicians from various parties – generally have their own intermediaries that engage with communities of urban poor. Within a given city, such communities tend to be divided into camps – one camp might 'belong' to the ruling party, for instance, whereas another might belong to the opposition. Politicians like to have one-on-one ('bilateral') relationships with community leaders, enabling them often to take a 'divide and rule' approach in dealing with their constituents and so maintaining power. But if this kind of patron–client relationship and its division between powerful 'benefactor' and lowly 'petitioner' is to change, such exclusive bilateral ties must be challenged. Development interventions can play an important supporting role in such a challenge by encouraging poor communities in a city to work together. The key goal is to foster city-wide processes that empower the urban poor not only to gain independence from the vertical strings of patronage that control their lives, but also to tap into them to advance their own interests.

A sharper focus on social cohesion: 'community-upgrading' versus 'slum-upgrading'

Within every community, even communities of the very poor, social gradients exist. Some individuals and families have better access to resources or social networks than others. Taking a sensitive approach to existing social gradients is crucial to the success of development interventions. 'Community-upgrading' emphasizes the restoration of shared space, shared resources and public goods, whereas 'slum-upgrading' is often a matter of improving only the poorest and perhaps excluded sections of a community. Thus the latter can be perceived as an assault on the very stability of a community, whereas community-upgrading can be a powerful intervention for rebuilding or reinforcing social cohesion. Social cohesion builds trust and creates opportunities for all individuals and families to take advantage of common resources and join social networks. Engaging the members of a community in these ways may further reduce poverty and support 'decentralization' – the shift away from dependence on the central city government and toward more community self-reliance and self-governance. CODI has done all this through subsidiaries and the financial incentives of a communal welfare fund and communal welfare facilities; the Institute calls the process 'collective equalizing'.

Another success story has been documented by the Self-Employed Women's Association (SEWA) in Gujarat, India. SEWA has provided opportunities for self-employment, but, more, the Association has joined other like-minded organizations to form a trust dedicated to promoting housing for self-employed women. The trust aims to provide technical support, research and advocacy for its members. These combined interventions have led to improvements in health and declines in morbidity.

The Orangi Pilot Project (OPP) in Pakistan is another organization that has developed 'networks of networks' of community organizations to improve the lives of the urban poor (see also Chapter 8). Begun in Karachi's Orangi squatter community in the 1980s after the central city government failed to address the low quality of local water and sanitation, the OPP simply organized the community to improve the systems on its own. One 'lane manager' would represent 15 households on a 'lane committee'; the committee in turn would include some 40 lane managers, thus representing a total of 600 households. The growth of these networks or organizations gradually gained enough political clout to persuade the municipal authorities to release funds for constructing primary and secondary sewers – which are now serving more than 600,000 Karachi residents.

Helping local governments learn to improve urban health and thereby hold themselves accountable for healthy urban settings

Decentralization has not been confined to the power relations between urban communities and the municipalities that encompass them. Many national governments in Asia are also decentralizing: transferring decision-making and spending powers to local governments. The shift tends to make city and municipal officials increasingly responsive to the needs of the urban poor. Those officials would, in any event, be the first to feel the heat from the political implications of rising inequity in their cities. But with new powers to do something about it (and the new incentive to earn political credit for their actions), local politicians are becoming less threatened and more open to engaging with their poorest constituents to find solutions. Increasingly, local governments of cities and municipalities are holding themselves accountable for health and its determinants. (The trend is perhaps best exemplified by the mayors, non-governmental organizations (NGOs) and civil-society groups that have been recognized as 'healthy cities' champions for their efforts to improve health in the urban setting.)

Decentralization policies have enabled local governments to break free from the stranglehold of national bureaucracies and hierarchies, even if in many countries the process is incomplete and poorly supported. But because they, too, still bear responsibility, national governments need to develop clear policies and strategies to manage rapid urbanization. Health and human development should be at the centre of their agenda. The drama will continue to be one in which central governments and local communities must learn to work together to balance priorities, allocate resources and manage personnel issues, as mayors, other elected officials and health-sector professionals and administrators play a growing role in health care.

City-to-city learning

As emerging health issues take on distinctly urban features, cities themselves have much to offer one another as they develop ways to reduce health risks. Many cities have already engaged in city-to-city exchanges on such topics as trade, economic development, environmental sustainability and finance. The phenomenon, known as 'horizontal assistance', already likely amounts to a shadow economy in knowledge exchange (Blanco and Campbell, 2006). The United Nations Development Programme (UNDP) estimates that between 15,000 and 20,000 intercity links have been forged in the past several decades (UNDP, 2001). City-to-city cooperation has become a recognized field of development assistance. Anecdotal evidence as well as systemic hard data for specific cities suggest a large, latent demand for arranging such cooperation and a strong willingness to pay for it. The formation of knowledge markets – complete with databases on good practices, websites that present case studies of effective urban health approaches, clearing houses for research on healthy cities, and the like – could be highly useful to cities as they seek to solve emerging health problems.

Learning through international networks of cities

The AHC is an international organization that aims to protect and enhance the health and quality of life of city dwellers. (Two co-authors of this chapter, Nakamura and Kiyu, are affiliated with the Alliance.) AHC is an autonomous organization, though it has a close relationship with WHO (indeed, WHO confers the name 'healthy city' on cities that are 'continually creating and improving those physical and social environments and expanding those community resources which enable people to mutually support each other in performing all the functions of life and in developing to their maximum potential'). AHC was founded in 2004 with 26 member cities, and by November 2010 it had grown to 121 member cities, from Australia, Cambodia, China, Japan, Republic of Korea, Malaysia, Mongolia, Singapore and Vietnam. That steady growth by itself reflects the high value cities place on city-to-city learning via international networks. The network fosters learning and capacity-building by publicly recognizing good practices. It has also helped cities pursue 'twinning'. For example, since 2005, Marikina City, Philippines, and Ichikawa City, Japan, have worked together to promote healthy diets and physical activity through urban planning. With WHO support, exchange visits between two twin cities enable city senior officers, technical officers, practitioners, community group leaders, teachers and children from both cities to gain insight and learn from one another.

The Asian Infectious Disease Project (AIDF) is another instructive example of city-to-city learning. Launched in November 2004 in response to the threats of SARS and avian influenza, AIDF was a health project of the Asian Network of Major Cities (initially, New Delhi, Hanoi, Jakarta, Singapore, Taipei, Tokyo and Yangon, though since that time the membership has grown). Its main contribution was to provide a mechanism for direct communication between cities about the spread of those diseases.

Working with local researchers to understand and address local problems

Solutions to local problems in cities require local evidence and the active participation of local researchers. Community participation in a research project on the health of communities living on boats in Hue, Vietnam, and research on drug abuse in Vientiane, Laos, show the importance of a community-level research capacity (Fujiwara *et al.*, 2005; Quang *et al.*, 2005). In the former case, for instance, outside researchers were unsuccessful in securing cooperation from the community. Only when local investigators joined the research teams did people begin to open up and participate. Research at the Healthy Urbanization Project of the WHO Centre for Health Development is an essential tool for understanding how the active participation of urban poor communities has affected health inequities in six urban sites. (Three of those sites are in Asia: Bangalore, India; Suzhou, China; and Kobe, Japan.) (For a more extensive discussion of one important kind of participatory action – namely, participatory budgeting – see Chapter 4).

Benchmarking against a healthy city demonstration site

Kuching City in Sarawak, Malaysia, is a healthy city demonstration site that first applied the healthy city concept to its communities in 1994. Since then more than 1,000 observers have visited Kuching City to see how a healthy city can be established. What visitors also see are 'process indicators' (such as improvements in local living conditions) and the establishment of 'elemental settings' (healthy marketplaces, schools that promote health), all attesting to the effectiveness of the healthy city approach. Senior officers of Kuching City also share their experiences at seminars, meetings and consultations with other cities.

*Exchanging information with other cities in the same country to
bridge language barriers*

Although international networking and exchange have many benefits,
language barriers can also keep local officials from learning much about
the experience of foreign cities. Domestic networks of healthy cities give
secondary and smaller cities a fairer chance to gain access to knowledge
about healthy urban governance. For example, the Mongolian Association
of Urban Centres (MAUC), established in 2003, is an NGO that demonstrates how cities can learn from each other within Mongolia.

Working with the private sector to promote health in cities

In the Asia-Pacific region, corporate social responsibility efforts directed
toward improving health and reducing the vulnerability of groups in the
urban setting is on the rise.

Independent media groups such as the Corporate Social Responsibility
Asia Magazine provide a clearing house of information, news and reports
that are relevant to business-initiated and supported projects on compliance
with labor law, occupational health, environmental and health issues and
the alleviation of poverty. In China, for example, a partnership between
academics and NGOs, and a consortium of export-processing companies
including Ford Motor Company, Gap Inc., Hewlett-Packard Company, Liz
Claiborne Inc., MeadWestvaco Corporation, Pfizer Inc. and Target Corporation launched the Global Supplier Institute to offer training on management, health and safety, HIV/AIDS and other topics (Yan, 2005).

In 2002 the first Asian Forum on Corporate Social Responsibility
(AFCSR) was convened by the Ramon V. del Rosario, Sr. Center for Corporate Responsibility (a center within the Asian Institute of Management). The
forum now meets annually to encourage social investment by corporations
in low-income housing and the delivery of health services, as well as corporate partnerships with health professionals.

Taking advantage of infectious disease outbreaks to promote healthy settings over the longer term

In the past decade outbreaks of infectious disease in Asia have prompted national
authorities and ministries of health to pay closer attention to health risks and
vulnerabilities created by such urban conditions as high density, crowding,
increased mobility, connectivity and diversity. Both the SARS and avian influenza outbreaks led to improvements in public health infrastructure and promotion of healthy settings in Asia. Shigeru Omi, Regional Director of the WHO
Western Pacific Region, nicely summarizes the positive outcomes in the book
SARS: How a Global Epidemic was Stopped (WHOWPRO, 2006, pvii):

SARS shook the world. By some standards, the first emerging and readily transmissible disease of the twenty-first century was not a big killer, but it caused more fear and social disruption than any other outbreak of our time... I don't know if one can decently say that SARS had a silver lining, but if it did, it was that it awakened the global public-health community from a kind of slumber... Since those days many countries and cities have invested extensively in public health... Health care workers have been drilled in infection-control measures. Better surveillance systems are in place. And research has been intensified. SARS, for all the fear and suffering it caused, has left public-health systems greatly improved.

Two tactical initiatives that emerged from the outbreaks deserve special mention. One is the Hygiene Charter, a document circulated by Hong Kong's health promotion sector while the bold and effective responses to SARS were still fresh in people's minds. Those responses had come from national governments and affected cities throughout Asia, which, despite tremendous political pressure and often adverse public opinion, mustered the political will to enforce strong surveillance, quarantine and isolation measures to control the spread of the disease. The Hygiene Charter put forward suggestions and guidelines on hygiene practices. Individuals, as well as representatives from business, industry, education, medicine and a number of other sectors were asked to sign the Charter as a pledge of their commitment to creating a new culture of hygiene in Hong Kong.

The second tactical initiative that owed its political acceptance to the disease outbreaks was the establishment of healthy marketplaces and safer food systems. The spread of the H5N1 virus in Vietnam and Hong Kong was linked to the unrestricted movement of poultry both within and between countries and, in particular, to the role of wet markets (fresh food) in that movement. Because marketplaces in Asia serve multiple cultural, economic, political, religious and social functions, closing the marketplaces was not an option. Instead, countries such as Vietnam invoked the avian influenza epidemic as a rallying cry to reform the poultry production and distribution systems. Before the epidemic, most Vietnamese markets did not have separate areas for different kinds of food. Fresh meat, fresh poultry and cooked food were often sold in the same stall. A lack of basic infrastructure for hygiene meant that the food sellers' hands were seldom clean.

Under the WHO's guidelines for healthy marketplaces, poultry sellers were given gloves, boots and aprons to protect them from the virus and prevent them from handling live chickens with their bare hands. They also underwent monthly preventative health check-ups. Most important, they were ordered to keep sick poultry out of market stalls. Sick or dead poultry were no longer allowed to be sold secretly, and an official stamp of approval was required for all poultry intended for sale. Healthy marketplaces have been successfully set up in the popular tourist area of Ha Long Bay, inspiring public admiration from officials in Quang Ninh and Thai Binh provinces. When new markets are built, the officials say, the two provinces may decide to duplicate the measures demonstrated in Ha Long Bay.

Improving the efficiency of financing health promotion in cities

In Asia and the Pacific it is estimated that less than 10 per cent of all national health expenditures are allocated to prevention or promotion.[2] Considering the magnitude of public health challenges that could benefit from prevention and promotion, the funds available for such attention to population health are a pittance compared with what is spent on hospital services, treatments and cures for acute medical conditions. Innovations in the financing of health promotion – public health insurance and 'sin taxes' on tobacco and alcohol – can ensure better health promotion and protection for people up and down the urban social gradient.

Upping the ante for tobacco and alcohol taxes

In 2006, the Thai government approved a budget of 5 billion Thai baht (US$125 million at then-current exchange rates) to support sports and cultural events, but that was only half the story. Much of the funding for those events was to come from a 2 per cent annual sin tax on tobacco and alcohol, based on the amounts spent per year to import those products (including insurance and freight), thereby paying for appealing public events by discouraging the use of unhealthy products. (In April 2011, the cost basis for the cigarette tax was changed to the retail value of the product, making it a simple sales tax.) Today ThaiHealth spends 6 per cent of its budget on raising awareness of health issues associated with tobacco and alcohol, and conducting an annual seminar on 'Cigarettes versus National Health'. The seminar is designed to facilitate regular exchanges among researchers, campaigners and the general public. ThaiHealth has also established an academic centre to train health care workers in the risks of cigarette smoking to health, to conduct further research on that topic, and to support legal and economic measures that will help expose unethical practices by the tobacco industry. The breakthrough by ThaiHealth in taxing tobacco to discourage its use has inspired other countries in the region, including Malaysia, Mongolia, the Philippines and Tonga. All are now in various stages of setting up autonomous infrastructure and financing for promoting health.

In the Republic of Korea, a national tobacco tax accounts for 14.2 per cent of the total price of a package of cigarettes, but, under the Local Tax Law, local governments are allowed to impose additional tobacco taxes that bring the total tax to as much as 32 per cent per package. One city taking advantage of this law is Wonju City. In 2005, its local tobacco tax accounted for 19.6 per cent of all city revenue, Wonju City's second largest revenue source. The tobacco-tax revenue was used for expanding and improving the housing supply and the supply of clean water, and providing free health care to low-income families.

Applying information technology to population health activities

Information technology can also benefit population health – by improving the efficiency of health systems, creating a more equitable distribution of health resources and providing access to information for planning and decision-making.

Geographic information systems (GIS) for city health programmes

In the Philippines, a number of local governments are leading the way in exploiting GIS technology. In the province of Capiz, for instance, a 'backyard GIS' system – running on low-end computers and using data already collected in government surveys – helped policy-makers and community members to take part in what was billed a 'Participatory Planning Budgeting Workshop'. Because provincial leaders and their constituents were looking at the same GIS picture and standing over the same GIS page, all the stakeholders had an overview of the community's infrastructure, investment plans and projects. Developing a list of funding priorities was then relatively straightforward.

In Cebu City, Philippines, the city government has exploited GIS technology to quickly identify 'disparity areas' or undertake 'poverty mapping' – graphical information displays that can call officials' attention to problem areas much more compellingly than can a written report. In health care, for instance, GIS maps enable city planners to monitor at a glance the spread and distribution of programmes for maternal and child health. Colour-coded representations of, say, the city's various *barangays* (villages) graphically and immediately show where health workers are scarce, or where infant mortality rates are high or low. This information guides policy and helps the city to direct its limited resources as beneficially as possible. Cebu officials credit GIS technology with helping them to narrow the gap between the health realities of 'disparity areas' and those elsewhere – in the larger, surrounding region or even in the nation as a whole. With GIS, officials can quickly determine where immunization is not being delivered or is still urgently needed.

Seeking to optimize the social determinants of health in urban settings

Social health issues need to be recognized and addressed in many different types of urban activities. Interventions that build social cohesion and address the social determinants of health point to a growing recognition of the links between social norms and fairer health opportunities.

Offering life skills and pre-employment training programmes to give the urban poor a fairer chance of employment

Marikina City, Philippines, has been a designated healthy city for more than 15 years; it is now recognized both locally and internationally for its successes in population health. In 2004, it embarked on a project known as 'The Marikina City Volunteer Corps', which sought to overcome social barriers to formal employment among the urban poor. The programme provides 'transformation and preparation of the poor for regular employment'. The 'volunteers' are engaged in training programmes on life skills such as how to budget a minimum wage for nutritious meals for a family of five, how to write a curriculum vitae, how to prepare for a job interview and the like. In addition, the volunteers receive health training that enables them to serve as volunteer health workers. They also get the job experience needed for them to rebuild confidence in their own ability to take on productive work – as clerks, as community health workers or as greeters for the local tourist programme. For four hours a day they earn a wage of 100 pesos (roughly $2).

The programme has helped add more than 4,000 volunteers to the city's health workforce – with an immediate, positive impact on its health systems. And though it is hard to attribute the subsequent reduction in diarrheal disease or the lower rates of dengue to this single intervention, the approach demonstrates how much local government accountability for the development of its human resources can accomplish at the municipal level. But even beyond this, Marides Fernando, a former mayor of the city, says the programme was also about 'creating opportunities for the people' – giving her constituents a greater capacity to compete in the job market. The Marikina government allots some 15 million pesos (US$350,000) a year to maintain the programme. From the perspective of the local government, the dividends, clearly, far outweigh the cost.

Implementing a fuel regulation policy to create healthier city air for all

'New Delhi was choking to death,' says Sunita Narain, director of India's Center for Science and Environment. 'Air pollution was taking one life per hour.' Bhure Lal, chairman of New Delhi's Environment Pollution (Prevention and Control) Authority, agrees: 'The capital was one of the most polluted on earth. At the end of the day your collar was black, and you had soot all over your face. Millions had bronchitis and asthma' (Perry, 2006).

For the past decade and a half, local advocates and champions of clean air from civil society have worked to pass regulations that would force Delhi's buses, taxis and rickshaws to convert to cleaner burning compressed natural gas (CNG). In July 1998, the Indian Supreme Court ruled largely in favor of the CNG proposal and ordered a ban on leaded fuel, the conversion of all diesel-powered buses to CNG, and the scrapping of old diesel taxis and rickshaws. But the powerful lobbying of bus manufacturers and oil companies – supported by government ministers – threw up serious obstacles to implementing the law. Bus companies took vehicles off the road, stranding angry commuters. Endless queues of rickshaws formed at the handful of gas stations with CNG pumps. Oil companies trotted out scientists who claimed that CNG was just as polluting as diesel. But Narain and Lal fought back. By December 2002, the last diesel bus had left Delhi. Ten thousand taxis, 12,000 buses and 80,000 rickshaws were powered by CNG (Perry, 2006). The city now stands as the world's best test case for CNG.

Conclusions

Globalization, urbanization, decentralization, democratization and advances in information technology, among the great forces in the world's economic development of the past several decades, have created a new political space. It should come as no surprise, then, that innovations in population health affecting Asia's urban poor have been driven by players and stakeholders who have learned how to use those forces in the service of the most vulnerable populations. They have been able to create opportunities, build capabilities, achieve greater security, empower, engage and mobilize support for policies and actions that improve the urban living environment. Thus, even from the necessarily limited set of examples we have cited in this chapter, it should be clear that a strong social movement is confronting the stark inequities in cities that not only create and perpetuate themselves, but also render the poor highly vulnerable to poor health.

Our survey of local innovations leads us to highlight three strategic entry points for scaling up actions:

1   Engage with the key players of existing social movements. As in any social movement, there are recognized political leaders at all levels (local, national, global) who have gained credibility over many years of staying focused on issues. Engagement with these key actors requires an appreciation of the asymmetry of the movements and skill in maneuvering through the networks and power nodes of governance.
2   Support the creation of 'global knowledge markets' for healthier cities. In many instances, the *effective* sharing of knowledge about municipal policy options may be all that is needed to solve what seem to be intractable problems. Previous work done by UN-Habitat and UNDP demonstrates how deploying the tools of urban governance, promoting systems for recognizing good practices and facilitating the mechanisms for cities to learn from each other can bring about a critical level of change. Global coalitions and alliances of cities such as United Cities and Local Governments, Metropolis and the Cities Alliance can strengthen their focus on health as part of their current agenda. There is clearly a demand and willingness among cities to pay for understanding how

practical interventions can be applied to specific contexts. Of course, these knowledge markets need not be confined to Asia: they could have a global reach.

3   Partner with global media to define more 'responsive forums' that can help the key actors reach a tipping point together. The global media – which have a natural interest in transparency and accountability – reach huge audiences, and engaging with them can create enormous opportunities for political mobilization. The threats of SARS and avian flu demonstrated the power of the global media in helping to control an epidemic, albeit indirectly.

We have stressed the need for a broad perspective on urban health in making interventions aimed at economic development. We have also argued that the goal of healthy urban governance, a constantly evolving and self-correcting emphasis on reducing the health vulnerabilities of the urban poor in Asia, is attainable. But to achieve that goal, the principles of good governance must be continually applied to the promotion and protection of health. There is no 'one-size-fits-all' solution, and those working toward any solution will need to continuously navigate a fast-changing environment in order to achieve results. Nodes of power and influence among the urban poor, within local governments and inside the public health sector itself are multiplying and discovering their counterparts and natural allies across geopolitical regions. In Asian cities, as in other cities in the world, there are countless examples of living networks of people, communities, organizations and institutions with the knowledge, skills and resources to scale up change. They could certainly benefit from a more supportive and enabling environment for achieving fairer health opportunities for all. Focusing attention on the health vulnerabilities of the urban poor by skillfully framing them as issues of public policy seems to be an effective starting point.

Acknowledgment

This chapter draws on a background document prepared by the World Health Organization (WHO) Centre for Health Development in collaboration with the Alliance for Healthy Cities (AHC) and in cooperation with the Southeast Asian Press Alliance for the Global Urban Summit, Rockefeller Foundation, 2007.

Disclaimer

This research was undertaken as work for the Urban Summit, Rockefeller Foundation, 2007. The views presented herein are those of the authors and do not necessarily reflect the decisions, policies or views of the WHO.

Notes

1   There is no universal agreement on the definition of what a 'slum' is, but for
purposes of this paper, the general definition used by UN-Habitat denotes 'a
wide range of low-income settlements and/or poor human living conditions.'
(UN-Habitat, 2003).
2   Email exchange with Dr D. Bayarsaikhan, Regional Adviser for Health Financing,
WHO Western Pacific Region, on April 27, 2007.

References

Barten, F., Mitlin, D., Mulholland, C., Hardoy, A. and Stern, R. (2007) 'Integrated
approaches to address the social determinants of health for reducing health
inequity', *Journal of Urban Health*, vol 84 (Suppl 1), May, pp164–173
Blanco, H. and Campbell, T. (2006) 'Social capital of cities: emerging networks of
horizontal assistance', *Technology in Society*, vol 28, no 1–2, Special Issue on
Sustainable Cities, Elsevier
Boonyabancha, S. (2005) 'Scaling up slums and squatter settlements upgrading in
Thailand leading community-driven integrated social development at city-wide
level', *New Frontiers of Social Policy: Development in a Globalized World*, World
Bank, Arusha, Tanzania
Burris, S., Drahos, P. and Shearing, C. (2005) 'Nodal governance', *Australian
Journal of Legal Philosophy*, vol 30, pp30–58
Burris, S., Hancock, T., Lin, V. and Herzog, A. (2007) 'Emerging strategies of healthy
urban governance', *Journal of Urban Health*, vol 84, May, pp154–163
Fujiwara, T., Takano, T., Nakamura, K. *et al.* (2005) 'The spread of drug abuse in
rapidly urbanizing communities in Vientiane, Lao Peoples' Democratic Republic',
Health Promotion International, vol 20, pp61–68
Garau, P., Sclar, E.D. and Carolini, G.Y. (2005) 'A home in the city', report from the
UN Millennium Project, Earthscan, London
Kawachi, I. and Wamala, S.P. (2007) *Globalization and Health*, Oxford,
New York
Ling, O.G. and Phua, K.H. (2006) 'Urbanization and slum formation', thematic
paper for the Knowledge Network on Urban Settings, WHO Centre for Health
Development, Geneva
Marmot, M. (2006) 'Social determinants of health', first meeting of the Social
Determinants of Health for the Asia Network, Asia Network, Tokyo
Perry, A. (2006) 'Delhi without diesel', *Time International*, vol 48, April 3, http://
www.proquest.com, accessed May 1, 2007
Quang, N.K.L., Takano, T., Nakamura, K., *et al.* (2005) 'Variation of health status
among people living on boats in Hue, Vietnam', *Journal of Epidemiology and
Community Health*, vol 59, pp941–947
Rakodi, C. (1995) 'Poverty lines or household strategies? A review of concep-
tual issues in the study of urban poverty', *Habitat International*, vol 19, no 4,
pp407–426
Satterthwaite, D. (1997) 'Urban poverty: reconsidering its scale and nature', *IDS
Bulletin*, vol 28, no 2, April, pp9–23

Satterthwaite, D. (2005) 'Housing as an asset and as an arena for developing social policy: the role of federations formed by the urban poor', *New frontiers of Social Policy: Development in a Globalized World*, World Bank, Arusha, Tanzania

Sen, A. (1999) *Development as Freedom*, Knopf, New York

UNDP (United Nations Development Programme) (2001) 'Linkages in cities', UN report on city-to-city cooperation, UNDP, New York

UN-Habitat (2003) *The Challenge of Slums: Global Report on Human Settlements*, UN-Habitat, Nairobi

WHO Centre for Health Development (2005) 'A billion voices: responding to the health needs of slum dwellers and informal settlers in the urban setting', strategic and analytic paper for the Knowledge Network on Urban Settings, WHO Commission on Social Determinants of Health

WHO Centre for Health Development (2007) 'Report of the Knowledge Network on Urban Settings to the WHO Commission on Social Determinants of Health', unpublished

WHOWPRO (2006) *SARS: How a Global Epidemic was Stopped*, WHO, Geneva

Wratten, E. (1995) 'Conceptualizing urban poverty', *Environment and Urbanization*, vol 7, no 1, April, pp11–36

Yan, S. (2005) 'Corporate social responsibility in China', *China Daily* (North American edition), May 13, http://www.proquest.com, accessed May 22, 2007

Chapter 6

The need for shelter finance improvements

Diana Mitlin

The need for shelter improvements

Shelter finance is critical to enhancing access to affordable housing (Renaud, 1999, p761). The development of urban areas reflects who has money and how much: both the scale and nature of shelter opportunities depend in large part on the scale and modalities of the available finance. For residential urban development in the Global North, people typically purchase housing as a complete unit in a single financial transaction – the dwelling, the services or utilities associated with the dwelling site, and tenure to the land. Even if people rent, the landlord of the dwelling they move into generally has formal title to the complete unit, in compliance with existing regulations. In the Global South, by contrast, this form of shelter investment is simply unaffordable. Most urban households in the Global South live in settlements and homes that have been developed incrementally, a process also known as progressive or phased development. Incremental housing development requires much more than financial investment alone; providing basic services and infrastructure to the site and creating land-tenure security entail collective social and political processes as much as they do financial transactions.

Loans whose financial structure meets the needs of low-income households for investments in incremental dwellings are rarely available through the formal commercial financial sector. In the vast majority of cases, these households, whose income comes from the informal economy, are ineligible for commercial mortgage finance and fall outside the regulations governing most microfinance loans. Households that want to invest in their own shelter (housing, infrastructure and land) are forced to rely on limited personal savings; to seek additional resources from family and friends; or to borrow – either through informal credit markets or, in some cases, from organizations such as credit unions. But all sources of finance are severely limited, and interest rates on such loans can be high. Yet without loans, construction is slow and sporadic.

Mortgage finance

These issues are particularly serious with mortgage finance. Mortgages are typically available only for completed legal dwellings (i.e. not for incremental development), yet most incomes in the Global South are too low to pay for completed dwellings built by the formal construction industry to approved regulatory standards. In many countries of Latin America and Asia, substantially less than half the population can afford formal loans for conventional housing. Among somewhat more affluent countries such as Mexico and Colombia, this proportion rises to about 60 percent, whereas in the Philippines and Suriname it falls to less than 30 percent. In Africa the use of mortgage finance is even more limited. Studies suggest that less than 10 per cent of households can afford to purchase complete homes through mortgage finance. (These circumstances remain broadly unchanged despite the recent crisis in housing finance in the North.)

Furthermore, widespread poverty combined with low levels of economic development virtually guarantee that the financial sector itself will remain weak. With many people on low incomes that barely cover their subsistence needs, savings are small and formal financial institutions that can service these savings are lacking. Such low incomes, along with endemic macro-economic instability, have prevented the development of institutions that could address immediate needs and facilitate the flow of long-term funds.[1] Financial institutions in the Global South also face high costs of administration relative to loan size, partly because of the small number of transactions (Ferguson, 2003, p25; Lall and Lall, 2003, p16).

Another major problem with mortgage finance is that the creditworthiness requirements of a traditional mortgage are incompatible with the high degree of informality associated with urban land, employment (labour markets) and incremental property development in the Global South. For many homeowners, titles are problematic; formal registration systems may be lacking, or there may be multiple claims to the land. And many homeowners – squatters, buyers of informally divided agricultural land and the like – have no title at all. Local customs for determining land tenure may be hard to reconcile (or even conflict) with Western land-tenure systems, further exacerbating the problems associated with titling. Even measures to improve access to titles have not necessarily resulted in increased access to mortgage finance.

Incomes from informal employment are also a continuing and significant obstacle to accessing mortgage finance (Buckley and Kalarickal, 2004, p22; Calderon, 2004), according to research on a state programme for issuing land titles in Peru. Indeed, mortgage companies generally refuse to provide financing to those who do not work in the formal sector or who cannot verify their incomes. One recent study suggested that the size of the informal economy measured by percentage share of gross national product (GNP) is 41, 42 and 26 per cent for Africa, Latin America and Asia, respectively – huge numbers that indicate the scale of the problem (Schneider, 2002).

Even if land titles and formal employment are in place, 'informal' property development presents a third obstacle to traditional mortgage finance:
formal financial institutions seem nervous about lending for anything other
than a completed modern residential unit. The Kenyan Banking and Building Societies Act, for instance, explicitly forbids financial institutions from
making loans for plots of land with no or only partly constructed housing
on them (Malhotra, 2003, p225). Such resistance to incremental housing
arises from the perceived risks of construction and the potential for contra-
vention of building regulations.[2]

Those who can afford complete homes and mortgage finance, and who
can offer acceptable collateral (either through titles or employment status),
may still face substantial barriers. Banks are so far away from low-income
settlements that settlement residents are hard-pressed to reach the banks
during business hours (Biswas, 2003). Sex discrimination makes it particularly difficult for women to secure formal housing finance (Datta, 1999,
pp192–3). And the formal requirements of financial institutions can be challenging to navigate for anyone, let alone those with limited literacy or limited familiarity with formal processes.

The mortgage industry's perspective on these problems is epitomized
in the findings of a study in Angola, which showed that, in 2002, banks
rejected 82 per cent of all applications for housing loans.[3]

Few government programmes

Governments have made numerous efforts to help the urban poor secure
adequate shelter. Yet not only have those efforts been generally ineffectual,
but, worse, they have aggravated the problem in several other ways. They
have failed to support housing itself at the necessary scale. They have reinforced the dominant idea that the only housing worth supporting is the
complete modern housing unit. They have failed to reform ineffectual legal
and regulatory systems. In fact, state-financed housing programmes in the
Global South have offered little but false hope to the urban poor. Many were
never intended for any but limited groups of workers, and, even though
such programmes did provide newly built, complete public-housing units at
a considerable discount in exchange for promissory notes, they can hardly
be called successful: many of the promissory notes were never repaid (Alder
and Mutero, 2007; Hardoy and Satterthwaite, 1989, pp107–111; Ogu and
Ogbuozobe, 2001, p477). Some countries, notably in Latin America, have
tried introducing financial processes that would at least help formal workers invest in housing, with some success. And it is true that some efforts
have provided good housing to the poor. In India, for instance, the Housing
and Urban Development Corporation (HUDCO) has funded the construction of 14.4 million modern dwelling units, 95 per cent of which have been
allocated to low-income and otherwise disadvantaged households. But the

success of such programmes must be judged limited in the broader regional or national context of Indian housing needs. The HUDCO programme required a significant transfer of public funds to the few who received complete, modern dwellings, leaving little for the many who remained without adequate housing. Indeed, through their additional support for site and service programmes, even official actions have recognized the inadequacy of the state's strategy of supporting only completed housing units. The site-and-service approach is a bare-bones strategy to increase the limited supply of legal land titles at minimal cost, and to restrict services only to such basic ones as water connections and graded, unpaved roads, in the hopes that urban dwellers could then secure adequate shelter more speedily. Although such programmes have been effective, the supply of land has been inadequate, location has not always been well selected, the real beneficiaries have often not belonged to the intended target group, and the dwellings eventually constructed have often been in violation of local building regulations. Site and service programmes are no longer in wide use.[4]

Incrementalism – the housing reality

How, then, do low-income residents incrementally finance their homes? For relatively high-income households, the land purchase may come first; further investments are made as incomes increase and assets accumulate. For lower-income families, the first investment may be in the dwelling itself, on a piece of land with uncertain security of tenure. As families feel more secure, they may make further investments. A shack is transformed into a more robust dwelling, rooms are added, flooring and roofing are improved. Households frequently work together to achieve tenure security and to obtain state investment in infrastructure improvements and connections to bulk, public networks (water, sanitation and so forth). Once those connections are made, individual families may install their own infrastructure. It should be noted that these improvements to the original dwelling often do not comply with building regulations. Many incremental shelters are built cheaply with temporary materials, and require frequent repairs – from storm damage, for instance. In Hyderabad, India, a quarter of a sample of 224 households had recently repaired their houses (Smets, 2002, p77). In spite of such drawbacks, though, incremental development is affordable because investments can be made in small steps, as funds become available, and without the interest costs associated with larger loans.

The major source of finance for incremental developments is savings. In India, more than 80 per cent of housing finance comes from private savings, via the sale of assets, or from informal sources of credit (Biswas, 2003). Only 5 per cent of those moving from informal into formal settlements obtain formal housing finance (Lall *et al.*, 2006, p1031). Likewise, in Botswana, savings are a critical source of funding for housing investment (Datta, 1999, p203). In Angola less than 2 per cent of a family's investment in housing comes from banks. Instead, most funding for housing is borrowed from the extended family (62 per cent) or from friends (27 per cent).[5]

Because both the construction of their homes and the land they occupy have uncertain legal status, the urban poor live with the constant risk of eviction. For many low-income residents, such illegality simply reinforces their status as second-rate citizens. It increases their vulnerability to threats of eviction, thereby fostering corruption in the form of bribery and extortion. Ostensibly, the lack of legal land tenure is the reason governments fail to provide, or at least underprovide, services to poor neighbourhoods, further exacerbating the difficulties faced by the poor in gaining access to adequate housing. Moreover, illegality can create a sense of 'otherness' among poor people, a feeling reinforced in some neighbourhoods by the stigma of living in perceived association with crime. (Henry-Lee, 2005; Lall *et al.*, 2006). The eviction of low-income residents from low-income settlements is done in a context that emphasizes formality as a necessary condition for urban 'citizenship'. The result is that a single dimension of poverty (low income) becomes compounded by social and political exclusion based on residency in a particular neighbourhood and accommodation in a particular type of dwelling.

Rental sector

One alternative to building one's home incrementally is to rent. In many large cities, land is in such short supply that households must choose between acquiring a plot in a remote location or finding rental accommodation. Temporary migrants and occasional workers also create an ongoing demand for rental lodgings (UN-Habitat, 2003, p110). Thus, a vibrant, informal rental market has grown up in many low-income settlements in most cities of the Global South. The arrangements vary widely. Small-scale landlords rent rooms on land they already occupy. But when dwellings are rented by absentee landlords with little incentive to invest in their properties, the low quality of accommodation can lead to serious problems – as they have, for instance, in Nairobi, Kenya.

Tenants can be particularly vulnerable to exploitation: rentals often come with difficult terms and conditions, even restricted access to services (Mohamed, 1997; Smets, 2002, p75), yet poor tenants have few affordable alternatives. Their preference for home ownership becomes evident once affordable programmes are put in place. In Goiania, Brazil, a successful grassroots movement shifted 10 per cent of the city's population – nearly 100,000 people – from the rental sector to secure land through appropriations of public common land (Barbosa *et al.*, 1997).

There is great current interest in the development community in understanding the dynamics of housing investment in private rental accommodation, particularly in Africa. A study in Dar es Salaam, Tanzania, noted that rental income is an important motivator for housing investment (Sheuya, 2007). Surprisingly, however, the study also reported that a major factor holding up rental investments is a shortage of capital.

In a small number of countries, the state supports low-income rental markets directly. Yet despite their recognition of these needs, governments have been reducing their investment in public-housing stock intended for rental. Like the European transition countries, China has relatively recently begun to transfer to homeowners dwellings that had previously been rented – primarily from state-owned enterprises but also from other state housing providers. The alternatives to providing rental housing include encouraging housing cooperatives, providing subsidies to housing providers and to those with formal employment, and making available 'housing provident funds' (funds accumulated through mandatory contributions by formal workers), which can offer assistance to house buyers and builders alike (Ping Wang et al., 2005, pp1875–6). But none of these 'solutions' really address the problem of housing for informal workers and for others surviving at the lowest income levels.

Summary

The scale of the problem of inadequate urban shelter in the Global South is so enormous that one of the UN Millennium Development Goals (MDGs) singles it out for special attention. Even with this emphasis, addressing half of the present need by 2015 is considered overly ambitious; instead, the goal is to reduce by 100 million the estimated 900 million people living with insecure tenure and inadequate services.

Unfortunately, as I elaborated earlier, market transactions can only partly address the need for investments in housing, infrastructure and services. State agencies are needed (and where they exist, they need to act) to ensure an adequate supply of serviced land, and to facilitate saving and lending for housing. Absolute poverty levels highlight the need for additional support to the lowest income households. Improving access to credit that can help spread income across the life cycle of residents will enable some households to invest in housing, but focusing on credit access is not always appropriate. After all, there is not much point in encouraging those with very low incomes into debt. One of the challenges of housing finance is how to set up processes that are realistic about its constraints yet nimble enough to tap its potential for creating opportunities.

Urban poverty, causes and consequences

As I outlined in the preceding section, urban poverty is a major reason people lack adequate shelter. Low-quality shelter, furthermore, compounds the problems of poverty: one of several vicious cycles associated with being poor. In particular, poor-quality shelter is associated with substantial health risks, including greater morbidity and increased chances of premature death (for further discussion, see Chapter 2 of this volume, by Gordon McGranahan). Poor health starts another vicious cycle, since it is widely acknowledged that poor health also increases the likelihood of being (or becoming) impoverished, which, in turn, further reduces the chances of improving one's housing.

There is also a strong association between living in chronic poverty and being unable to work (or to work only at considerable competitive disadvantage) in labour markets. Two recent studies in Dhaka, Bangladesh found that the primary reason for households to suffer deteriorating financial circumstances was that the principal income earners became ill or incapacitated (Kabir *et al.*, 2000, p709; Pryer *et al.*, 2005).

After such an illness, both the income and the assets of the earner's household declined, since for an informal worker days not worked are days not paid. Such households typically reduced expenses to save money, took out loans and mortgages and sold assets. Some households even took up begging.

The adverse locations of low-income neighbourhoods also lead to severe hardships for the poor. (Low-income neighbourhoods occupy adverse locations almost by definition, since their residents cannot afford to live elsewhere.) Adverse locations often pose health risks – and residents who are sickened, say, by toxic fumes or contaminated soil often suffer further impoverishment. The locations occupied by low-income residents also directly reduce job opportunities for wage-earners, exacerbating low incomes and reducing the family resources available for shelter improvements. For example, residents may be barred from jobs simply because of their address in an illegal settlement or 'slum' and a supposed association with criminality. For those who occupy homes on the city periphery, where land is cheaper and more plentiful, transportation can take up a substantial portion of income – often as much as 10 per cent. Informal enterprises within a slum may lose business because of poor-quality infrastructure or natural disasters (such as flooding) associated with the location that bar or deter customers from visiting.

A study of improved road networks in one low-income settlement in Luanda, Angola, highlights how infrastructure investment can also improve local incomes. Before the improvements, the study identified ten enterprises along one road. Yet after two years of improved access, 44 new income-generating activities had appeared along the same road, generating additional income of US $124,080 a year. That yearly gain was nearly equal to the total cost of the improvements.

If there is a strong nexus between urban poverty, inadequate shelter and poor health, how might climate change interact with these realities? The changing pattern of environmental assets is likely to result in transitional problems: reduced economic growth in the short and medium term and hence fewer market-led employment and income opportunities. Although some areas may have new economic opportunities as a result of climate change, tapping into them will require investments as well as time. Reduced macroeconomic growth will lead to job losses among many of the urban poor and so reduce their ability and that of state agencies to invest in improved housing.

Hundreds of millions of urban dwellers are at risk from the direct and indirect impacts of climate change (McGranahan, 2007). Most of this risk is associated with development failures, especially the incapacity of local governments to ensure provision for (for instance) all-weather roads, piped water, sanitation, waste collection, drainage and disaster preparedness – in particular, their refusal to do so in 'illegal settlements'. Much of the urban population and most urban governments have a very low capacity to deal with any environmental hazards – thus a low capacity to adapt to climate change and variability. In particular, they are highly vulnerable to any increase in the frequency or intensity of extreme weather events or to increased risk of disease. Pro-poor adaptation strategies are not possible if the city government refuses to work with the poor, or sees their homes, neighbourhoods and enterprises as 'the problem'.

Settlements in low-lying locations face particularly acute difficulties. Many low-income residents live on flood-prone sites; such land is cheap because the costs of landfill or drainage make it undesirable for higher-income housing. But the increased frequency and intensity of storms and the rise in sea levels associated with climate change will increase the costs of maintaining such places (through, for instance, greater required investments in drainage) and intensify the hardships of living there – including greater loss of life, more economically damaging illness and injury, more frequent damage to possessions, and more disruptions to local business.

It should be noted, however, that the risks associated with climate change are only a few of the many potential risks from adverse environment changes that endanger the health and well-being of the urban poor.

Understanding the role of shelter finance in addressing vulnerabilities

Both the number and diversity of institutions engaged in shelter finance have increased in recent decades. To understand how these changes may affect access to housing, it is useful to analyze four kinds of institutional funders and the role they play (if any) in making systemic improvements in shelter finance for the poor: traditional mortgage finance companies, public housing agencies ('social housing'), microfinance institutions and community funds.

Mortgage finance

Broadly speaking, the history of mortgage finance in the past two decades has been dominated by financial deregulation, growth in the number of financial agencies and intensifying competition among financial-service providers. Government measures have focused primarily on reducing the cost of borrowing and on supporting the system of mortgage finance (by fostering the extension of the secondary mortgage markets and by promoting initiatives for managing risk) – all within the broader context of financial deregulation. In some countries, governments have made capital grants (direct-demand subsidies) available directly to developers of low-income housing or to the households themselves, enabling them to borrow the rest of the financing they need from conventional mortgage lenders.

One significant trend emerging in both Latin America and Asia is the effort to enable lower-income groups to secure mortgage finance from private lenders, thereby expanding the market for commercial housing finance and increasing formal home ownership. Notable successes have been realized in such lower-income Asian countries as Indonesia and India. In Indonesia, housing finance grew at annual rates of more than 20 per cent between 1993 and 1996 (Seki and Watanabe, 1998, pp118–9). Following the financial crisis in Asia in 1997, the significance of mortgage finance briefly declined, but then expanded once more. According to Marja Hoek-Smit, outstanding mortgage credit in Indonesia increased from close to 20,000 billion rupiahs in 1997 (nearly US $2.3 billion at 2011 exchange rates) to more than 50,000 billion rupiahs (nearly US 5.7$ billion) by mid-2005. 'Indeed,' Hoek-Smit notes, 'growth in mortgage credit has exceeded growth in other types of credit. However, expressed as a percentage of gross domestic product (GDP) mortgage credit is still only 1.83 percent compared to 3.12 percent before the crisis of 1997' (Hoek-Smit, 2005). In India, following slow growth in the decades prior to the 1990s, the number of specialist housing-finance institutions has increased, and the housing-finance market grew at an annual rate of 32.1 percent between 1999 and 2005 (see Box 6.1).

Box 6.1 Down-marketing in India

Since the late 1990s, the housing-finance market in India has undergone considerable growth and penetration. Several non-banking financial companies (NBFCs) have entered the market, and between 1999 and 2005 (the latest period for which reliable data are available) the market grew at an astonishing annual rate of 32.1 percent. In March 2006, the outstanding portfolio of retail housing finance by commercial banks alone stood at US $42.3 billion (Reserve Bank of India, 2006); housing-finance disbursements by all types of finance institutions have continued to increase consistently, and by 2008–09 had reached 2900 billion rupees (the equivalent of US $61 billion at September 2011 exchange rates). Outstanding housing loans as a percentage of GDP reached 7.25 percent in 2008, compared with 3.44 percent in 2001. (The comparable numbers are 80 percent in the US and 86 percent in the UK.) (Nenova, 2010)

To expand their client base, mortgage lenders have increased their loan terms from 25 to 30 years and have diversified their products to include loans for home improvements, bridge loans and construction finance. The reasons for substantial growth in the commercial housing-finance market include:

- financial-sector liberalization and greater competition
- high liquidity in the market
- reduction of interest rates from 18 percent in 1997–98 to 8.5 percent in 2005–06
- increased household incomes, especially among middle- and higher-income borrowers, as well as higher rates of national domestic savings
- fiscal concessions in the form of income-tax exemptions to individuals on mortgage payments of both principle and interest
- laws to help to foreclose properties in default
- policy formulation to allow foreign direct investment (e.g. investment from overseas) in housing and real estate
- a mandate by the RBI that (a) requires so-called scheduled commercial banks to lend at least 3 percent of their incremental deposits for housing; and (b) declares housing to be 'priority sector lending'[6]
- amendment of National Housing Bank Act in 2000 to allow NHBs to establish special-purpose vehicle trusts to undertake mortgage-backed securitization; and
- establishment of credit-information bureau to track information on customers in 2005.

The increase in housing finance, however, apparently helped to fuel inflation in the real-estate market in the period 2004–07. In several cities even most middle-income households could not afford a decent house. Urban housing prices have sky-rocketed primarily because of inefficient land utilization and lack of infrastructure.

Source: Satyanarayana, 2007, p4.

More recently, despite the global financial crisis, financial indicators suggest that mortgage markets continue to grow in significance. In Brazil, for example, outstanding mortgage debt increased from 1.4 percent of GDP in 2005 to almost 5 percent in 2011 (*The Economist*, 2011). Despite the recent crisis in the mortgage markets, quasi-governmental programmes to increase mortgage lending appear to be continuing. A loan by the Asian Development

Bank (ADB) to Indonesia, for instance, to help expand mortgage finance remains in the pipeline.[7] That is not to say there is no evidence of a downturn in mortgage lending in the Global South.[8] But the overall effects of the crisis may be relatively low in the Global South because, as W.B. Gwinner and J. Sanders argue (Gwinner and Sanders, 2010), mortgage expansion to lower-income groups there never did reach the levels it had reached among lower-income groups in some countries of the Global North.

Indeed, there has been no subprime mortgage crisis in emerging markets because there has been no subprime mortgage lending. Instead, as I noted earlier, mortgage lending is still typically made on conservative terms to middle- and upper-income households employed in the formal sector. Because of the overall lack of access to credit in emerging markets, the predominant lack of access to financial services there and the relatively high cost of registering and enforcing a mortgage lien, banks in such countries have been slow to move down-market with mortgages.

Despite the growth in mortgage finance, problems remain in reaching those with informal employment or low incomes. In Mexico, housing-finance institutions are potentially relevant to only two-thirds of the nation's households (Mulas, 2005, p30). In South Africa, only 5 percent of the population has taken out mortgages; another 20 percent could qualify for a mortgage but are not taking advantage of that option (Baumann, 2007, p4). One notable attempt to increase the relevance of mortgage finance to low-income households has been to enhance access to property titles. For example, programmes in Peru, Tanzania and elsewhere have sought to provide low-income residents living in informal areas with title to their properties, in anticipation that loans for shelter improvements and entrepreneurial activity, collaterized by the titled properties, would ensue. As I noted earlier, however, these programmes have not been successful.

Lenders have also been encouraged to extend mortgage finance to non-traditional, informal markets by approving loans for the construction of incomplete units. Construction quality must be high enough to be legal and hence eligible for traditional mortgage finance, and the new units are intended to be occupied before they are completed. Residents are then expected to finish the construction once their incomes increase – paid either from personal savings or with additional loans approved because of the homeowner's increasing creditworthiness. Thus, unfinished, low-cost units have opened up in Ahmedabad, India,[9] and in Manila, the Philippines.[10]

Another strategy, adopted in Tanzania, has been to reduce the size of the house that qualifies for a mortgage.[11] And in some countries greater competition among lenders does seem to have benefited consumers: loan-to-value ratios on mortgages issued have risen and profitability margins on loans have declined – though these indicators by themselves do not prove that mortgages have become more accessible to the poor.

To what extent, then, have the foregoing changes in the mortgage market enhanced the access of the urban poor to shelter finance? Perhaps their greatest impact has come indirectly: by meeting the housing-finance needs, not of the poor, but of lower-middle-income households. More specifically, the market changes have made it less likely that lower-middle-income households will occupy housing intended for low-income households. For low-income households, however, mortgage finance remains just as unaffordable and inaccessible as ever, both because of its long-term cost and because of the cost of housing itself.

Public and government initiatives

Public-policy initiatives addressing low-income housing ('social housing') in the past two decades have centred on the state as enabler rather than as provider. That shift was catalyzed by the recognition that traditional government strategies – building limited completed units, subsidizing mortgage finance – proved ineffective in reaching those with low incomes. The new generation of 'direct-demand' subsidies are often modelled after the Chilean housing-subsidy system, which provides a capital contribution (along with a loan) directly to beneficiary households to purchase dwellings from commercial developers or non-profit agencies, usually with the proviso that the households also contribute from their own savings. With these subsidies, households themselves can pay commercial housing developers or non-profit agencies for the dwelling. Owner-oriented direct-demand subsidies were introduced in Costa Rica in 1986 and almost immediately replicated in Colombia, El Salvador, Paraguay and Uruguay in 1991 (Mayo, 1999, p36). Two features of the Chilean programme are regarded as essential to its success: the clarity of the conditions it imposes on households and the transparency of its selection process. Both are intended to ensure that no one abuses the programme to buy political support, reward corrupt officials or simply meet the interests of specific or non-needy groups (Gilbert, 2004, p15; Gilbert, 2002a, p310).

Another trend in housing policy, as in mortgage lending, has been a willingness to support incremental housing.[12] For example, a new subsidy, savings and loan programme in Mexico includes an option for incremental improvements, though it should be noted that 92 percent of the programme's funds (about 60 percent of its loans) are earmarked for buying completed, albeit minimal, housing.

State financing may also benefit community-managed construction, generally as part of a larger housing-subsidy programme. In India, state subsidies are supporting an alliance of the Society for the Promotion of Area Resources Centre (SPARC, a non-govermental organization [NGO]), the National Slum Dwellers Federation and *Mahila Milan* (a network of women's collectives), which builds the capacity of local communities to manage a comprehensive upgrading and redevelopment process. Additional funding for this initiative comes through loans taken by the communities and repaid by individual members of *Mahila Milan* (see Chapter 7). In South Africa, a related approach, the People's Housing Process (PHP), directs a stream of state housing subsidies to local communities, which then build for themselves.

In addition to supporting new building and greenfield developments (on previously undeveloped land), governments are also seeking to improve living conditions in existing low-income settlements. In these so-called slum-upgrading programmes, a state development agency, the central government and/or a municipality finances the upgrade process. The main goals are to regularize tenure and provide (or upgrade) infrastructure and services to the settlement. These programmes may be integrated with programmes to provide home-improvement loans; typically they involve both local government and public–private partnerships for housing and community development. Examples include the Local Development Programme (PRODEL) in Nicaragua; the Slum Networking Project in Ahmedabad, India (Cities Alliance, 2002); the comprehensive Kampung Improvement Programme (KIP), introduced in Surabaya, Indonesia; and the Programme for Integrated Urban Renewal, used in El Salvador to help rehabilitate *mesones* (Murcia de López and Castillo, 1997, p173). (*Mesones* are old, colonial-style houses originally built for the rich but now subdivided into one-room rentals for low-income families.)

How effective are social-housing initiatives in addressing shelter vulnerabilities? In reaching those with low incomes, they vary. The Chilean and Costa Rican programmes, for example, direct most of their funding into subsidy streams that include loan components; since loans must be repaid, they are suitable only for higher-income households (Fernandez, 2004; Stein, 2007, p7). For reaching low-income or informally employed households, subsidy programmes less dependent on loan finance are more successful. But even the largest and most successful programmes are small relative to the needs. In South Africa, government-housing initiatives have helped more than two million people to obtain secure housing, yet the 2001 census reported that some 1.9 million households, or more than 16 percent of them, were still inadequately housed. Moreover, it was estimated that between 3 and 4 million houses would be needed to keep pace with the population increase, urban migration and the formation of new households.

Quality concerns have been raised in some countries about large-scale low-income housing programmes that are heavily dependent on private-sector construction companies (Gilbert, 2002b, p1929; Mitlin, 2007). The companies' focus on maximizing profits, of course, encourages their decision-makers to minimize land and building costs. In Chile, that appears to have led to poorly located housing developments – a false economy that became widely recognized in 1997, when heavy rains damaged as much as 10 percent of the low-income housing stock. [13] In South Africa, some units were built so small that a corrective, minimum size requirement was set in the late 1990s; increased funding has now been allocated in that country to improve both size and quality.

Programmes for upgrading housing, services or tenure in existing neighbourhoods appear to be less problematic than new building programmes. Upgrading is more affordable and involves fewer formalities than new building does; a location targeted for an upgrade also has the advantage that it is already known to be reasonably suitable. In fact, upgrade programmes for infrastructure and services are often done at sites that are relatively well located, simply because the strain on services that leads to calls for an upgrade in part reflects the popularity of a site with local residents. Upgrade programmes generally subsidize support for tenure security and basic services, and so all residents benefit. But in some programmes there is the option to invest in upgrades of the housing stock itself, which makes such programmes more flexible and responsive to the needs of residents in the target settlement.

Shelter microfinance

Microfinance lending has developed more slowly for housing investment than it has for developing small business enterprises, in part because of the much larger loans – between US $500 and $5000 – needed for housing. But microfinance providers have also shied away from housing because of a belief that shelter investments are not productive, and so do not generate the income needed to ensure loan repayments. Over time that belief has been challenged.

Most microfinance housing loans are made for terms of between one and eight years, though usually at or near the one-year end of that range (CGAP, 2004). Security requirements vary considerably with local circumstances. Sometimes they resemble the requirements for enterprise-development loans – that is, the loan contracts insist on group guarantees and co-signers. In other cases, the microfinance agency may require at least minimal legal documentation declaring the property and other non-mortgage assets as collateral. Some shelter microfinance lenders issue a conventional mortgage for loans at or near the high end of the US $500–$5000 range. They often encourage the use of savings by the borrower as well, though this practice may be constrained by financial regulations.

These and other terms and conditions of microfinance lending favour households with some degree of tenure security – indeed, some degree of land security is generally a prerequisite. But even for these households microfinance lending for land purchase remains uncommon, because of the high costs and other problems associated with individualized solutions to tenure and infrastructure needs. Instead, microfinance loans are generally taken to build additional rooms, replace traditional building materials with concrete, improve roofs and floors, and add kitchens and toilets. Such investments are highly popular: India's Self-Employed Women's Association (SEWA) estimates that almost 35 percent of the housing loans from its bank go for installing infrastructure such as a private water connection or a toilet (Biswas, 2003, p51).

In addition to 'traditional' microfinance agencies and NGO lenders, a number of other institutional players are active in this market, or else considering entry:

- Commercial banks. The Banco de Desarrollo in Chile has a small housing-loan programme, with 15,000 loans, averaging US $1200 each, outstanding (Escobar and Merrill, 2004, p41). The Industrial Credit and Investment Corporation of India Bank (ICICI) in India has recently begun to make microfinance loans, including those for housing, though the supply of suitable housing is limited.[14]
- Building materials suppliers. Also in Chile, companies such as Easy, Homecenter and Home Depot that sell building materials extend credit to customers through easy-to-access systems, provided the customer can offer proof of income. Elektra, a large electrical-appliance chain in Mexico, has formed a bank providing credit for starter-home packages. Patrimonio Hoy, also in Mexico and run by Cemex (a building materials company), encourages women to save together. By 2009 it had reached 235,000 households.[15]
- Central governments. The state may also finance decentralized initiatives. In Peru the state housing authority is channelling housing funds to microfinance agencies, municipal savings and loan cooperatives, and some microfinance banks (Escobar and Merrill, 2004, p40).
- Traditional small lenders such as credit unions. The Kenya Union of Savings and Credit Cooperatives established a housing fund in 1998. Housing and/or savings and loan cooperatives and *mutuales* are further sources of loans in Latin America (Escobar and Merrill, 2004, p39).

There is now considerable experience with shelter microfinance. Small loans can make a big difference to low-income households with reasonably secure tenure, who are engaged in incremental development and who can afford to pay interest and make regular loan repayments. For example, the Peruvian-based MiBanco, one of the leading microfinance agencies in Latin America, reaches clients whose incomes are at or below the poverty line for Peru (where 50 percent of the population have incomes below the poverty line). Funhavi, a Mexican NGO that finances home improvements, serves relatively low-income clients who earn between two and eight times the local monthly minimal wage of US $125. SEWA Bank's clients are all poor, self-employed women, mainly street vendors, labourers or home-based workers. Fifty-nine percent of the clients of the Kuyasa Fund in South Africa earn between R1000 and R2500 (between US $140 and $360) a month (Mills, 2007). Clearly, all these groups are poor. But many other low-income households are not being reached by these lenders.

Microfinance agencies approach shelter lending in a way that is embedded in the informality of low-income settlements, and so they can avoid having to comply with the building regulations associated with many professional attempts to improve shelter. That gives them access to households that cannot be reached by housing cooperatives, which also make small loans for subdivided, phased improvements. The cooperatives are more likely to provide loans for work on greenfield sites, where building regulations are more likely to be enforced. Inevitably, having to comply with such costly standards makes it that much more difficult for cooperative housing loans to remain relevant to the poorest of those in housing need.[16]

Microfinance organizations, for the most part, seek to be viable commercial enterprises, and by that measure, broadly speaking, many are successful (Malhotra, 2003). Scale is critical to achieving this goal, however, and so microfinance agencies depend on securing adequate capital to expand their lending. Accessing that capital is often difficult.

Thus a widespread belief has developed in microfinance circles (a belief supported by much experience) that access to credit is more important than the price of credit. To ensure their continuing access to credit, many micro-lenders pay – and therefore must charge – relatively high interest rates compared with the cost of money in the formal financial markets (although low compared with what informal money lenders charge). But since housing loans are often considerably larger than the microloans made to small businesses, the interest charges to the borrower are more significant. In many cases, microlenders charge lower interest rates for specific housing products (Escobar and Merrill, 2004, p58).

Community funds

Because so many low-income residents of towns and cities in the Global South live without secure tenure, adequate services or safe housing, a tradition of building and maintaining community funds has developed, primarily to make loans to this group. Community funds are supported by a range of NGOs, social-service organizations and state agencies. For the last, these funds are, in a financial sense, social-housing programmes, but they are quite different from conventional government housing programmes: rather than dealing with individuals, they engage with collectives of the poor (see Box 6.2).

Box 6.2 Community Mortgage Program

The Community Mortgage Program (CMP), a low-income housing-finance initiative of the National Home Mortgage Finance Corporation (NHMFC) in the Philippines, enables an association of low-income, informal settlers to finance the purchase of an undivided tract of land. Typically, the settlers are occupying land without the permission of the owner, and so applications for CMP loans are often made when residents are threatened (or think they are about to be threatened) with eviction. To receive the loans, informal settlers have to organize themselves into community associations (they have ranged in number from nine to 300 households), because under the CMP it is the association that legally acts as the borrower. The individual household members of the community association make a commitment to amortize the loan, usually for a term of 24 years at an annual interest rate of 6 percent, but CMP requires no financial track record of them to do so.

Two kinds of projects can be funded under a CMP loan. On-site projects enable illegal settlers to finance the purchase of land they already occupy; off-site projects entail their relocation to another area. Between 1989 and 2001, CMP developed 883 community projects, benefitting 111,000 families, at a total cost of P3.14 billion (3.14 billion pesos, or US $70 million at 2011 exchange rates). Between 2002 and 2007, an additional 664 projects were undertaken, benefitting a further 78,000 families, at a total cost of P3.6 billion (US $80 million) (UN-Habitat, 2009). Of all government housing programmes in the Philippines, CMP has helped the greatest number of families in the shortest time with the smallest aggregate loans. It is also cost-effective, in that only a relatively small amount is needed to provide urban poor households with land-tenure security. According to NHMFC, the average loan made under CMP from 1989 to 2000 was P28,039 (about US $660) per beneficiary – only 15 percent of the average loan made by other government housing programmes. Moreover, the average monthly payment by a household on a CMP loan is P185.00 (less than US $4.50), a readily affordable amount even to very low-income households. From 1993 to 1998, CMP's collection efficiency exceeded that of the Unified Home Lending Programme (UHLP) and other Philippine publicly financed housing programmes, including those under the Philippine National Housing Authority.

Source: Llanto, 2007, p7.

The growth of community funds and the emphasis on socially oriented savings and loans has paralleled the growth of shelter microfinance. In essence, community funds are financial mechanisms that enable collective investments for shelter improvement, supporting any one or more of the following: land purchase, land preparation, infrastructure installation, service provision, and housing construction, extension and improvement. Their most visible distinguishing characteristic is how their funding is perceived. Community funds use savings and loans to trigger a development process that strengthens the social bonds among community members (building social capital). Stronger social bonds make it more likely that loans will be repaid, that existing finance within the community will be used effectively, and that other development objectives will be secured.

In practice, community funds and microfinance agencies share a good many overlapping interests. Like community funds, microfinance institutions are keen to find new ways of reducing poverty – many of them, after all, remain mission-led development agencies. At the same time, community funds face issues of loan- and debt-management similar to the ones that plague microfinance. Both kinds of institutions are eager to learn about new tools and mechanisms for addressing such challenges. Moreover, both kinds lie on a continuum that includes microfinance programmes emphasizing the collective features of a neighbourhood (strengthening local organizations, improving relations between them and political and state agencies, and the like) and community funds that emphasize market-oriented financial investments. Some agencies, including the ones specializing in microfinance, recognize that money is just one aspect of what is needed.

Yet despite their similarities, community funds and shelter microfinance do have distinct objectives, which explain their different loan orientations. Most microfinance initiatives emphasize integrating the borrower with the financial markets. By contrast, most community funds emphasize inclusive and equitable access to tenure security and basic services (IIED, 2005), which entails their close involvement (and that of the communities they work with) with local authorities. Thus, as I remarked earlier, improvements financed by community funds must comply with current laws, rules and regulations governing construction and land development.

Another important feature of community funds is that part of the funding they provide is subsidized – in other words, part of each loan they make comes either from the state and/or from international development assistance, and is not expected to be repaid. The subsidies may go to reduce interest rates, to extend funding to everyone in a community, or to reach low-income communities. It is important to recognize that subsidy providers view their subsidies not as money lost, but rather as social-protection funds that reduce poverty and promote social welfare, which are being used particularly effectively because they encourage strong local ownership (Mitlin, 2003).

Because of their emphasis on securing land and upgrading neighbourhoods, community-fund programmes work best with relatively stable communities of the urban poor, with some capacity for financial management. Communities in Thailand, for instance, were able to analyze the costs of buying land on the edge of Bangkok, and found that, though initially the land appeared affordable, in the longer term it was too expensive.[17] (A more effective strategy for acquiring title to land, they decided, was to join together into networks of urban communities and exploit their collective strength to negotiate for tenure to the land they already occupied.)

Unfortunately, however, community funds, like the other three kinds of institutions engaged in shelter finance for the poor, continue to have difficulties reaching the poorest of the poor. Research on the Community Mortgage Program (CMP), a Philippine community fund (see Box 6.2 on p119) shows that most neighbourhood associations able to secure CMP loans come from the second and third lowest income deciles; the lowest income groups struggle to be included.[18]

Yet there are promising efforts to bridge this gap. Shack/Slum Dwellers International (SDI), a network of grassroots organizations and support NGOs, has recognized that the monthly cycles imposed by loan providers have often been out of sync with the one- to five-day cycles within which the poor manage their livelihoods. SDI's member groups make widespread use of community funds, and their core activities have been organized around a daily cycle of saving, to ensure that even the poorest can participate.

In Kenya, a new policy has created Special Planning Areas to address another kind of mismatch between community-fund loan providers and the poor: the mainly informal organization of construction within low-income settlements and the very strict codes, rules and procedures enforced by governments and their agencies. In such Special Planning Areas, strict building regulations have been relaxed to enable communities to experiment with incremental upgrading of services and housing.[19] Elsewhere, the development of strong grassroots organizations has also helped the lowest income groups negotiate with the state to transform local planning rules and regulations, thereby making local improvements more affordable. But even when state support is secured, it remains vulnerable to changes in political priorities.[20]

Even as community-fund programmes evolve, they face the same fundamental threats to their long-term viability as they always have: the need for high enough rates of loan repayments to maintain capital in the programme, and the need for access to subsidy finance.

Conclusion

Upgrading is so important for the life of the urban poor, because they are 'illegal' they don't have security, they don't have rights. The poor are usually not considered as *bona fide* citizens – once you change their tenure status, their citizenship in the city also undergoes a change, through the upgrading process.

Somsook Boonyabancha, 2007, p8

Yet there are important limits to the contribution finance can make to addressing inadequate shelter. Lack of investment capital is part of the problem, but many housing inadequacies are hard to remedy even if finance is in place. Tenure and services cannot easily be 'bought' by individual citizens – they are collective goods. The absence of such secure tenure and services not only affects the health and security of the poor, but, as noted in the quotation by Somsook Boonyabancha, Director of Thailand's Community Organization Development Institute (CODI), it also creates social exclusion.

A strong emphasis has been placed in recent years on neo-liberal policies, along with their increased reliance on the market and its mechanisms. What is perhaps most visible in looking at markets, however, is who is being included and what they are receiving, rather than who falls into the cracks left behind: groups that cannot be reached by the kinds of support being provided.

Thus, for instance, there appears to be little concerted effort to extend the reach of mortgage finance to relatively neglected groups. Whereas opportunities to obtain mortgage finance may have increased, no comprehensive strategy seems to have emerged that could extend such finance to those who work in the informal sector in such a way that it reduces their house prices and costs of borrowing.

The growth of microfinance reflects a willingness to support households that can only afford small loans, but the emphasis on those with relatively secure tenure limits the value of this strategy. Perhaps the most notable shortcoming of microfinance is its inability to address access to sanitation and water (MDG targets in their own right) and secure tenure. Although community funds do seek to address these issues, they (like social-housing initiatives) must continue to find sources of subsidies if they are to maintain the scale and accessibility of their programmes.

More active engagement with citizens is evident across the housing sector. The shift to demand-driven subsidies (see Chapter 7) has helped to identify suitable beneficiaries and to broaden the options households have in choosing the kind and location of the homes they will receive under social-housing programmes. Neighbourhood upgrading, too, is generally associated with a participatory process, at least in name.

Private commercial companies are interested in both mortgage finance and microfinance lending for shelter when they believe it can be profitable. Governments, too – particularly in Latin America and Asia – continue to be engaged with the shelter sector. In some cases, states have made innovative attempts to work with commercial interests. The Slum Rehabilitation Scheme in Mumbai, India, offers free housing to slum dwellers, which is financed by permitting private developers to build at increased densities (thereby generating an additional surplus for the developers).[21] State support for mortgage finance also continues, as do government attempts to make mortgage markets more effective. Support for neighbourhood improvements in low-income settlements remains ongoing in many large cities, and that support appears to be growing. And the potential benefits of combining neighbourhood upgrading programmes with small loans for individual housing improvements are increasingly recognized (Satyanarayana, 2007, p6).

Notes

1 In Zambia, between 1985 and 2000, the average annual mortgage interest rate oscillated between 20 and 90 percent (Groves, 2004).
2 These perceived risks persist even when incremental housing is backed by the state, such as in Brazil (Rodrigues and Rolnick, 2007).
3 Ministério das Obras Publicas e Urbanismo, *A Privatização do Stock Habita-cional Público*, Luanda, 2003, quoted in Cain (2007).
4 See Alder and Mutero (2007), p4 for an example of their decline in Kenya.
5 MINUA, *Perfil Urbano em Angola*, Luanda, 2005, quoted in Cain (2007).
6 RBI regulations require that domestic commercial banks lend as much as 40 percent of net bank credit to 'priority sectors', including housing. The corresponding figure for foreign banks is 32 percent.
7 Project number 44936.
8 See, for example, Venter, P. (2009) 'Housing finance in South Africa', *Housing Finance International*, September, pp5–10.
9 Sources: Mukhija (2004); Discussions with Prof Madhu Bharati, Centre for Environmental Planning and Technology, Ahmedabad, quoted in Satyanarayana (2007).
10 Freedom to Build is an interesting example of a commercial building programme for low-middle-income households that has been operating for some years in Metro Manila.
11 According to Anyamba and Nordahl (2005), p25, houses as small as 25 square metres qualify.
12 Rojas, Eduardo, Presentation to the Woodrow Wilson Center, Smithsonian Institution, May 22, 2007
13 For South Africa, see Baumann (2007); for Chile, see Jiron and Fadda (2003) and Gilbert (2004), p28.
14 See http://hofinet.org/themes/theme.aspx?id=56
15 See http://www.unhabitat.org/downloads/docs/9123_82457_CEMEXPHSubmission.pdf
16 See, for example, the discussion of cooperatives in Senegal by Tall and Gaye, (2007).
17 In these first housing schemes funded by the Urban Community Development Office (UCDO) in Thailand (1992–96), some 54 percent had previously been renting land and the remainder had been squatters.
18 Porio *et al.* (2004), pp72–3; for discussion of the trend to formal sector employees, see Porio and Crisol (2004), p218.
19 Pamoja Trust, personal communication.
20 See, for example, the discussion of FONHAPO in Mexico in Connolly (2004a).
21 Between 1996 and 2006, permission for approximately 125,000 dwelling units was given, and some 65,000 housing units were constructed (*Times of India*, 2007, quoted in Satyanarayana, 2007, p6).

References

Alder, G. and Mutero, J. (2007) 'Housing microfinance in Kenya', background paper for meeting of the CSUD/Rockefeller Foundation Global Urban Summit

Anyamba, T. and Nordahl, B. (2005) 'Review of Women's Advancement Trust development programme and the partnership with NBBL', Project Report 393, Norwegian Building Research Institute Development Studies (PIDS)

Barbosa, R., Cabannes, Y. and Morães, L. (1997) 'Tenant today, posserio tomorrow', *Environment and Urbanization*, vol 9, no 2, pp17–46

Baumann, T. (2007) 'Shelter finance strategies for the poor: South Africa', background paper for meeting of the CSUD/Rockefeller Foundation Global Urban Summit

Biswas, S. (2003) 'Housing is a productive asset – housing finance for self-employed women in India', *Small Enterprise Development*, vol 14, no 1, pp49–55

Boonyabancha, S. (2007) 'Baan Mankong', background paper for meeting of the CSUD/Rockefeller Foundation Global Urban Summit

Buckley, B. and Kalarickal, J. (2004) 'Shelter strategies for the urban poor: idiosyncratic and successful but hard mysterious', World Bank Policy Research Working Paper 3427, World Bank, Washington DC

Cain, A. (2007) 'Housing microfinance in post-conflict Angola', *Environment and Urbanization*, vol 19, no 2, pp361–390.

Calderon, J. (2004) 'The formalisation of property in Peru 2001–2002: the case of Lima', *Habitat International*, vol 28, pp289–300

CGAP (2004) 'Housing microfinance, Donor Brief No. 20', CGAP, Washington, DC

Cities Alliance (2002) 'SEWA Bank's housing microfinance program in India', *Shelter Finance for the Poor Series*, Cities Alliance, Washington, DC

Connolly, P. (2004a) 'The Mexican National Popular Housing Fund', in D. Mitlin and D. Satterthwaite (eds) *Empowering Squatter Citizen*, Earthscan, London, pp82–111

Datta, K. (1999) 'A gendered perspective on formal and informal housing finance in Botswana', in G Jones and K. Datta (eds) *Housing and Finance in Developing Countries*, Routledge, London, pp192–212

[*The*] *Economist* (2011) 'Latin America's housing boom. It's not all froth: Big price hikes at the top end reflect a new, richer reality', May 5, http://www.economist.com/node/18651524, accessed September 11, 2011

Escobar, A. and Merrill, S.R. (2004) 'Housing microfinance: the state of the practice', in F. Daphins and B. Ferguson (eds) *Housing Microfinance: A Guide to Practice*, Kumarian Press, Bloomfield, NJ, pp33–68

Ferguson, B. (2003) 'Housing microfinance – a key to improving habitat and the sustainability of microfinance institutions', *Small Enterprise Development*, vol 14, no 1, pp21–31

Fernandez, V. (2004) 'Housing finance – the case of Chile', mimeo

Gilbert, A. (2002a) 'Power, ideology and the Washington Consensus: The development and spread of Chilean housing policy', *Housing Studies*, vol 17, no 2, pp305–324

Gilbert, A. (2002b) 'On the mystery of capital and the myths of Hernando de Soto', *International Development Planning Review*, vol 24, no 1, pp1–19

Gilbert, A. (2004) 'Helping the poor through housing subsidies: lessons from Chile, Colombia and South Africa', *Habitat International*, vol 28, pp13–40

Groves, R. (2004) 'Challenges facing the provision of affordable housing in African cities', *Housing Finance International*, June, pp26–31

Gwinner, W.B. and Sanders, J. (2010) 'The sub-prime crisis: implications for emerging markets', *Housing Finance International*, June, pp5–13

Hardoy, J. and Satterthwaite, D. (1989) *Squatter Citizen*, Earthscan, London

Henry-Lee, A. (2005) 'The nature of poverty in the garrison constituencies in Jamaica', *Environment and Urbanization*, vol 17, no 2, pp83–99

Hoek-Smit, M. (2005) 'The housing finance sector in Indonesia', Warton School, University of Pennsylvania, mimeo.

IIED (2005) 'Report of the International Workshop on Housing Finance', ACHR/IIED/CODI, Bangkok, June

Jiron, M.P. and Fadda, G. (2003) 'A quality of life assessment to improve urban and housing policies in Chile', paper presented to the *World Bank Urban Research Symposium 2003*, Washington, DC

Kabir, A., Rahman, A., Salway, S. and Pryer, J. (2000) 'Sickness among the urban poor: a barrier to livelihood security.' *Journal for International Development*, vol 12, pp707–722

Lall, S. and Lall, V.D. (2003) 'ITDG integrated urban housing strategy experiences of a secondary town – Alwar', paper presented to the International Workshop on Integrated Housing Development, Rugby, 16–18 March 2003

Lall, S.V., Suri, A. and Deichmann, U. (2006) 'Household savings and residential mobility in informal settlements in Bhopal, India', *Urban Studies*, vol 43, no 7, pp1025–1039.

Llanto, G. (2007) 'Shelter finance strategies for the poor: the Philippines', background paper prepared for the meeting of the CSUD/Rockefeller Foundation Global Urban Summit

Malhotra, M. (2003) 'Financing her home, one wall at a time', *Environment and Urbanization*, vol 15, no 2, pp217–228

Mayo, S. (1999) 'Subsidies in Housing', *Sustainable Development Department Technical Papers Series*, Inter-American Development Bank, Washington, DC

McGranahan, G. (2007) 'Urban environments, wealth and health: shifting burdens and possible responses in low and middle-income nations', Urban Environment Discussion Paper, London: International Institute for Environment and Development

Mills, S. (2007) 'The Kuyasa Fund: housing microcredit in South Africa', *Environment and Urbanization*, vol 19, no 2, pp457–469.

Mitlin, D. (2003) 'Finance for shelter: recent history, future perspectives', *Small Enterprise Development*, vol 14, no 1, pp11–20

Mitlin, D. (2007) 'Beyond win-win', in T. Bebbington and W. McCourt (eds) *Development Success: Statecraft in the South*, Palgrave Macmillan, London

Mohamed, S.I. (1997) 'Tenants and tenure in Durban', *Environment and Urbanization*, vol 9, no 2, pp101–118

Mukhija, V. (2004) 'The contradictions in enabling private developers of affordable housing: a cautionary case from Ahmedabad, India', *Urban Studies*, 41, no 11, pp2231–2244

Mulas, A. (2005) 'Setting the context: Mexico', *Housing Finance International*, September, pp27–33

Murcia de López, E. and Castillo, L. (1997) 'El Salvador: a case of urban renovation and rehabilitation of mesones', *Environment and Urbanization*, vol 9, no 2, pp161–179

Nenova, Tatiana. (2010) *Expanding Housing Finance to the Under-served in South Asia*, World Bank, Washington, DC

Ogu, V.I. and Ogbuozobe, J.E. (2001) 'Housing policy in Nigeria: towards enablement of private housing development', *Habitat International*, vol 25, pp473–492

Porio, E. with Crisol, C.S., Magno, N.F., Cid, D. and Paul, E.N. (2004) 'The Community Mortgage Programme: an innovative social housing programme in the Philippines and its outcomes', in D. Mitlin and D. Satterthwaite (eds) *Empowering Squatter Citizen*, Earthscan, London, pp54–81

Porio, E. and Crisol, C. (2004) 'Property rights, security of tenure and the urban poor in Metro Manila', *Habitat International*, vol 28, no 2, pp203–219

Pryer, J., Rogers, S. and Rahman, A. (2005) 'Work-disabling illness as a shock for livelihoods and poverty in Dhaka slums, Bangladesh', *International Planning Studies*, vol 10, no 1, pp69–80

Renaud, B. (1999) 'The financing of social housing in integrating financial markets: a view from developing countries', *Urban Studies*, vol 36, no 4, pp755–773

Reserve Bank of India (RBI) (2006) 'Report on Trend and Progress in Banking in India 2005–06', Reserve Bank of India, November 2006

Rodrigues, E. and Rolnick, R. (2007) 'Shelter finance strategies for the poor: Brazil', background paper for meeting of the CSUD/Rockefeller Foundation Global Urban Summit

Satyanarayana, S. (2007) 'Shelter finance strategies for the poor: India', background paper for meeting of the CSUD/Rockefeller Foundation Global Urban Summit

Schneider, F. (2002) 'Size and measurement of the informal economy in 110 countries around the world', presented at a Workshop of the Australian National Tax Centre, Canberra, July 2002

Seki, M. and Watanabe, M. (1998) 'Housing finance and capital markets in Indonesia', in M. Watanabe (ed.) *New Directions in Asian Housing Finance*, International Finance Corporation, pp113–126

Sheuya, S.A. (2007) 'Reconceptualizing housing finance in informal settlements: the case of Dar es Salaam, Tanzania', *Environment and Urbanization*, vol 19, no 2, pp441–456

Smets, P. (2002) *Housing Finance and the Urban Poor: Building and Financing Low-Income Housing in Hyderabad, India*, Vrije University, Amsterdam

Stein, A. (2007) 'Shelter finance strategies for the poor: Central America', background paper for meeting of the CSUD/Rockefeller Foundation Global Urban Summit

Tall, S.M. and Gaye, G. (2007) 'Housing finance in Senegal', background paper for meeting of the CSUD/Rockefeller Foundation Global Urban Summit

UN-Habitat (2003) *The Global Report on Human Settlements 2003: The Challenge of Slums*, Earthscan for UN-Habitat, London

UN-Habitat (2009) 'Community-based housing finance initiatives: the case of the Community Mortgage Program', UN-Habitat, Nairobi

Wang, Y.P., Wang, Y. and Bramley, G. (2005) 'Chinese housing reform in state-owned enterprises and its impact on different social groups', *Urban Studies*, vol 42, no 10, pp1859–1978

Chapter 7

Innovations in shelter finance

Diana Mitlin

Innovations in shelter finance

Innovations in addressing shelter needs are clustering around four basic approaches, which have different objectives and target groups and hence different funding modalities. Since the approaches target different groups, they should be regarded as complementary, each with an important role to play in any strategy that hopes to address the housing needs of low-income or disadvantaged groups. No group can meet its housing needs if the needs of other, more powerful groups are not also met – all that happens is that the more powerful groups 'crowd out' the less powerful. Hence, even if the basic objective is to target low-income groups, a range of solutions are needed that address the housing needs of all income groups.

The four approaches are as follows:

- Market led – bringing mortgage finance 'down-market'.
- Integrated neighbourhood development – upgrading existing settlements or developing greenfield sites, with optional housing microfinance for individual households.
- Comprehensive, inclusive, citywide development – multi-option development of low-income settlements.
- Federated, community-driven development – locally managed improvements done in alliance with state agencies and coordinated by an autonomous network of grassroots organizations.

All four approaches seek to work with demand, rather than simply supplying housing whether demand is present or not, as government programmes traditionally have done. Mortgage finance, of course, works with market demand, whereas citywide development and community-driven development respond to the willingness of local communities to organize themselves and draw down available funds. Integrated neighbourhood development is the only approach that is driven primarily by the willingness of the state to supply resources, and it responds to the almost constant, informal upgrading process.

Each approach seeks to ensure secure land tenure, gain access to services and make affordable home improvements for the groups they target. Each encourages resident contributions and gives as much choice as possible to the residents, in a non-directive system of allocation. Each approach provides a framework for combining public and individual investments, sometimes with the participation of commercial financial institutions. All four approaches, to some extent, try to recover costs, in part so that subsidy finance can be spread as widely as possible. The final two approaches, aimed at the lowest income households (as well as the second approach, albeit in a more dilute form) directly address the relations between asset accumulation and poverty, the problems of credit and poverty, and the non-material aspects of poverty.

Demand-led programmes can use finance in two distinct ways, termed here 'direct' and 'creative'. By direct, I mean financing provided for housing or infrastructure investments, rather than for other objectives such as social integration, peace, poverty reduction (beyond housing poverty) or economic development. Creative finance, by contrast, does address such broader social objectives, using finance (sometimes in conjunction with improvements in, for example, basic services) to catalyze change. In creative finance, for instance, community and individual savings and local fund management become strategic tools for changing social relations, both within low-income settlements as well as with outsiders. These changing social relations can amount to nothing less than a newly recognized role for low-income settlements in the economic prosperity of the city, enabling grassroots organizations of low-income households to negotiate for the necessary political support.

Box 7.1 elaborates some of the many ways in which finance can be an effective means to address shelter poverty.

Box 7.1   Finance as a tool for inclusion and to reinforce collective action: Baan Mankong

Collective finance – in which everyone in a community works together, as a group – is a means to secure greater financial security for all. If people don't have a savings group, if they don't have a communal financial-management system, only a few better-off people in the community will be able to work within the market system. But if we want to get everybody on board, we need a collective financial system that links everyone, no matter how poor they are. In that way, the entire community goes ahead as a group. Collective finance provides a mechanism for bringing people together from all the different economic levels within the community, and a means for addressing the economic needs of all those members. A communal financial system can act as a buffer between the outside financial system (which is very stiff and accessible only to the better-off), and the internal, people-owned financial system (which is highly flexible, informal, communal and constantly making adjustments to accommodate the crises that are part of poverty).

Having a collective financial system means having collective decision-making. Collective decision-making is never easy. There are always those troublesome community members who don't cooperate or don't follow the rules, or make off with money. But if the requirement is that everybody is part of the project, as with the Baan Mankong ['Secure Housing'] Programme [in Thailand], the not-easy process of dealing with these people and these problems becomes a very important social-development opportunity.

Once people can manage their finances and can start upgrading their community collectively, a lot of communal creativity is unleashed. You start creating a lot more other communal activities. Now, for instance, because the community organization owns the land, you activate creative thinking about how people will live together as a group, how they will help each other, how they will collect loan repayments from everybody in such a way that people in subgroups can help each other? They have to figure out how to ensure that anyone who has problems or defaults on their payments gets taken care of, because the community still has to repay its loan collectively. They have to have a system of support. So little by little, through all these activities and all these systems, you foster more and more collectivity. And this collectivity can be channelled in many ways to meet people's various needs. When people are linked together through the kind of collectivity that is built in to the Baan Mankong process, they almost automatically start dreaming up, and then putting into practice, ideas about how to resolve their needs – and they do so in highly creative ways. This is what I call human culture!

Somehow in recent decades, changes in the world have eroded this collective culture, so we are more likely to think of individual culture – especially in cities. So what we are trying to do in this collective system is bring back this human culture, which is so rich, which is limitless, which has such a lot of warmth, friendliness and flexibility in it. And it is still there, especially in poor communities – it's only a question of how to tap it, to revive it and strengthen it

Source: Boonyabancha, 2007

Each of the four approaches to shelter that I listed earlier responds to a distinct combination of political and social pressures. Ideology clearly plays a role in the choice of approaches and mechanisms. Yet, at least among the three approaches that aim to address the needs of the lowest income households, ideology is not the outstanding feature. Rather, their differences appear to be related to the scope and orientation of the sponsoring agencies.

The four approaches all lie along a continuum of responses, both individualized and collective, to the needs and demands for housing: a core challenge for humankind in the twenty-first century. The approaches also reflect the spectrum of political responses to some of the broadest questions we face in the twenty-first century, issues of environmental sustainability, security, identity and values: which problems can best be solved with individually held assets, through the market, and which need to be addressed through other institutional mechanisms and frameworks, with different actors and alternative logics of operation?

Today's dominance of neo-liberal policy and planning reflects the belief that individual choices are, if not the best, then the best possible. That view, which came to the fore in the 1980s and is still powerful today, holds that collective mechanisms are prone to free-riding and corruption, that they encourage people to act in their own self-interest even if they are exploiting others, and (as a result) that they lead to citizen disengagement. Accordingly, neo-liberal policies have promoted markets wherever possible, using state regulation only to control negative consequences. More recently, attempts have been made to strengthen collective endeavours, but society has been struggling to find an appropriate form for exercising collective choice and action. Many still argue that the state is the institution through which collective choice should be made and collective action taken. And, at least in modern advanced capitalist societies, it usually is – for instance, the state provides basic services such as police and fire protection. But the enormous scope of the modern state, its capture by elite groups and its recognized willingness to operate in its own interests rather than in the interests of those it allegedly seeks to represent and serve, all raise serious questions about its ability, acting alone, to represent and address issues of collective choice. Thus a number of alternative proposals and actions have sought to recapture citizen collectivity at a local level, through a range of measures that can loosely be termed 'participatory governance'. All the demand-led approaches to shelter finance (except the efforts simply to bring mortgage finance down-market) seek to support the challenge of engaging collective action, in various ways and at various levels. Further examples of participatory governance are elaborated in David Vlahov and Waleska Caiaffa's contribution to this volume (Chapter 4).

Down-marketing mortgage finance

The economies of scale that attract suppliers of construction and financial services to 'down-market' households are present primarily in economies that include a substantial lower-middle-income group. Thus, as I noted in the preceding chapter, (Chapter 6, p112), the relevance of down-market mortgages for low-income households (as opposed to lower-middle-income households) remains limited, since low-income households usually cannot afford a complete house. Because of the stress on lower-middle-income households, the growth of down-market mortgage lending varies widely by region. Most of it is taking place in relatively high-income countries of the Global South, or in countries with rapidly growing economies. Some countries have sought to link the urban poor to the formal financial sector through support for housing provided through financial packages that combine both subsidies and loans – but this strategy does not appear to have been particularly successful. Two recent studies of South Africa suggested that borrowers who could afford a choice preferred to take several smaller loans instead of one large mortgage, to minimize their risk (Tomlinson, 2007). As I noted in Chapter 6 (p105), there is a well-recognized group of potential borrowers who might be able to afford mortgage finance but who are denied access to it – because, for various reasons, financial institutions perceive them to be high-risk investments. Banking institutions may feel that poor families with low incomes cannot be trusted. Or the banks may be reluctant to loan to informal workers with unverifiable incomes, from which deductions cannot be made directly. Yet some innovative institutions are seeking to extend finance to these groups. One is SOFELES (*Sociedades Financieras de Objeto Limitado*), in Mexico, now estimated to be the main source of private home lending in that country (World Bank, 2004, p4). SOFOLES appears to be particularly successful in reaching out to informally employed households. It has maintained steady collection rates as well as an average default of only 2.4 per cent per year on total outstanding mortgage balances. Aggregated levels of non-repayment were lower than those of either public lenders or banks. This sterling performance is the result of a number of specific strategies: requiring borrowers to have enough savings to make the mortgage repayments for a period of time, making 'in-person delivery of statements' and accepting 'payments at on-site locations and outside of traditional business hours' (Joint Center for Housing Studies, 2004, p35). Recent evidence, however, suggests that families have been struggling to repay their loans since 2008 because the global recession has reduced earnings both in Mexico and from Mexican migrants working overseas.

Integrated neighbourhood development

One set of housing programmes, notable for their national scale as well as for the depth and complexity of the integrated development options they offer to informal settlements, has been established in each of five countries in Central America (Costa Rica, El Salvador, Guatemala, Honduras and Nicaragua), with the financial and organizational support of the Swedish International Development Cooperation Agency (Sida). The programmes seek to address the lack of decent shelter (housing as well as land services) by improving 'the living conditions of the urban poor, especially of families living in slums, tenements, unplanned and informal settlements and precarious neighbourhoods'.[1] Although Sida's own emphasis is on shelter improvements, its funding for these programmes also supports upgrades of existing low-income areas – upgrades that may take the form of obtaining tenure security through participatory planning, making investments in basic services and infrastructure, and, to a limited extent, making investments in new housing. Sida justifies this broadening of its usual investment strategy on the grounds that democratic processes need to be strengthened and peace agreements reinforced, goals the Central American programmes seem to support by improving governance and reducing conflict.

The catalyst for each national programme has been a specialist agency, created in some cases through negotiation between Sida and the various central government ministries. In Honduras, an existing government programme was transformed into a not-for-profit foundation. Nicaragua took a slightly different path, first establishing a government programme and then transforming it into a not-for-profit foundation. In Guatemala, a commercial trust fund was created. All these programmes deliberately bring together a number of different institutions: central and local government; non-governmental organizations (NGOs); conventional and non-conventional (microfinance) agencies; and community-based organizations. Development-assistance funds are allocated to three components of each programme:

- Technical assistance – in providing services and securing land tenure (that is, assistance both to the executing agencies and to the target populations).
- Loans – including microloans, for housing improvement, new housing construction and income-generating activities.
- Institutional capacity building and development – particularly for intermediary institutions (those that provide basic services, new housing and housing improvements).

Investments in land vary considerably with differences in local attitudes and laws. Costa Rica, for example – unlike other countries – tolerates insecure tenure: the investment process can begin even if the borrower has not acquired title to the land, but titles are required to secure mortgage loans for housing investments or for infrastructure upgrades. Thus the Foundation for Housing Promotion (FUPROVI), a non-profit Costa Rican development organization, focuses on providing technical assistance in legalizing tenure to low-income communities and households. The organization also pre-finances shelter investments made during the legal process of securing tenure, then reclaims its subsidies once tenure is secure. In Honduras, Nicaragua, and, to some extent, El Salvador, tenure is not required either for infrastructure investment in state land or for small housing loans, provided there is no evidence of any conflicting land claims. Still, the agencies all support legalizations and provide technical assistance to low-income households and communities.

Infrastructure finance is secured through central government agencies (with some development assistance), municipal authorities and local residents; for example, in Nicaragua, infrastructure improvements to a community are financed jointly by the Local Development Programme (PRODEL) (50 percent), the municipality (35 per cent) and the community (15 percent, through savings, repayments and in-kind contributions).

Loans for individual home improvements are available, usually through microfinance institutions (MFIs) or, in some cases, through the specialist central government agencies. Interest rates are set just high enough to cover administrative costs, insure against default, technical assistance and inflation; in 2003–04, for instance, interest rates were between 18 and 24 per cent. The size of the typical loan for new housing varied between US $1500 and $3000 and averaged US $800 for housing improvement. The programmes accept a wide variety of collateral and securities from households (for mortgages in particular, pawning valuables to use as collateral and the cosigning of loans are common practices). In Costa Rica, El Salvador and Honduras, state housing subsidies are available to help consolidate assets, though legal tenure is usually required to receive a subsidy. Pilot schemes in Nicaragua and Guatemala are also exploring subsidies.

The contribution of these programmes to addressing shelter needs has been small but significant. By the end of 2010, they had benefited approximately 153,000 low-income families, representing some 3.3 per cent of the total urban population of the five countries and about 9 per cent of the total urban poor. The impact of the various national programmes has varied, but it is estimated that they have reached about 18% of the urban poor in Costa Rica, 14 per cent in Honduras and 10 per cent in Nicaragua. According to the Costa Rican Ministry of Housing, from 1987 until 2004 nearly 220,000 families received state subsidies, making FUPROVI responsible for about 10 per cent of the new housing and improvements in the country. A strong, consistent commitment by the state to allocate resources for the past 20 years, as well as higher incomes in Costa Rica than in its neighbouring countries, has made finding housing solutions there easier.

Taking national prosperity into account, perhaps the most notable successes have been in the lower-income countries of Honduras and Nicaragua. About 20 per cent of those assisted there receive housing loans, a figure that holds across various income levels.

Across the five countries, the average investment cost per person is about US $100. Most low-income families that participated in the lending programmes earned at least one minimum wage per month (US $90 in Nicaragua and US $150 in Costa Rica). Of course, there are always households whose incomes are too low to take out loans. Some MFIs prefer to lend to families with very low but steady incomes, rather than to those working in the informal sector; repayments can simply be deducted from the wages of the former. Other families are helped mainly through financing for infrastructure and basic services. The intention is to reach very low-income households with basic services alone, and to provide mortgage or home-improvement loans to higher-income families.

This Central American model has been applied in a number of other Latin American countries (IDB, 2006, p1). The model has three integrated core components: financial assistance to secure land tenure, infrastructure improvements (perhaps with a community contribution), and microfinance loans for housing improvements to those households that can afford to take out loans. Subsidy finance can be easily blended into this model at a number of stages, as in some of the Central American countries.

But the model has been less widely used outside of Latin America. Sida tried and failed to replicate it in South Africa during the second half of the 1990s. (More recently, the Kuyasa Fund in Cape Town has developed a microfinance programme for housing to enable households to gain additional finance to the state subsidy (Mills, 2007)). The model has not been applied in Asia, either, at least at full scale – though its elements are present in a number of programmes in countries such as India, Indonesia, and the Philippines.

Comprehensive citywide strategies

There has been some recognition of the need to upgrade all informal settlements citywide, and considerable efforts to do so have been made in Brazil and India. One notable recent example is the *Baan Mankong* ('Secure Housing') Programme in Thailand, which the Thai government announced in 2003 as one of two then-new programmes for the urban poor. The government's goal was to reach 1 million low-income households within five years. Baan Mankong, according to its website, 'channels government funds in the form of infrastructure subsidies and [housing] loans directly to poor communities'. (The second programme is the *Baan Ua Arthorn* – 'we care' – programme, within which the National Housing Authority designs, constructs and sells ready-to-occupy flats and houses at subsidized rates to lower-income households. This programme has had some problems in scaling up.)

Under the Baan Mankong Programme, the communities themselves – low-income households, their community organizations and networks of those organizations – plan, design, manage and implement improvements to their housing and to basic services. The programme is managed by a government-financed programme known as the Community Organization Development Institute (CODI; see Box 7.1 on p128, which is in turn a branch of Thailand's Ministry of Social Development and Human Security. The community organizations and networks also work with local governments, professionals, universities and NGOs in their city to survey all the low-income communities, and then formulate a plan to upgrade conditions within three to four years. To oversee the plan's implementation, each city establishes a joint committee made up of representatives from all these groups. This committee seeks to build new, cooperative relationships, integrate housing for the urban poor into the city's overall development and create a mechanism for resolving future housing problems. Once the upgrade plan has been finalized, CODI channels the infrastructure subsidies and housing loans directly to the communities.

The Baan Mankong Programme places few conditions on its participants, thereby allowing communities of the urban poor, their networks and other stakeholders in a city freedom to design and lead their own projects. These upgrade projects build on the community-managed programmes that CODI and its predecessor, the Urban Community Development Office (UCDO), have supported since 1992, as well as on people's capacity to manage their own needs collectively. They also build on what 'slum' communities have already developed, recognizing the large investments the communities have already made in their homes. The projects upgrade existing settlements whenever possible, but, if residents must be relocated, a site is sought close by to minimize the economic costs and social upheavals to households.

Infrastructure subsidies of 25,000 Baht (US $715) per family are available for communities doing upgrades in situ, and 35,000 Baht (US $1000) per family for relocations. CODI makes bulk housing loans to community cooperatives at a subsidized annual rate of 2 per cent, and communities add their own margin (for management, community activities and welfare) and on-lend to families at 4 per cent. (CODI's usual housing loan rate is 4 per cent, but under the Baan Mankong Programme the government subsidizes half this interest rate.) Individual communities can access a grant equal to 5 per cent of the total infrastructure subsidy to help fund the project development and management costs.

The programme initially set a target of improving housing, living conditions and tenure security for 300,000 households in 2000 poor communities in 200 Thai cities within five years. In August 2005, the Thai government approved US $240 million to support this programme. Between 2003 and 2010, within the Baan Mankong Programme, CODI approved 745 projects in more than 1300 communities (some projects cover more than one community) spread across some 249 urban centres and covering more than 80,000 households. CODI plans a considerable expansion of the programme within the next few years. Slightly less than two-thirds (64 per cent) of the beneficiaries belong to communities that were upgraded in situ and negotiated long-term secure collective tenure on that site. Fourteen per cent of the beneficiaries relocated to new sites within two kilometres of their former homes. Those communities that moved to public land negotiated long-term collective leases to that land; the ones that moved to private land purchased the land at prices they negotiated with CODI with loans made to the community cooperative. By 2010, the total number of households reached by the programme had grown to more than 25 per cent of the numbers that Baan Mankong targeted, but they still represented only about 13 per cent of the 600,000 families in need within towns and cities in Thailand. During the same period, grants for infrastructure upgrading exceeded US $46 million; and loans for land and housing exceeded US $52 million. More than 82 percent of households are now living in settlements that have also achieved tenure security, via long-term leases or collective land ownership.

The Baan Mankong Programme also seeks to enhance the collective understanding by the poor of their own city as well as their own neighbourhood. By collaborating on the management of the programme, groups of urban poor can not only strengthen their interrelationships, but also gain a better understanding of their collective asset, the land on which they live (see Box 7.1 on p128). Indeed, the CODI board includes representatives from community organizations and government, thus further opening up communications channels that have the potential to transform the way the poor connect with their own local governments.

CODI also supports community-managed savings-and-loan groups, as well as the community networks to which these groups belong. Savings groups, and the savings on deposit with them, are key elements in the community's management of its own affairs. They enable communities to take the lead in defining and realizing their own development options, using the land they live on as collateral for home-improvement and new-housing loans. Such decentralization, or local management, is seen as critical, since local groups are clearly in the best position to work out the most effective strategies for getting the most from the financing they have secured. CODI's support of the community networks is vital, too, because they enable local groups to couple their ideas with the necessary skills, capacities and support to see the ideas through to a successful conclusion.

Community-driven neighbourhood development

Shack/Slum Dwellers International (SDI) is an alliance of NGOs and federations of the homeless or landless poor, which is seeking new ways to eradicate homelessness, landlessness and poverty. The federations affiliated with SDI are engaged in many community-driven initiatives to upgrade slums and squatter settlements, improving tenure security and offering residents new development opportunities. Their goals will by now be familiar to the reader: developing new, affordable housing for low-income households, and installing infrastructure and services. The members of the federations are so-called savings schemes – not to be confused with the savings groups in Thailand supported by CODI – local groups that draw together residents (mainly women) of low-income neighbourhoods to share resources and address their common and collective needs. By pooling their financial resources first at the neighbourhood level and then at the city level, low-income residents can build relationships of mutual trust, and their collective savings become a strategic tool for attracting the resources and attention of the state.

SDI was launched in 1996, building on existing relationships between federations of savings schemes in Cambodia, India, Namibia, Nepal,

South Africa, Thailand and Zimbabwe. The alliance now includes 15 federation affiliates. Grassroots savings groups are also emerging in ten other
countries. SDI believes it has achieved some success with its methodology,
mobilizing more than two million women slum dwellers in 24 countries
of the Global South. These individual savers interact daily in a context of
savings and loans. With their own savings, along with a range of loan
and subsidy finance to which the women gained access as a result of their
enhanced financial sophistication, more than 150,000 families have secured
formal tenure to land with services, and about half of these have also been
able to improve their housing. Negotiations led by the savings groups have
helped many more families avoid eviction or secure other services.

Another advantage of community-driven development is that its priorities
are those of the members of local savings organizations, such as low-income
women living in informal and underserviced urban neighbourhoods. Organization through collective savings is particularly attractive to such women,
whose need for secure tenure, services and housing reflects their daily strug-
gles to take care of themselves and their families. Insecure tenure and inadequate housing become a way in which more powerful social actors and
agencies frame and construct the disadvantage of the poor. To counter this
image of the urban poor as impotent victims, one priority is to consolidate
a process whereby the poor, through federated organizations, can take an
active role in addressing all aspects of their inequality. For example, through
their collective strength, they can and should negotiate on their own behalf
for state support of development initiatives that they have designed for
themselves.

In Namibia, the first groups involved in the SDI process were women
living in the shacks of the former black township of Katatura, in a northwest quarter of the capital city, Windhoek. The women began exploring the
possibilities for self-help housing through credit unions in the late 1980s,
motivated by the opportunities that independence and democratic government would offer. In India, women living with their families on the pavements of Mumbai were the first group to organize to improve their housing.
In 1985, the Supreme Court provided further impetus for the women to find
safe housing locations, when it ordered that pavement structures in the city
be demolished.

The Shack Dwellers Federation of Namibia (SDFN) and its supporting
NGO, the Namibian Housing Action Group (NHAG), now include 607
savings schemes involving 18,000 Namibian households. The two organizations work closely together to promote shelter opportunities. One project is
an urban-poor fund, the Twahangana Fund, which lends at low, concessional
rates to savings groups undertaking development. The Namibian government has invited NHAG to sit on the Habitat II Committee, a government
stakeholders' forum. Windhoek also contributes to the Twahangana Fund
from the central government's Build Together Programme, which makes

subsidized home-improvement loans to individual homeowners. The government supports the fund directly as well, currently with an annual contribution of a million Namibian dollars (NAD 1 million, or US $140,000 at current exchange rates), to support SDFN's core organizational and federating expenses.

Local savings groups access finance for land and housing developments through the Twahangana Fund. Funding is available for greenfield development (on previously undeveloped land), as well as for upgrading. But to date there has been relatively little experience with upgrading. Land is sold without a subsidy at the cost of its development (though clearly there is scope for negotiation about the buyer's share of bulk service costs). Local authorities offer communities the option of repaying land costs over several years. The cheapest land is sold as a block, with bulk infrastructure connections only. Communities can borrow from the Twahangana Fund to develop infrastructure, but many choose to use the savings accrued within their savings group instead. Costs are further reduced because households manage the land development and contribute unskilled labour to the effort. The authorities permit them to remain in the shacks they have already built if they cannot afford the additional costs of development. All these factors substantially reduce the costs of basic shelter improvements, and households can join one of these programmes at a monthly cost of less than NAD 100 (US $14). Those who wish to improve their housing can borrow (through Twahangana) for housing developments. The maximum housing loan is NAD 20,000 (US $2800) with an annual interest rate of 5 per cent and repayable over 11 to 20 years. This finance is managed by NHAG but is actually provided directly by a central government programme that uses the Twahangana Fund as one of a number of conduits.

What have these programmes accomplished in Namibia so far? First, 3100 members of SDFN have secured land. (To put this in perspective, SDFN now counts about 18,000 members, or 15 per cent of shack dwellers in the country.) Of the 4646 landed members, 2542, or 55 per cent of them, have also accessed loans for improved services and infrastructure; the other 62 per cent have secured access to services by purchasing serviced land through local financing and/or personal savings. Slightly more than 1200 members have taken loans for housing development and improvements.[2] The federation can acquire a plot of land with access to bulk infrastructure, suitable for a family, for between NAD 1500 and NAD 3000 (US $200–$400). Many savings schemes that want to invest in infrastructure and services (e.g. extending piped water and sanitation to each house from a central supply point) simply save the money to meet the costs: typically about US $20 to $40 per household.

In India, the alliance includes three organizations: Mahila Milan ('Women Together,' a collective of women's savings schemes); the Society for the Promotion of Area Resource Centres (an NGO known as SPARC); and the

National Slum Dwellers Federation. In 1998, the alliance formed a non-profit company called SPARC Samudaya Nirman Sahayak ('SPARC's assistance to collective construction,' usually known as SSNS or 'Nirman'), to manage large-scale construction projects. By 2004, the Indian Alliance was working with more than 200,000 families in Mumbai alone, a scale of effort that has spurred interest from other cities. The alliance works closely with central, state and local government; SPARC, for instance, has been invited to sit on a number of government bodies, including the $12 billion Jawaharlal Nehru National Urban Renewal Mission (JNNURM). The breadth of the alliance's activities in India and the magnitude of its potential are reflected in its ability to collaborate with a wide range of development-assistance agencies and to play a major role in large-scale urban-development programmes, notably those with funding from a bilateral development agency (a donor agency set up by a donor government, such as USAID) and the World Bank.

The work of the Indian Alliance has strengthened local community organizations in their negotiations with all levels of state officials, and the alliance itself has been quite successful in obtaining state subsidies for housing development. In the past decade, SPARC has worked closely with commercial financial institutions that want to reach the urban poor: Unit Trust of India, the Housing and Urban Development Corporation (HUDCO), the National Housing Bank (NHB), Citibank and the Industrial Credit and Investment Corporation of India Bank (ICICI). It is worth emphasizing, however, that a financial package for the poor is useful only if it recognizes how little the lowest income households can afford.

The alliance has negotiated a number of financing options for land development. One notable example has been its effectiveness in helping groups in Mumbai eligible for benefits from transferable development rights (TDR). TDR is a cross-subsidy system that enables low-income families to secure resources from the redevelopment of designated slum areas. Households in Mumbai belonging to groups that successfully apply for TDR benefits receive a complete, finished unit in a medium-rise block free of charge. The groups obtain financing for the new housing units from commercial developers in exchange for the groups' development rights. (Developers value those rights because they allow higher density, hence more profitable, housing construction.)

Householders' groups without such rights to sell receive subsidies from the central and state governments, and make up the rest of the cost themselves. For example, in one case, units costing 75,000 rupees (Rps 75,000, or about US $1650 at current exchange rates) qualified for a Rps 50,000 (US $1100) subsidy. Of the Rps 25,000 remainder, Rps 7500 (about US $165) came from the group's savings and the remaining Rps 17,500 (US $385) was paid with funds loaned to the group at 12 per cent annual interest by SPARC. The financing to SPARC was, in turn, provided by the commercial bank ICICI, so the members repay SPARC and SPARC repays the bank.

An estimated 67 million urban poor residents of Indian cities lack adequate housing; that means India now needs to build or upgrade some 22 million housing units. Moreover, those figures do not take account of all informal settlements; if they did, the figures could be significantly higher. The Indian Alliance has secured land for about 80,000 families; of these, 6000 are living in self-built units and a further 30,000 are living in units constructed by commercial contractors and then allocated to families belonging to the federation. This building programme is actively being extended: 2200 new units are currently under construction, and negotiations are underway for 4400 more. In the experience of the alliance, household contributions must be kept as low as possible, since loans can be hard to repay. It is also important to have the collective as a buffer to assist families that have difficulties paying in any single month.

Conclusion: Mapping out questions and next steps

Constraints on the players

All the players in the effort to improve shelter for the urban poor face constraints on their actions. A review of those constraints will help set the stage for a summary of what is needed to catalyze effective responses and then scale them up, and which research questions should be given highest priority.

The urban poor themselves, both as individual households and as organized collectives, face two serious constraints. The first is the inability of state agencies to provide the poor with adequate land and access to basic services, without subjecting the poor to a regulatory system that penalizes them for their inability to invest in housing assets. The second constraint for the poor is, obviously, their income poverty and their limited ability to invest in shelter. Organized groups of the urban poor can reduce their constraints by negotiating with state agencies (or by bringing pressure on them) to create programmes that offer affordable access to housing. Organized groups can also pool resources, and so gain leverage in negotiating for additional resources. In some contexts, groups of the poor can collectively purchase private land for community-managed development: large blocks of land may be more affordable than smaller parcels. Occupancy on the land, however, is likely to remain illegal, at least for some time. In sum, despite the advantages of organizing, the resource problems of the poor remain significant.

Civil-society agencies seeking to assist the urban poor face constraints that depend to a considerable extent on the kind of assistance they offer. The three most common assistance strategies are land-rights advocacy, shelter microfinance and support to federated social movements. In addition, some agencies have a strong focus on a particular sector, such as water or housing. The most effective models are fairly well established in each case, and knowledge and tools are not lacking. But there is no agreement about how particular strategies compare in effectiveness. Strong differences of opinion persist, for example, about the relative significance of policy change versus increased pressure for implementing existing policies; the value of legal or other professional interventions versus grassroots capacities; the effectiveness of savings-based organization versus other modes of organization; and the advantages of individual versus collective finance.

Civil-society agencies, like everyone else, must live within the constraints of limited resources. But perhaps equally damaging (and frustrating!) are some of the conditions grant-makers impose, reducing an agency's flexibility in offering support to local groups. In many cases, agencies also have limited institutional capacities: civil-society agencies with appropriate skills do not exist in many relatively small urban centres. Agencies can also limit themselves: many act without effective strategies, and so end up pursuing project-based initiatives that do not grow into any significant or coherent activity. One stumbling block of civil-society organizations appears to be their limited capacity to work in genuine partnership with the urban poor. On many occasions their programmes fail to engage significant numbers of the poor – and so, predictably, the outcome is a transfer of minimal resources to a few.

One important kind of civil-society agency is the foundation. Foundations have very little interest in supporting work on urban poverty related to shelter. In Europe, the few foundations that support development tend to focus on particular countries or particular themes (e.g. children, HIV/AIDS). US foundations are more active overseas than their European counterparts, but they tend to concentrate on rural development, the environment, health and international relations – rather than on shelter for the poor.

Private-sector capacities also face constraints. Clearly the limits on what the poor can afford act as a considerable constraint that reduces anticipated profits and deters investments. Several country studies (of India, the Philippines and South Africa) suggest that in the current investment climate private companies have only limited interest in low-income construction, simply because of opportunity costs: the rates of return (albeit positive) are not as great as they are in alternative investment opportunities. That said, there are a number of indications that the private commercial sector is responding to the down-marketing of mortgage finance and the provision of capital for microfinance. As I argued earlier, however, such strategies have limited relevance for those living with insecure tenure. For the latter, the private informal sector is far more important: informal housing is often commissioned by local residents, and the dynamics of that market has received relatively little attention from the development community.

Finally, even governments face considerable constraints. A number of innovative projects and programmes initiated by government entities have been successful and reached a significant scale. In general, however, governments fail to act when they could and often fail to deploy existing resources effec-tively. Experience shows that governments are most likely to respond with progressive policies if one or more of the following conditions are met:

- Demonstrated community capacity in relevant areas. In India, the Rail-way Slum Dwellers Federation organized people living alongside the railway tracks to substantiate their claims of the need for resettlement. The organization also built up a capacity for independent verification, which was critical in persuading the government to provide alternative shelter when railway redevelopment took place.
- Evidence of community capacity to co-finance. In Windhoek, Namibia, local savings schemes demonstrated the residents' willingness and capacity to finance shelter improvements both collectively and indi-vidually. As a result, municipal regulations were rewritten to standards affordable low-income residents.
- Sustained community pressure for improvements. The political dimen-sion is highly important in gaining government support, because politi-cians require a level of confidence that there will be electoral rewards for promoting resource-intensive programmes. Political engagement is particularly necessary in gaining resources for incremental development programmes, simply because politicians and officials perceive them as less attractive: less of a 'showcase' for the politician's efforts.
- Evidence of the need for improvements within existing programmes. Project reports and academic documents convinced both the Chilean and South African governments of the need to improve the quality of contractor-built and publicly financed housing.
- Additional support for implementation. In a number of cases, state agencies appear to lack confidence in their own implementation capaci-ties. They seem to respond well to coordinated lobbying that includes the promise of technical support.
- The presence of catalyst funding to demonstrate projects that can be scaled up. Workable examples provide the state with confidence in the acceptability and affordability of the project and can be a lobbying point.

What about donor agencies? What constraints are keeping them from get-ting involved in housing? Part of their reluctance stems from early problems with low-income shelter finance and a notable lack of success in reaching the target group. The political dimension is particularly difficult for major donors to navigate. They are aware that they lack legitimacy to intervene politically, and so they tend to be overly involved in technical, 'neutral' interventions. (even though the evidence that such interventions are effec-tive is limited). Moreover, donor agencies are under increasing pressure to get 'quick' results – yet, as described earlier, there is broad agreement that effective programmes take time. They depend on building relationships so that they can include community-led activities. They rely on support from civil-society organizations, from local government and from (sometimes reluctant) state agencies, all of which has to be negotiated. Demanding quick results for impatient donors runs directly contrary to these hard-won lessons.

In spite of all these constraints, there have been successful attempts, through specific sectoral interventions, projects or, in some cases, larger scale programmes, to address shelter needs. Those successes point to the following general guidelines:

- Improvements require the participation of various different agencies which – depending on the improvement in question – may involve just one, or a combination, of these actors: the national government, the private sector, development assistance, organized local people, local government and civil-society support organizations. Involving the private sector in construction can make a significant contribution to building capacity – the speed and volume of construction activity – and sometimes to financial resources, but the activities of private companies need to be managed.
- Subsidy finance is required if improvements are to be inclusive. The poorest cannot afford adequate housing at open-market (or even informal-market) prices – particularly if state regulations require plot services (water, wastewater drainage and the like to individual buildings) and concrete dwellings. Yet programmes cannot be driven by subsidy finance alone. Successful programmes include options to blend sweat equity, savings and subsidies with optional loan opportunities.
- Development and/or improvements must address land, infrastructure *and* dwelling. Hence programmes need strategies to ensure that each of these is available. In some cases, gaining legal land title is an essential step, but in other contexts title requirements are less rigid.
- The greater the commitment to address the needs of the lowest income households, the greater the need to make them central to the programme design. Professional agencies tend to skew designs towards their own perspectives and requirements. And professional designs often become *less* suitable (and *more* irrelevant) the farther down the economic ladder the intended 'improvements' are applied. The lives of the poorest people are embedded in informality.

What is needed to catalyze more effective shelter finance for the poor?

Any project that hopes to realize its goals requires a champion ready to build an idea into an operational form. And projects in shelter finance are no exceptions. But what else is required?

Critically important appears to be a vision that not only recognizes the multiplicity of problems – dealing with land, infrastructure and dwelling improvement – but also has a strategy to address all of them. Such a vision must be attractive both to the various groups who live together in local communities and to politicians.

Flexibility in making financial allocations is important, since any of a number of tactics may be required as the times dictate. A willingness to change financial priorities so as to reflect realities on the ground helps to ensure that what is catalyzed continues to flourish. As programmes become more established, they can draw on an increasingly large repertoire of activities, and so the need for flexibility in any particular instance becomes easier to manage.

The trust of local people, which always takes time to earn, is also essential. Successful shelter-finance programmes all depend on recipients' own resources, and recipients are hardly likely to spend their scarce resources on programmes that seem unlikely to meet their shelter needs. Gaining trust, and the resources that go with it, also requires the ability to act effectively within an environment of cynical but conventional land-accumulation practices that may secure only partial, poor quality and incomplete shelter opportunities in return for votes.

Savings-based organizations have been widely used, particularly in Africa and Asia, to catalyze shelter improvement (saving is a less straightforward route to shelter improvement in Latin America, partly because of past experiences with inflation). Still, effective housing programmes for the poor usually encourage savings because they recognize the importance of savings as a source of investment capital for shelter improvements.

Finally, it is important to recognize that there are many catalysts: there are lots of small-scale successes. What is much more difficult is to take a small programme to the next level, with larger scale finance and the required institutional capacity.

What is needed for scaling up?

Each of the programmes I have highlighted in this chapter began small and were scaled up over more than a decade. Even CODI, which drew on earlier investments made by the UCDO, was nurtured through a slow investment phase. A commitment to such slow initial growth seems an essential attribute.

Shelter-finance programmes need large-scale funding to scale up their activities. In each of the programmes I outlined, there are two major sources of funds: state funds and the people's (i.e. the recipients') funds. How these sources balance and what particular form they take vary considerably from programme to programme. For example, funds may be lent and returned through service charges and loan repayments; funds may be provided as subsidies; funds may be drawn from people's personal savings, acquired over many years; or funds may come from cross subsidies (secured when one part of the development is sold to higher-income residents or to private commercial developers).

Acquiring people's funds is relatively easy, so long as a programme is working for them. Securing large-scale state funds, by contrast, requires careful planning and execution. Engagement with the political process is imperative, and, for the promoters of a new project, that entails moving beyond professional 'comfort zones' into mass movements that offer a potential advantage in electoral politics. A completed demonstration project is also extremely helpful, since it shows what a programme may offer and builds momentum for change both within the state and without. Experience suggests that considerable care must also be given to envisioning what form state support will take and through which institutions it will be provided – not to mention the attention paid to the operational and the financing role of the state.

No matter what the nature of the funding, once a project has gained political momentum, its champions need to address any technical constraints likely to emerge. For example, how will the project deal with the frequent – even inevitable – shortage of suitable professionals with appropriate skills, including the ability to work with local residents and their organizations? Programmes that have scaled up have sought to address this problem through collaboration with such agencies as the local government, NGOs and private companies.

Experience shows that most aspects of large-scale development can be driven locally, including the surveying and subdivision of suitable land. Hence local actions, either by the community committee or by a local authority, can make substantial improvements, since in many locations some land is available. If the land lacks bulk infrastructure, however, the community faces a serious problem that cannot easily be addressed at the local level.

What are the priorities for research?

There seems to be greater need for research analyzing the effectiveness of existing approaches to shelter finance than for research into developing new approaches. Investigators have made considerable progress, but shelter-finance strategies are still often challenged because of suspicions about incremental improvements or about the many self-interested actions taken by higher-income and more powerful groups. In particular, there appears to be a need for evidence-based studies comparing the effectiveness of various financing strategies in securing land tenure (paying attention to the direct and indirect costs of tenure security). There is a similar need for studies assessing the effectiveness of incremental or phased shelter development, as a cost-effective and low-risk route to improved shelter.

In extending mortgage finance to lower-income groups, there is a need to continue innovating, so as to reduce the cost of housing and basic services. Technical innovations are also needed that reduce both costs and the use of resources at the same time. Many environmentally sustainable practices add substantially to the cost of housing, but low-cost, environmentally sustainable technologies do not seem out of reach.

Mortgage finance raises another research question that could have important practical consequences: how can conventional housing finance reach those employed in the informal sector? As I noted earlier, some of these households earn enough to be able to repay mortgages, yet they are denied access to mortgages because of traditional requirements for qualifying such loans.

In moving beyond the individual dwelling to questions about the neighbourhood and city, there appears to be a need to do more research into processes that could ensure that cities inclusively serve *all* their citizens with comprehensive upgrading and improved provision of housing.

Even beyond housing, there is considerable merit in countering the strong inclination among city politicians to adopt a style of city development modelled on Dubai, U.A.E. Developing other more inclusive and less environmentally damaging models than Dubai could offer an alternative vision to city planners and politicians.

Research focusing on city inclusivity will seek to understand which groups are being reached by city services and which are being neglected. Central to that discussion is the level and nature of gender discrimination encountered by those seeking shelter finance and shelter. The analysis of inclusivity, however, needs to extend well beyond gender, to take into account the needs and perspectives of a range of discriminated and otherwise disadvantaged groups.

In relation to the challenges of understanding how to sustain income growth and reduce income volatility, there is a need to articulate a strong argument in favour of integrated poverty reduction, with measures that address incomes, assets (including shelter) and rights. Developing such measures may require further research to determine the most effective strategies across a range of contexts: a theme directly linked with the complex issues of citywide upgrading and redevelopment.

Finally, there is value in considering more explicitly the strategies that can be used by governments to support shelter improvements, including extending access to secure tenure and services. As I argued earlier, governments have continued to support shelter subsidies, both to respond to widely recognized needs and for political advantage. Official development-assistance agencies have criticized subsidy strategies for being ineffective in reaching target groups and addressing the needs of the poor. Nevertheless, a key role of the state is to redistribute resources, and it is not at all clear how the needs of the poorest can be addressed without effective state subsidies. Many current trends suggest that some 3 billion people will be living in inadequate, unsafe and insecure accommodation by 2030. If the world is to avoid such a global calamity, both governments and citizens will have to build on their past experiences to work out how the state can support improvements. There is no question that when subsidy programmes have been designed to support people's own efforts to create homes for their families, the money has been used to good effect. Governments and citizens must work together to encourage local investment, increase tenure security and ensure that our neighbourhoods are nurturing the next generation of citizens, and not adding to regional and social inequalities.

Notes

1 See Stein (2007), p8; 'precarious' is a term used to describe poor-quality housing with insecure tenure.
2 SDFN can build houses of 34 square metres (366 square feet) for NAD 15,000 (US $2000), about 75 per cent of equivalent government estimated costs (Habitat Research and Development Center, 2006, p13).

References

Boonyabancha, S. (2007) 'Baan Mankong', background paper for meeting of the CSUD/Rockefeller Foundation Global Urban Summit

Habitat Research and Development Center (2006) 'Report on secure land tenure and the conditions of low-income groups is Namibia'. Report prepared for the Habitat Sub-committee on Secure Land Tenure (a stakeholder panel coordinated by the Ministry of Regional and Local Government and Housing and Rural Development, Windhoek

IDB (2006) 'Sharpening the bank's capacity to support the housing sector in Latin America and the Caribbean', background paper for the implementation of the Social Development Strategy, Inter-American Development Bank: Washington, DC

Joint Center for Housing Studies (2004) *The State of Mexico's Housing Finance*, Joint Center for Housing Studies of Harvard University, Cambridge, MA.

Mills, S. (2007) 'The Kuyasa Fund: housing microcredit in South Africa', *Environment and Urbanization*, vol 19, no 2, pp457–469

Ogu, V.I. and Ogbuozobe, J. E. (2001) 'Housing policy in Nigeria: towards enablement of private housing development', *Habitat International,* vol 25, pp473–492

Okpala, D. (1994) 'Financing housing in developing countries: a review of the pitfalls and potentials in the development of formal housing finance systems', *Urban Studies,* vol 31, no 9, pp1571–1586

Porio, E. with Crisol, C.S., Magno, N.F., Cid, D. and Paul, E.N. (2004) 'The community mortgage programme: an innovative social housing programme in the Philippines and its outcomes', in D. Mitlin and D. Satterthwaite (eds) *Empowering Squatter Citizen*, Earthscan, London, pp54–81

Porio, E. and Cristol, C. (2004) 'Property rights, security of tenure and the urban poor in metro Manila', *Habitat International,* vol 28, no 2, pp203–219

Pryer, J., Rogers, S. and Rahman, A. (2005) 'Work disabling illness as a shock for livelihoods and poverty in Dhaka slums, Bangladesh', *International Planning Studies*

Renaud, B. (1999) 'The financing of social housing in integrating financial markets: a view from developing countries', *Urban Studies,* vol 36, no 4, pp755–773

Rodrigues, E. and Rolnick, R (2007) 'Shelter finance strategies for the poor: Brazil', background paper for meeting of the CSUD/Rockefeller Foundation Global Urban Summit

Satyanarayana, S. (2007) 'Shelter finance strategies for the poor: India', background paper for meeting of the CSUD/Rockefeller Foundation Global Urban Summit

Schneider F. (2002) 'Size and measurement of the informal economic in 110 countries around the world', Presented at a Workshop of the Australian National Tax Centre, Canberra, July 2002

Seki, M. and Watanabe, M. (1998) 'Housing finance and capital markets in Indonesia', in M. Watanabe (ed) *New Directions in Asian Housing Finance,* International Finance Corporation, pp113–126

Shenya, S.A. (2007) 'Reconceptualizing housing finance in informal settlements: the case of Dar es Salaam, Tanzania', *Environment and Urbanization,* vol 19, no 2, pp441–456

Smets, P. (2002) *Housing finance and the urban poor: building and financing low-income housing in Hyderabad, India,* Vrije University

Somik V Lall, Suri, A. and Deichmann, U. (2006) 'Housing savings and residential mobility in informal settlements in Bhopal, India', *Urban Studies,* vol 43, no 7, pp1025–1039

Stein, A. (2007) 'Shelter finance strategies for the poor: Central America', background paper for meeting of the CSUD/Rockefeller Foundation Global Urban Summit

Stephens, M. (2004) 'Housing Finance, "Reach" and Access to Owner-occupation in Western Europe', University of York, mimeo

Tall, S.M. and Gaye, G. (2007) 'Housing finance in Senegal', background paper for meeting of the CSUD/Rockefeller Foundation Global Urban Summit

Tomlinson, M. (2007) 'The development of low income housing finance sector in South Africa: have we finally found a way forward', *Habitat International,* pp77–86

UN-Habitat (2003) *The Global Report on Human Settlements 2003: The Challenge of Slums,* Earthscan for UN Habitat, London

UN-Habitat (2005) *The Global Report on Human Settlements 2005: Shelter finance,* Earthscan for UN Habitat, London

Weru, J. (2004) 'Community federations and city upgrading: the work of Pamoja Trust and Muungano in Kenya', *Environment and Urbanization,* vol 16, no 1, pp47–62

World Bank (2004) 'IBRD program document for a proposed programmatic loan to the amount of US $100 million to the United Mexican States for affordable housing and urban poverty sector adjustment loan', Report no. 27627-MX, World Bank, Washington, DC

Chapter 8

Investing in urban water and sanitation systems

Sophie Trémolet, Rachel Cardone and Catarina Fonseca

Introduction

Providing water and sanitation services (WSS) to the urban poor in developing countries is a daunting task. Urbanization continues unabated, and more people now live in urban areas than in rural ones (World Bank, 2009). Extending services in large urban areas to keep up with demand is challenging enough: growth in small towns and intermediate-size cities that require new infrastructure increases the complexity for delivering, and financing, services for all (UN-Habitat, 2010).

Water and sanitation infrastructure is expensive. Establishing and sustaining services over time that meet the needs of all requires financing – especially if those services are to reach vulnerable groups. Yet in many cases, traditional approaches to development finance have reached their limits or need to be re-thought. 'Free' money, for instance, such as cash grants or gifts in the form of donated equipment or installations from overseas donors or philanthropic organizations, has sometimes proved more a curse than a blessing. Too often, this kind of financing has resulted in service providers that are simply unsustainable. Countries are left with oversize or poorly maintained facilities that cannot be operated because funds are lacking for recurring expenses. At the same time, the accumulation of debt, even at concessionary terms, has weighed heavily on the finances of developing country balance sheets. As a result, there is insufficient funding to upgrade or manage existing services.

Inadequate financing for urban WSS has also made it hard to expand networks beyond core urban centres. Unserved groups – newcomers to urbanized areas, slum dwellers and small-town inhabitants – have only limited access to formal WSS services, which in turn limits their access to better health, education and economic activities. Of course, lack of finance is only one of many factors contributing to this predicament. Lack of awareness of the positive impact that adequate WSS can have on human development; weak governance; graft and corruption; inadequate technical solutions; and inadequate human resources are some of the other factors that have so far prevented the development of WSS in line with rapid population growth and urban expansion. Yet, though financing is not a sufficient condition for extending services, it is a necessary one. There is therefore a need to better understand where financing for WSS should come from and in what form, in order to address the vulnerabilities and make improvements at the required scale.

Financing urban water and sanitation

What needs to be financed?

Adequate WSS can be seen as a loop between upstream and downstream services, as shown in Figure 8.1.

Providing access to water is usually considered the main entry-point in describing the delivery of WSS – typically from a well or a hand pump or via a reticulated network system (either through a house connection, a yard tap or a standpipe). To ensure water quality in line with World Health Organization (WHO) guidelines (WHO, 1997) for urban drinking-water quality), water treatment is necessary. Investing in upstream water-resource management is also critical, so that sufficient water resources of adequate quality are continuously available with limited negative impact on other uses of water.

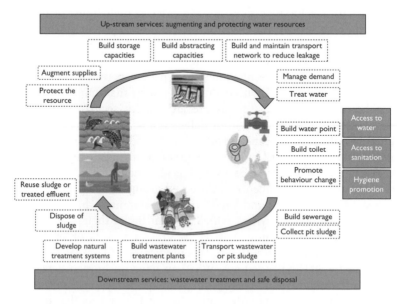

Figure 8.1 The value chain of sustainable water and sanitation services
Source: OECD, 2011b.

Sanitation as a whole is defined by the WHO-UNICEF Joint Monitoring Programme (JMP) (WHO/UNICEF, 2010) as the 'methods for the safe and sustainable management of human excreta, including the collection, storage, treatment and disposal of faeces and urine'.[1] Providing access entails investment in the first segment of the sanitation value chain – that is, ensuring that people are adequately separated from their excreta. Two main kinds of collection facilities exist: on-site sanitation systems (such as dry-pit latrines or ventilated, improved pit latrines) and waterborne, network-based systems. For both kinds, adequate investment in treatment and disposal is necessary to control the impact of the wastewater (the residual sludge on the environment, for instance) and to maintain the good quality of the other water resources. The recycling or reuse of treated wastewater can also reduce water consumption and generate by-products useful in agriculture or energy production.

What are the costs of providing WSS in low-income urban areas?

Water and sanitation services typically require substantial up-front capital investment in long-term assets. If adequately maintained, those assets can provide benefits for several decades. The bulk of the investments are for underground infrastructure (particularly piped networks), which complicates monitoring the condition of the assets over time. Without sustainable systems for continuing repair and maintenance, even such relatively simple equipment as a hand pump can fall into disrepair. Overall, it is estimated that annualized operations and maintenance (O&M) costs add between 20 and 40 per cent of the capital expenditures (Shugart and Alexander, 2009; Fonseca et al., 2011). The common failure to provide and pay for these O&M costs leads, in practice, to WSS providers that are financially fragile and unable to provide good quality services to customers.

Providing WSS to the urban poor using conventional, networked approaches requires financing not only for individual connections, but also for extending the primary distribution networks – since unserved communities usually lie at the periphery of cities, physically far from the bulk water-supply network. Furthermore, informal communities are often situated on marginal lands, steep hillsides or, more generally, where construction is complicated and expensive. Cost estimates for new connections vary widely, depending on technology. In many places, the poor must pay the costs of the household connection as well as a portion of the cost of the primary network, if they are to get the service extended into their neighbourhood. Those costs are beyond the reach of what a poor household can afford.

Figure 8.2 shows the costs of providing service at each stage of the value chain. They include capital expenditures (CapEx), the capital invested in constructing or purchasing fixed assets such as concrete structures, pumps, pipes and latrines. All the remaining costs are recurrent and include O&M, capital maintenance (CapManEx), the cost of capital (CoC) and direct and indirect support costs.

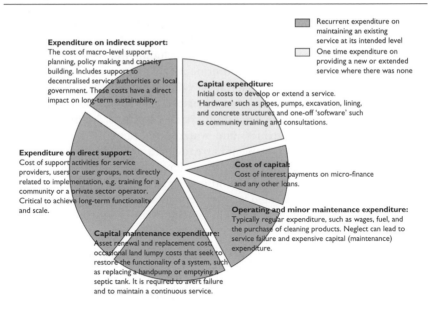

Expenditure on indirect support:
The cost of macro-level support, planning, policy making and capacity building. Includes support to decentralised service authorities or local government. These costs have a direct impact on long-term sustainability.

Recurrent expenditure on maintaining an existing service at its intended level

One time expenditure on providing a new or extended service where there was none

Capital expenditure:
Initial costs to develop or extend a service. 'Hardware' such as pipes, pumps, excavation, lining, and concrete structures and one-off 'software' such as community training and consultations.

Expenditure on direct support:
Cost of support activities for service providers, users or user groups, not directly related to implementation, e.g. training for a community or a private sector operator. Critical to achieve long-term functionality and scale.

Cost of capital:
Cost of interest payments on micro-finance and any other loans.

Capital maintenance expenditure:
Asset renewal and replacement cost; occasional land lumpy costs that seek to restore the functionality of a system, such as replacing a handpump or emptying a septic tank. It is required to avert failure and to maintain a continuous service.

Operating and minor maintenance expenditure:
Typically regular expenditure, such as wages, fuel, and the purchase of cleaning products. Neglect can lead to service failure and expensive capital (maintenance) expenditure.

Figure 8.2 Cost components for delivering water and sanitation services defined by WASHCost, IRC International Water and Sanitation Centre
Source: Fonseca *et al.,* 2011.

Who pays?

Finance for the water sector traditionally comes from three sources: 'tariffs', including payments from customers to service providers, as well as households' own investments; 'taxes' (i.e. allocations from domestic government budgets); and 'transfers' from external development agencies and philanthropic organisations (OECD, 2009). Financing can also come in the form of loans from commercial banks and development banks, or as investment income (structured as a bond or as shareholders' equity) from domestic or international private operators. The latter type of financing must ultimately be repaid out of the primary sources of income, such as tariffs, taxes and transfers (OECD, 2010).

Users contribute a substantial amount, and not only through user fees

User fees are the main financing source for WSS, either through fees for network services or through users' own investments in sanitation (latrines and septic tanks) (Ghosh Banerjee and Morella, 2011). User fees are often not enough to finance capital expenditures required to extend network services to (poorer) unserved areas. Notably, contributions are typically inequitable: better-off users pay less for high-quality piped water, whereas poor users pay higher tariffs for poor-quality water sold from street vendors (UN-Habitat, 2010).

The financing of water services via user charges is usually marred by a well-documented 'vicious circle' that plays out in numerous countries in the Global South. Tariffs are typically kept low for 'social' or political reasons – in other words, for fear of triggering social unrest or losing elections following a water rate increase. As a result, tariff revenues usually do not cover capital maintenance expenditures or expansion costs – and in some cases do not even cover O&M costs. A study of seven African countries found that operating cost-recovery ratios ranged from 65 per cent in public companies in Zambia to 160 per cent in Senegal, where services are run by a public–private partnership (Ballance and Trémolet, 2005). When tariff revenues fail to cover operating costs, the existing service deteriorates and funds for extending services dry up, hurting the groups that need them the most: typically those living on the fringes of urban centres or in slum areas in the centre. The same vicious cycle operates even more acutely for sanitation services: in that case, funds may not even be clearly earmarked, because of fragmented institutional arrangements and difficulties in charging for sanitation services.

For these reasons, a broad consensus has developed at both national and international levels that it is unrealistic to rely exclusively on user finance for full cost recovery. The costs are simply too high for user fees alone to sustain service levels for existing customers and to achieve universal coverage.

Public finance is almost always needed to plug the gaps

Although there are no reliable ways, yet, to estimate how much governments allocate to the WSS sector, the Global Annual Assessment of Sanitation and Drinking Water (GLAAS) (WHO, 2010) found the governments surveyed allocated roughly 0.48 per cent of their GDP to WSS annually. Foster and Briceño-Garmendia (2010) provide a highly detailed overview of investments and needs for various infrastructure sectors, including WSS, but only for Africa. These data show that the contribution of public investment in water and sanitation is higher than previously thought. Domestic public-sector financing usually includes matching funds from overseas aid. When WSS are managed by public-sector entities (as they are for the vast majority of urban WSS in developing countries), public-sector financing can fund the utility's operating deficits or subsidize new investments, including those for new connections (paid to the utility or, in some cases, to customers directly).

Official development assistance is on the rise but not optimally allocated

Official development assistance (ODA) provides substantial funding to the WSS sector. Aid to WSS declined temporarily in the 1990s, but it has risen sharply since 2001. In 2008–09, the total annual average aid commitments to WSS were US$8.1 billion (OECD, 2011b). Between 2002 and 2009, the average annual increase in bilateral aid (aid from a government agency of a single donor country) for WSS was 18 per cent; the corresponding increase in multilateral aid (aid from an agency that pulls resources from several governments) was 10 per cent (OECD, 2011b). According to the 2010 report by the Development Assistance Committee (DAC) of the Organisation for Economic Co-operation and Development (OECD) (OECD-DAC, 2010), the share of aid to water and sanitation in the aid programmes of DAC member countries has also risen since 2001, though at a more modest pace. In 2008–09, aid to water and sanitation represented 8 per cent of DAC members' bilateral sector-allocable aid (OECD, 2011b).

Between 2003 and 2008, loans represented slightly more than half the total aid for WSS. Projects for 'large systems' in urban areas were predominant and accounted for 57 per cent of total contributions to WSS in 2007–08. Out of that total ODA for large systems, 68 per cent were concessionary loans. By contrast, financing for basic drinking water and on-site sanitation was almost exclusively in the form of ODA grants (90 per cent of the total ODA). In that same period (2003–08), the primary targets for aid to water and sanitation were regions most in need of improved access: the poorest countries received 43 per cent of total WSS aid, two-thirds of it in the form of grants (OECD-DAC, 2010). Substantial aid for WSS also goes to middle-income countries, where unserved populations are relatively low. Finally, aid allocations tend to stress drinking water over sanitation, though it remains difficult to assess the relative allocations with precision. Certainly, when development projects combine both water and sanitation, drinking water tends to receive the lion's share.

The large-scale capital investment on which external financing tends to focus often goes to water-production facilities (dams, reservoirs, wells or canals), water and wastewater treatment facilities and network upgrading. Donors may even come together to share the costs of such large projects. The Ziga dam, which supplies water to Ouagadougou, the capital of Burkina Faso, and the enlargement of the Ngith conduit, which guarantees Dakar's long-term water supply in Senegal, were both built with shared donor funds. For donors, large-scale capital projects can be easier to manage, because transaction costs can be shared over a large project and because relatively few interlocutors are involved. Governments also tend to prefer large-scale capital projects: they are highly 'visible', and so better than smaller projects for building political capital. That is particularly true for the WSS sector, where most of the assets are underground and therefore more difficult to account for (or take credit for) politically.

The limited role of private financing

In poor urban areas of developing countries, local private providers have made an important contribution by self-financing with personal or family income, and taking out commercial bank loans when needed. Often, these smaller providers partner with other businesses: local private water providers, for instance, typically have interests in construction businesses.

In small towns in Cambodia, for example, local private operators routinely make an initial investment of as much as US$10,000 in a small water-treatment plant and a distribution network within an urban centre. Under the MIREP programme, a public subsidy was added to local private investment, bringing the total initial investment as high as US$33,000 per small town (on average, fewer than 3000 inhabitants). (MIREP is a French acronym for a programme designed and implemented by GRET, a French non-governmental organization (NGO) with French government support in Cambodia.) Similar examples are well documented in Mauritania (Cardone and Fonseca, 2003) and in Maputo, Mozambique (Trémolet, 2006a). The World Bank estimates that small-scale providers serve about 25 per cent of the urban population with water in Latin America and East Asia, and 50 per cent in Africa. As for sanitation, such providers serve as much as 80 per cent of the population in African cities (Bill and Melinda Gates Foundation, 2006). Unfortunately, though, because small-scale providers usually operate in the informal sector and crucial information about their activities is lacking, it is extremely difficult to obtain aggregated data on which to base a market analysis.

The international private sector also plays a role in urban WSS, but its ability to bring in financing is limited. A review of 15 years of private-sector participation in infrastructure in developing countries (Marin, 2009) points out that private financing of urban water utilities (i.e. new capital brought in by private operators) represented only 5.4 per cent of the total investment commitments in private infrastructure between 1990 and 2000. Based on figures from the Public – Private Infrastructure (PPI) database,[2] Marin found that investment commitments by private operators (made in the year of financial closure) fell sharply in the wake of the Asian financial crisis, from a peak of US$10 billion in 1997 to a low of US$1.5 billion in 2003, and have not recovered since. Furthermore, private-sector investment commitments are highly concentrated in a few countries such as China, Malaysia and the Arabian Gulf states; only a handful of projects have been undertaken in low-income countries. Private operators are reluctant to take over the entire management of a utility (particularly in countries that are seen as risky); they are more interested in investing solely in water- or wastewater-treatment facilities. In riskier countries, private operators are turning to management or lease contracts, with minimum financing requirements but high expectations for the returns on their equity.

How existing financing fails to reach the urban poor

We discuss four reasons for this failure under the subheadings in this section.

Subsidies are inadequately targeted

It might seem straightforward to subsidize those too poor or vulnerable to afford user fees. In practice, however, problems abound in structuring effective programmes for allocating subsidies. Allocation by geography ignores the reality that in urban areas the boundaries between poor and non-poor areas are not clear cut. Allocation by amount of living space overlooks the fact that poor people tend to live in crowded homes. According to a study done for the African Development Bank, 'One of the reasons for failure in the [WSS] sector has been the unwillingness by direct providers to segment customers to a sufficient degree ... and then to target services accordingly' (Franceys et al., 2006, section 3.4, p24).

On one principle, however, there is unanimous agreement: the most efficient way to deliver subsidies for water to poor households is to subsidize the charges for a connection to the water distribution network (Water and Sanitation Program, 2002). High connection charges usually represent the single greatest obstacle to the poor in gaining access to reliable, affordable services. A connection also reduces costs associated with the negative impact of non-piped water on health, because piped water is usually safe to drink. (Vended water may be contaminated at various points along the transport chain.) A 2005 study found that the total costs of acquiring a private water connection could be the equivalent of between four and six months' income in India, 12 months' income in Ghana and as many as 43 months' income in Uganda (Franceys et al., 2006, section 9.9). Connection subsidies can be transferred directly to the household or channelled to the service provider, based on the provider's output. Subsidies to providers can be designed so as to incentivize them to extend their services to poor areas, and, at the same time, to leverage any private financing available. In addition, the water connection cost can be billed in small instalments, along with the charge for monthly usage. There is no reason to require these costs to be paid up front, as a heavy lump sum, which would keep the poorest of the poor from accessing the service. Similar connection fees for sanitation can be useful, to offset the lump-sum costs households must bear for toilets. In urban areas, however, charges for sanitation services must account for the costs of collecting and treating fecal sludge or wastewater, as well as for the various ways sanitation services are delivered (e.g. via household toilets or by providing community or public toilets). In spite of this complexity, eliminating sanitation subsidies is not the answer; instead, new designs are needed for effectively allocating them.

Land tenure remains a prerequisite for financing

People who lack title to their land are usually excluded from subsidy programmes financed by their government or utility. For related discussion of the difficulties of securing affordable housing finance where title to land is missing or uncertain, see Chapter 6. There may be some valid reasons for this: water and sanitation policy may need to be aligned with broader urban planning and housing policies to prevent the consolidation of slums into more permanent housing areas. The land title may need to be used as collateral for securing the payment of the connection charge. Programmes run by NGOs or philanthropic organizations have sought to address this problem by providing subsidies for connections to users without land title, but the scale of these programmes remains limited.

Large service providers receive the bulk of available financing

The channels for collecting and transferring public funds vary by country, but, in general, international donors provide funds for WSS through a ministry of finance. From there, the funds are allocated to ministries of water or sanitation, which then distribute WSS funds, typically to national or municipal utilities. Funds in the form of concessionary loans are guaranteed by the ministry of finance on behalf of the ministry of water and the utility. Given this pattern, it is easier (and perceived as less risky) for larger WSS utilities to receive the bulk of public financing available for WSS. ODA flows tend to be centralized, and go to the service provider in the capital city. Yet most WSS financing needs are in peri-urban areas (usually not served by the main utility) or in small and medium-size towns (or other decentralized entities).[3] This mismatch can lead to a number of difficulties – for example, the adoption of inadequate or overdesigned technological solutions; long time lags between the investment decision and its implementation; and an inability to allocate funding in small, targeted amounts, rather than only to one-off, bulky, capital-intensive projects.

This funding pattern persists even though large utilities operating in a capital city may serve only a small proportion of the city's total population. Throughout the Global South, small-scale independent providers (usually referred to as SSIPs) often lack access to formal sources of finance, for any of several reasons: because WSS loans are simply unavailable in their regions, because the SSIPs lack credit history, because interest rates are too high (reflecting the relatively high perceived risk), or because local financial markets are not geared up for financing them.

Small and medium-size towns attract less funding than cities do

As noted earlier, even though WSS funding is mostly centralized, funding needs are increasingly decentralized. Water and sanitation services themselves tend to be decentralized, and are managed at the municipal (city) or regional level. The decentralizing trend in WSS services is based largely on the assumption that a local government (town, municipality or district) understands local needs better than the central government does. But it also stems from the fact that a high percentage of urban growth is expected to take place in small and medium-size towns (see Pilgrim *et al.*, 2004). Decentralization also holds local officials transparently accountable to consumers (Helmsing, 2002; WaterAid, 2008; Lockwood and Smits, 2011).

This decentralized structure complicates the ability for central governments to allocate funding to WSS effectively. Allocating funds to decentralized service providers requires support structures in the central government and a financial-allocation mechanism, such as a challenge fund, to give relatively small cities and towns the incentive to compete for access to public finance. Much remains to be done to understand how such support structures can be designed and executed effectively.

Reaching the poor: the role of financial innovation

In light of the financial crisis that has crippled public finance in many global markets, it is important to define innovation in the context of WSS financing. In some cases, innovation is as simple as dividing the lumpy connection charge into instalments. Other innovations require a shift in assumptions about who can provide finance for WSS and who can obtain it. The generic assumption that finance is about providing infrastructure loans to national governments, for instance, has shifted to focusing on how to improve services for consumers in low-income areas. Broadly speaking, financial innovation to reduce poverty has been accompanied by a policy shift from supply-driven approaches to demand-led ones.

Several long-term trends have contributed to financial innovation. Decentralization has been one important factor. A raised awareness at a global level of the scale of the WSS challenge has also contributed to the sense of urgency, along with the realization that international aid and subsidies as designed may be both inadequate and ineffective in addressing the coverage deficit and the poorest individuals. Professionally, the water and sanitation sector, which was focused in the past on civil engineering solutions, has begun to attract a wider diversity of expert interest. In particular, a more recent influx of expertise in the social sciences and economics has led to efforts to balance supply-side approaches with financial innovations that focus on understanding and stimulating demand. More recently, advances in access to information and to mobile technology, including the ability to transfer money electronically, have led to unprecedented real-time collection of information and outreach to even the poorest urban dwellers (Hughes and Lonie, 2007; Ivatury and Mas, 2008; ITU, 2010). As a result, new opportunities, previously not possible, are emerging for a wider range of stakeholders to participate and affect positive change. Slum dwellers are forming federations to upgrade their communities; solidarity mechanisms are arising that enable individuals and businesses in the Global North to provide grants and loans to individuals and businesses in the Global South (Akvo, 2011) Likewise, those taking part in developing financial aid to the WSS sector are increasingly looking for ways to leverage market-based (i.e. commercial) mechanisms. For example, though development finance has traditionally been applied to capital investment, donors are now working to apply grants and even concessionary loans for such purposes as strengthening the operational efficiency of a utility, building business-development skills for non-utility service providers, financing connection fees for the poor and facilitating scalable models of service delivery.

In what follows, we identify several innovations in finance for WSS in poor urban and peri-urban areas, with brief case studies that exemplify the spectrum of arrangements and activities taking place. At this stage, experience is still too meagre to determine which approaches work better than others, or whether any of them are applicable in more than one context: success is typically contingent on local factors. Table 8.1 presents a framework for understanding the dynamics of innovation for urban WSS.

Table 8.1 Sources of finance for the urban water and sanitation sector

	Sources of finance	Traditional	Innovative
Public	Government	Fiscal transfer Cross subsidy Latrine subsidy Connection subsidy	Debt/equity swap Means-tested subsidy Municipal credit pool
	ODA grants	Direct grant Technical assistance	Revolving fund Seed finance Output-based aid Project development facility Partial risk/credit guarantee Credit enhancement
	ODA loans	Concessionary loan	Municipal development fund Line of credit Output-based aid
	Non-ODA grants (NGOs, philanthropic organisations)	Technical assistance Solidarity mechanism Direct grants	Revolving funds Microfinance start-up
	Non-ODA loans (IFIs and others)		Microfinance Municipal bond Working capital loan Solidarity mechanism Line of credit
	Private equity	Direct foreign investment Local private sector	Seed capital
Private	Individuals/users	Revolving funds Microfinance Tariffs Direct equity (self-financed)	Remittances

Source: OECD (2011a).

The importance of household-level finance

Although the financial contribution to WSS from households is often not captured in global figures, consumers – and especially the poor – pay more than any other group of consumers for WSS. For example, GLAAS (WHO, 2010) showed that households' own investments (particularly in on-site sanitation and water storage facilities) were the largest source of financing for WSS in Africa.

That statement holds whether the measure is simply cash outlays (e.g. the daily costs of water) or the health, education, social and economic losses that result from a lack of safe and clean services. The examples in Boxes 8.1 and 8.2 highlight some of the ways household-level finance is being leveraged to improve services.

Box 8.1 Demand-led approaches in urban slums

In many countries, federations of urban poor and slum dwellers are working to address issues of poverty, including WSS. These federations are deeply involved in community-led schemes, and at their core are community-based savings groups, formed and managed by the urban poor themselves. Women in particular are attracted to doing business with savings groups because such groups provide flexible terms on loans, which are often taken to deal with family crises. But savings-group loans are also used for longer term housing improvements and income-generating activities. When clusters of savings groups federate, their capacity to support broader changes also increases. Not only can they become effective advocates for slum upgrades, they can also implement them across an entire city, and sometimes even at national and international levels. Shack/ Slum Dwellers International (SDI) is a good example of what is possible.

Although such federations are 'demand-led', they are by no means isolated from government or from international agencies. In many cases, city and national governments and international agencies have acknowledged and supported the federations because of their success in addressing urban poverty. Federations typically seek partnerships with local governments to achieve secure land tenure, and street numbers and addresses for the poor, which empowers slum dwellers to take advantage of their rights as citizens, such as voting.

All federations apply the savings model – that is, they create individual savings accounts for their members – as a means to provide credit for housing and other upgrading. The savings accounts demonstrate to local and national governments the ability of the poor to mobilize and overcome extreme poverty, often at a lower unit cost than government or international agencies can achieve. Further, the savings model depends on a cost-recovery philosophy that holds even the poorest and most marginalized people responsible for their accounts. Importantly, the federations work to ensure that poor people are dissuaded from taking loans whenever possible, and, if they do, to minimize the size of the loans. This effort contrasts sharply with supply-oriented approaches, which tend to maximize loan sizes: indeed, staff performance in donor and other agencies is often measured by the number and amounts of loans signed.

Source: d'Cruz and Satterthwaite, 2006

Even as the role of savings is growing, NGOs have been testing microfinance in recent years, and in particular microlending as a means to finance household connections to utility networks. In general, microfinance institutions (MFIs) are not well versed in how to develop specific products aimed at sustainable WSS delivery. But they do have experience with short-term loans for such products as household water filters, water storage devices, some kinds of latrines and hygiene products. Beyond that, MFIs do have experience in managing credit, but many have only limited understanding of the nature of demand for WSS finance, or of how to help poor communities finance projects that do not have a straightforward way of generating income.

Among the barriers to microfinance for water and sanitation are high transaction costs (given the small size of dedicated WSS loans) and the relatively large need for follow-up during the loan cycles. When these costs of capital are included in the loan, they only increase interest rates.

Box 8.2 Sanitation surcharges in Burkina Faso

Discussions of innovative finance tend to focus on drinking water and its delivery; investments in sanitation are typically considered too expensive, and with too little cost recovery, to attract commercial finance. In Burkina Faso, the National Water and Sanitation Office (ONEA) is responsible for water and sanitation in urban and peri-urban areas throughout the country. Faced with limited effective demand for sanitation services and limited funding, ONEA imposed a surcharge on the water bills of its existing customers to extend services to the poor.

The scheme has a 27-year history. In 1985 the Ministry of Water authorized fees for sanitation services through a water surcharge. A similar surcharge was also imposed on water usage in Ouagadougou, the nation's capital, in order to develop a strategy for on-site sanitation, school latrines and a sewerage network for the city centre. One key point of the strategy that was finally approved was that households are expected to finance their own latrines.

ONEA, through its sanitation surcharge, finances such activities as training masons in building on-site sanitation facilities, or providing supplies of construction materials at appropriate quality standards. ONEA also finances campaigns to promote sanitation and social mobilization to generate demand. Where necessary, poor households get small capital subsidies, but the goal is to minimize government funding of capital costs. ONEA does not apply the sanitation surcharge to building networked sewerage, but does use it to fully fund hygiene education in schools and to construct school latrines. (Parents pay for latrine maintenance.) ONEA subsidies are available to all urban households, whether or not they are connected to the network.

Source: Savina and Kolsky, 2004.

Indeed, there is some question whether the MFI approach to WSS is even sustainable. Many microfinance institutions claim they are – and that their default rates are lower than those of large banks. But their financial health is hard to document: many MFIs are non-governmental or not-for-profit organizations, lacking transparent monitoring systems, and their overheads are highly subsidized by their donors.

A more localized way to leverage household funds for WSS connections is through cross subsidies and surcharges to utility bills. One example of a surcharge is described in Box 8.2.

Supporting domestic private-sector investment in WSS

Traditional models for financing WSS have tended to ignore domestic firms in the private sector, including SSIPs, MFIs and commercial and cooperative banks. The reason is that urban SSIPs tend to operate informally and outside the scope and recognition of the formal utility and government. Likewise, microfinance and commercial banking activity in the WSS sector has been largely non-existent. But in many cities, SSIPs are an integral part of the service provision, particularly in low-income areas (utilities in those areas usually have a mandate to provide services, but lack the financial and technical capacity to do so).

SSIPs operate as service providers, but they can also do the drilling and construction work (employing masons, artisans and so forth) that are critical for service delivery, sometimes in formal partnership with a utility. Not surprisingly, informal SSIPs operate under greater regulatory uncertainty than their formal counterparts, but both are constrained by their limited ability to access finance. One way to improve the operating environment for SSIPs is to develop opportunities for collaboration with utilities and NGOs, in which a common goal is to extend services to the poor. In recent years, several examples of such partnerships have emerged; one example is described in Box 8.3.

Box 8.3 Use of design-build-lease contracts in Vietnam to support small-scale providers

In Vietnam, a design-build-lease project was undertaken in two towns, each with a population of about 10,000. Under this scheme, private contractors design, build and operate the town water system, borrowing funds from the water utility. After a grace period, which enables the contractor to build up cash reserves in case of a shortfall during the design and construction phases, the contractor repays the utility, with interest, out of revenues from the new system.

To avoid costly delays, all stakeholders are encouraged to take part early on in determining the feasibility of the design and the reliability of the cost estimates, as well as in reaching agreement on tariffs. Although the tariffs are not high enough to recover the full cost of the system, it is important for the contractor and the long-term viability of the scheme that the local authority (and the users) agree to a minimum consumption of five cubic metres (about 1320 U.S. gallons) of water per billing period. To cover connection costs, users have preferred a higher monthly tariff over a larger up-front charge; likewise, they agree to small but relatively frequent tariff increases over time rather than larger but less frequent increases. After addressing issues such as these, the local authority must vote on whether the plans are viable, and whether the utility is allowed to buy shares in the new system in order to kick-start investment.

This approach has several benefits. The contractor who builds the system must operate it, which counters any inclination for overdesign. Because revenues are directly tied to tariffs, the operator has an incentive to provide network connections for customers, as well as a good service, including billing and collections. For the utility, the risk of fronting an equity investment (usually a 15 per cent stake) is managed because the assets – which are likely to grow in value under the scheme – belong to the utility, providing the utility with an incentive to maintain oversight over the contractor. Likewise, the contractor is bound by a performance bond, which is forfeited if the contractor does not meet its obligations. Importantly, a competitive market for operators thrives in Vietnam, which increases the likelihood of success for the utility and the local government. Towns smaller than the ones discussed here may offer provincial or regional utilities – or even a local utility in a nearby urban centre – a chance to invest profitably in piped connections for the townspeople, while supporting local economic development. Preliminary observations suggest that stakeholders in these schemes may need help understanding the implications of their contractual rights and obligations. But, happily, research findings also suggest that a small-town water supply can be profitable for small enterprises, provided the players do the advance work needed to get the incentives right and properly address the risks.

Source: adapted from Cardone and Fonseca, 2006a. Reprinted with permission from UN-Habitat.

Strengthening the financial health of utilities

As the main service providers in urban areas, municipalities and utilities face considerable pressure to extend WSS to ever-growing neighbourhoods. Even well-managed utilities cannot maintain the pace of urban expansion, in part because most new urban residents are poor and lack secure land tenure.

In the late 1990s it was expected that the international private sector could and would fill the investment gap – the difference between WSS needs for universal service coverage and what local utilities could provide. Since then, experience with large-scale private-sector investment has not been particularly successful, especially in low-income countries. The reasons include mismatched expectations, lack of a transition strategy to implement tariff reform, and a lack of tangible successes by private operators in extending WSS (for a myriad of reasons not entirely under the control of the private operators). Meanwhile, a consensus has developed that, though water and sewer utilities should be publicly owned and controlled, they should also operate according to sound business principles: strong revenue management, efficient customer service, competent operations and structures for maintaining accountability. If a utility can effectively recover its costs and, ultimately, finance itself, the government and ODA funds that would have subsidized it should, at least in theory, be freed up to focus on other targeted, pro-poor activities.

The strongest utilities tend to be found in capital cities, though in many countries a single utility is responsible for all water services at the state or national level. In some cases, the strategic use of external, private-sector expertise can help to catalyse shifts to autonomous utilities (see Box 8.4).

Box 8.4 Transforming water services through a public–private partnership

In anticipation of the shift to democracy in South Africa, the City of Johannesburg created a contract management unit (CMU), which focused on how to rapidly transform public services, including water supply and sanitation. Johannesburg Water was created as a 'ring-fenced', public company from the city's seven dispersed water utilities and departments.[4]

The CMU sought to 'reboot' the utility as a professional and competent company with a single operating culture, and to rebrand it to its customers. To that end, the CMU engaged a consortium of Suez Water, a multinational corporation based in Paris, and several local private companies, in a five-year management contract. From 2001 until 2006, the consortium refocused the company through staff training, customer service, revenue management and measures to operate more efficiently and expand programmes for the poor.

Source: Cardone (2006).

Enabling local governments to support the local water sector

At a national level, the innovation with the greatest impact in most low- and middle-income countries and across all regions has been the decentralization of service delivery. What hasn't followed in many cases is fiscal decentralization to support these new responsibilities for officials at the local district, municipality, town, village or community levels. The result is that many such decentralized water services are financially weak, and particularly so when they must rely on transfers from the national government to complement tariff revenues from users.

Traditionally, utilities have been run as an extension of national or local governments, and utility budgets have been combined with those of other urban departments. Their governance has been dominated by political appointees. In the urban setting, a shift from a public water department to a 'ring-fenced', publicly owned water utility is a challenge. Many governments are loath to give up control of the utility's revenues. For their part, however, many utilities see the value in distancing government from their day-to-day activities, say, through corporate governance structures.

National governments often meet calls to decentralize fiscally with the retort that local governments lack the capacity to absorb – meaning spend – what budgets they have. And it is true that the 'absorption capacity' of local levels is a problem, even in middle-income countries.[5] But the mismatches between budgeting and actual spending often grow directly out of the allocation process of the central government.

This traditional, supply-side attitude of national governments toward localized service delivery has recently evolved into new thinking about the role of fiscal transfers and how they might stimulate market approaches to improved delivery of public services. For example, given a clear policy toward the WSS sector (and an accompanying framework for guiding expenditures), fiscal transfers that enable local governments to meet their responsibilities to deliver WSS can empower those governments. The transfers can be direct, or they can take the form of debt repayments or guarantees – and they can be earmarked to improve access and services for the poor.

When services are decentralized via fiscal transfers, the absorptive capacity of local governments has been shown to improve when elements of direct democracy are introduced. A good example is participatory budgeting, in which representatives of poor communities take part in planning and budgeting for services to their own communities (for in-depth discussion of this topic, see Chapter 4. Participatory budgeting has expanded in many areas throughout Brazil as well as elsewhere in Latin America, including Argentina, Bolivia, Colombia, Ecuador, Mexico, Peru and Uruguay, as well as in Africa and Europe).

Another mechanism for national government to support networked WSS infrastructure finance at the municipal level is through Municipal Development Funds (MDFs) (see Box 8.5).

Box 8.5 Using Municipal Development Funds to stimulate innovation

Municipal Development Funds (MDFs) can either work as substitutes for grants and fiscal transfers to local authorities, or act as a bridge for local authorities to access private credit markets. Under the first model, the MDF, funded by the government and donors, on-lends to the local authority at concessionary rates, often in conjunction with subsidized loans and grants (again, from donors and/or the central government).

The objective is to stimulate a market for domestic finance, while introducing local authorities to the uses of municipal borrowing. In developing countries where the market is relatively weak, the MDF can seek to incorporate investment priorities of the central or state governments, and work with the local authority to ensure that preparation for a project is robust and thorough.

One MDF, in the Philippines, the Local Water Utilities Administration (LWUA), is a specialized lending institution mandated by law to promote and oversee the development of provincial waterworks systems throughout the country. LWUA extends financial, institutional development, technical and watershed management assistance to water districts and to Rural Waterworks and Sanitation Associations (RWSAs). LWUA secures its funding by selling equity subscriptions to the national government, as well as through concessionary loans or grants from International Finance Institutions (IFIs) and bilateral agencies.

Under the second model, which is perhaps more appropriate only in further-developed countries, an MDF can work to strengthen both the municipal and financial sectors to support transactions between the two. Here, the MDF tends to lend at commercial interest rates, and works with commercial banks and other private-sector lenders to inform its funding decisions. The MDF typically requires that private lenders assume the credit risk of the municipal loans, in order to help the municipality develop a credit history.

Source: adapted from Cardone and Fonseca, 2006a. Reprinted with permission from UN-Habitat.

Another mechanism that has become common in developing countries is the creation of dedicated water-sector funds managed at a national or a district level. These funds are often created for a social purpose, as part of broader water-sector reform. They can be structured either as sinking or revolving funds, depending on their objectives, and they can often be disbursed more rapidly and flexibly than funds made available through the budgeting process. Such water-sector 'piggy banks' can also pay for elements of infrastructure that communities cannot afford. But national funds face challenges similar to those faced by the proliferation of other funds: a lack of 'good' projects and channels for disbursing the money.

From the perspective of international agencies, decentralization has raised practical questions. Traditionally, a donor agency seeking to implement urban WSS projects would obtain a memorandum of understanding (MoU) from the central government, then work with the national utility or transfer money through the government or the relevant sector ministry. Interaction between the donor and local government was minimal, and for good reason: at local levels of governance, administrative, financial and technical constraints loom large. Many district, municipal and town officials simply lack experience – technical or otherwise – in WSS. These constraints become even more pronounced in small urban and peri-urban informal communities, which have traditionally been overlooked – and even ignored – by central governments as well as donors.

Conclusions: How can financial innovation be scaled up?

Despite the many examples of innovations, they remain islands of success. Greater dissemination of experience and information about successes, failures and lessons learned is needed across all regions, particularly in the use of innovative approaches. To achieve sustainable financing for urban WSS, one must recognize the linkages between water, sanitation, housing and other factors in the urban environment.

One common problem is that financial innovations have been put in place only as pilot projects or case studies, often implemented by outside agencies that are superficially connected with local governance. Such arrangements make scaling up impossible, even citywide.

The challenge of scaling up infrastructure services stems from a lack of understanding about how to effectively and appropriately coordinate the parallel financial buildup to a scale that both works and is big enough to yield measurable improvements. Support and coordination structures are needed to ensure that whatever factors led to success at a small scale can be replicated at the larger one. Those factors might include the status of health and level of education in the target communities, or the amount of 'capacity building' needed for the target service providers and local governments.

In urban areas, providing access to WSS must also be seen in a broader context of improving shelter and livelihoods among the poor. Thus in evaluating the costs associated with WSS, it is also important to remember what else those costs are buying: a reduction in the costs of healthcare, improvements in housing and education and an increase in economic activity, all made possible by providing safe and secure access to WSS – and impossible without it.

Acknowledging contextual elements when considering scaling-up

All the regions considered for this report – Asia, Africa and Latin America/Caribbean – have experience with innovative finance mechanisms, and all those regions encompass low- and middle-income countries. On the whole, regional differences do not seem to matter to the success of one approach or another,[6] but success does seem highly context-specific. For example, the ability of one South African utility to issue a bond does not necessarily mean that all South African utilities can do so – or even that issuing bonds is an optimal approach to finance services for poor people in urban areas in all regions.

Strengthening the overall capacity of local governments

To extend WSS to small and medium-size towns in a decentralized context, a key prerequisite is that the local governments can already carry out such critical tasks as water resource management, the planning of extensions to the service, contracting service providers and monitoring their performance. How much financial support these activities will need depends on the initial strength of local government and its ability to take on new tasks. If municipalities initially lack the capacity to take on these tasks, or are laden with responsibilities without finance to match, a first step may be to reinforce them through separately funded local government reform, synchronized as far as possible with reforms in the water and sanitation sector.

But what happens if towns are simply too small to acquire and maintain the capacities needed to manage WSS on their own? Then pouring additional funds into local WSS for capital-intensive projects and technical assistance may only dilute the funds' effectiveness. This risk is particularly high if staffing at the local level is too small to fully assume WSS capacities, or if staff, once trained, is lured away by more attractive employment elsewhere (DFID-IWA, 2011; Lockwood and Smits, 2011). One solution to this need for 'critical mass' may be to modify the structure of various small WSS markets by finding ways to aggregate.

For example, in Hungary, small towns are encouraged to form an association to access financing from the European Union for upgrading water facilities. In Brazil in the 1970s, the National Water Supply and Sanitation System (PLANASA) created state-level water companies in each Brazilian state; the companies took charge not only of providing infrastructure, but also of operating the systems nominally owned by the municipal governments.

Formalizing small-scale providers

Similar issues emerge in scaling up a successful pilot project in slums. Here, however, market forces may have more leeway, because informal, private operators are already providing whatever services exist. These small, private operators can be encouraged to move into the formal sector and, perhaps, to form associations to obtain financing. The process was tested with good results in Asunción, Paraguay, where small-scale water service providers known as *aguateros,* operating in previously unserved areas of the city, were encouraged to bid for output-based aid contracts in small towns and rural areas. To do so, they associated themselves with formally established construction companies and complied with a formal method of contracting.

It does little good to scale up distribution without a compensatory increase in operating capacity. Financing is needed to grow informal providers into medium-size enterprises able to take on new businesses and penetrate new markets. This aspiration underlies the appeal of the franchising model, whereby established companies roll out operating models in smaller towns.

Developing a strategic approach to introducing innovation

Donors often focus too much on single points of engagement, rather than commit to a long-term programme with a transition period that includes consideration and sensitivity to political and economic reality. Traditional finance mechanisms and their accompanying supply-side thinking are often deeply entrenched in the incentives and structures of the institutions that 'do' development finance, in national governments and in other external support agencies. Perhaps most difficult to change is the mindset about the poor – both by 'outsiders' and among the poor themselves – who are traditionally viewed as beneficiaries of aid, rather than empowered agents of change. Consequently, achieving success with innovative mechanisms simply takes longer, requiring learning, coordination, patience and a consistent local presence in poor communities to take root. The trade-off is that once an innovative mechanism does take root successfully, experience suggests it multiplies and spreads to other communities and institutions.

Providing capacity building and support to access finance

In nearly all of the successful cases outlined in this report, external support agencies provided transaction support and helped to build up the technical and financial skills of project implementers, whether individuals, communities or private operators. In some cases, such as the work of the Water and Sanitation Program in Kenya, this transaction support is institutionalized: each pilot project aims to build a new, local cadre of business-development specialists who can provide technical and financial audits, as well as support when the pilot is scaled up.

Many facilities and funds exist whose mission is compatible with improving WSS – there is plenty of financial supply. Only a few, however, mainly international organizations, are able to capture those funds. To enlarge the recipient base, project preparation costs should be minimized and the application process should be simplified as much as possible. Standard operating procedures for assessing the viability of projects should be developed. And wherever possible, community members should take part in project development. The goal is to make facilities and funds accessible to a much wider range of stakeholders than before, particularly to locally based institutions and groups.

Additional financing is only part of the solution to provide sustainable services

Scaling up WSS finance is often misunderstood to mean only the mobilization of additional resources to finance water services. A more correct understanding begins by stressing its goal, the scaling up of service delivery of safe water and sanitation. The additional finance (most likely innovative finance) then serves as a catalyst for reaching that goal.

In scaling up, it is important, too, to recognize that, though demand-led approaches work more effectively than one-off, supply-driven approaches, the most successful of the former also retain the key elements that grounded their successful origins as small, pilot projects: proximity to customers, mechanisms for cost recovery, community-led decision making and effective management. Finally, finance should be considered a means to an end, not an end in itself. The real goal is adequate, accessible, affordable and sustainable water and sanitation for all.

Notes

1   This definition excludes other environmental health interventions such as solid-waste management and surface-water drainage.
2   http://ppi.worldbank.org
3   Only certain lending organizations, such as the European Bank for Reconstruction and Development, active in Eastern and Central Europe, can provide financing at the municipal level.
4   A 'ring-fenced' utility would have its own set of financial accounts so as to increase financial transparency.
5   See, for example, www.dplg.gov.za/speeches/21Sep2005PR_imbizo.doc and www.dwaf.gov.za/Communications/MinisterSpeeches/2005/MinMEC5Jul05.doc.
6   The Latin American/Caribbean region could be an exception, where direct democracy and social movements may influence approaches to community mobilization and development, seen most prominently in the use of participatory budgeting.

References

Akvo (2011) 'See it happen', http://www.akvo.org, accessed July 3, 2011
Ballance, T. and Trémolet, S. (2005) 'Private sector participation in urban water supply in sub-Saharan Africa', a study financed through German Development Cooperation, commissioned by KfW and GTZ
Bill and Melinda Gates Foundation (2006) 'Landscaping and review of approaches and technologies for water, sanitation and hygiene: opportunities for action, main report', http://www.irc.nl/page/35950, accessed March 31, 2012
Cardone, R. (2006), Studies on financial instruments to facilitate investment for water infrastructure, African Development Bank, Mimeo
Cardone, R. and Fonseca, C. (2003) 'Financing and cost recovery', IRC thematic overview paper (TOP), http://www.irc.nl/page/7582, accessed March 31, 2012
Cardone, R. and Fonseca, C. (2006a) 'Experiences with innovative financing: small town water supply and sanitation service delivery', background paper prepared for UN-Habitat global report *Meeting Development Goals in Small Urban Centres: Water and Sanitation in the World's Cities*, UN-Habitat, Nairobi
D'Cruz, C. and Satterthwaite, D. (2006) 'The role of urban grassroots organizations and their national federations in reducing poverty and achieving the Millennium Development Goals', *Global Urban Development Magazine*, vol 2, no 1, http://www.globalurban.org/GUDMag06Vol2Iss1/d'Cruz%20&%20Satterthwaite.htm, accessed March 30, 2012

DFID-IWA (2011) 'Mind the gap! – Assessing human resource capacity shortages in the water and sanitation sector', DFID (Department for International Development) and IWA (International Water Association), London

Fonseca, C., Franceys, R., Batchelor, C., McIntyre, P., Klutse, A., Komives, K., Moriarty, P., Naafs, A., Nyarko, K., Pezon, C., Potter, A., Reddy, R. and Snehalatha, M. (2011) 'WASHCost briefing note 1a: Life cycle costs approach – costing sustainable services', IRC International Water and Sanitation Centre, The Netherlands

Foster, V. and Briceño-Garmendia, C. (eds) (2010) *Africa's Infrastructure. A Time for Transformation*, Agence Francaise de Développement in association with the World Bank, Washington, DC, http://siteresources.worldbank.org/INTAFRICA/Resources/aicd_overview_english_noembargo.pdf, accessed August 2, 2011

Franceys, R., Perry, C. and Fonseca, C. (2006) *Guidelines for User Fees and Cost Recovery for Water, Sanitation and Irrigation Projects*, IRC/Cranfield report for the African Development Bank, unpublished

Ghosh Banerjee, S. and Morella, E. (2011) 'Africa's water and sanitation infrastructure: access, affordability, and alternatives', Directions in Development, DID – Infrastructure, World Bank, Washington, DC

Helmsing, A.H.J. (2002) 'Decentralisation, enablement, and local governance in low-income countries', *Environment and Planning C: Government and Policy*, vol 20, no 3, pp317–340

Hughes, N. and Lonie, S. (2007) 'M-PESA: mobile money for the "unbanked". Turning cellphones into 24-hour tellers in Kenya', *Innovations: Technology, Governance, Globalization*, vol 2, nos 1–2, pp63–81

ITU (International Telecommunication Union) (2010) 'ITU estimates two billion people online by end 2010', press release, October 19, 2010, http://www.itu.int/net/pressoffice/press_releases/2010/39.aspx, accessed August 2, 2011

Ivatury, G. and Mas, I. (2008) 'The early experience with branchless banking', Focus Note No 46, April, Consultative Group to Assist the Poor, Washington, DC, http://www.cgap.org/gm/document-1.9.2640/FN46.pdf), accessed April 4, 2012

Kiva (2011) http://www.kiva.org

Lockwood, H. and Smits, S. (2011) *Supporting Rural Water Supply: Moving Towards a Service Delivery Approach*', Practical Action Publishing, Rugby

Marin, P. (2009) 'Public – private partnerships for urban water utilities: a review of experiences in developing countries', *PPIAF Trends and Policy Options No 8*, Washington, DC

OECD (2009) *Managing Water for All: An OECD Perspective on Pricing and Financing*, OECD, Paris

OECD (2010) *Innovative Finance Mechanisms for the Water Sector*, OECD, Paris

OECD (2011a) *Benefits of Investing in Water and Sanitation: An OECD Perspective*, OECD Publishing, http://dx.doi.org/10.1787/9789264100817-en, accessed March 30, 2012

OECD (2011b) *Meeting the Challenge of Financing Water and Sanitation: Tools and Approaches*, OECD, Paris

OECD-DAC (2010) *Financing Water and Sanitation in Developing Countries: The Contribution of External Aid*, OECD, Paris

Pilgrim, N., Roche, B., Revels, C., Kingdom, B. and Kalbermatten, J. (2004) 'Town water supply and sanitation' Bank-Netherlands Water Partnership, Project 43. World Bank, Washington, DC

Savina, A. and Kolsky, P. (2004) 'Mobilizing resources for sanitation', WSP-Africa Field Note, WSP (Water and Sanitation Program), Nairobi

Shugart, C. and Alexander, I. (2009) 'Tariff setting guidelines: a reduced discretion approach for regulators of water and sanitation services', World Bank Working Paper No 8/2009, World Bank, Washington, DC

Trémolet, S. (2006a) 'Adapting regulation to the needs of the poor: experience in four East African countries', BPD Research Series, May, http//:www.bpdwater-andsanitation.org/web/d/DOC_109.pdf, accessed March 30, 2012

UN-Habitat (2010) 'The right to the city: bridging the urban divide', report of the fifth session of the World Urban Forum, Rio de Janeiro, Brazil, 22–26 March, United Nations Human Settlements Programme, Nairobi

WaterAid (2008) *Think Local, Act Local: Effective Financing of Local Governments to Provide Water and Sanitation Services*, WaterAid, London

Water and Sanitation Program (WSP) (2002) *Water Tariffs and Subsidies in South Asia: Understanding the Basics*, http://web.mit.edu/urbanupgrading/waterand-sanitation/resources/pdf-files/WaterTariff-1.pdf, accessed March 30, 2012

WHO (World Health Organization) (1997) *Guidelines for Drinking-water Quality, 2nd Edition, Volume 3: Surveillance and Control of Community Supplies*, WHO, Geneva

WHO (2010) *UN-Water: Global Annual Assessment of Sanitation And Drinking-Water (GLAAS) 2010: Targeting Resources for Better Results*, WHO, Geneva

WHO/UNICEF (2010) 'Progress on sanitation and drinking-water: 2010 update', World Health Organization and UNICEF, Geneva, http://www.wssinfo.org/fileadmin/user_upload/resources/1278061137-JMP_report_2010_en.pdf, accessed July 5, 2011

World Bank (2009) *World Development Report. Reshaping Economic Geography*, World Bank, Washington, DC

Perceiving the social and economic consequences of natural disaster shocks or getting ready for climate change

John C. Mutter

Introduction

Climate change is now inevitable. Even if, by the wave of a magic wand, we could somehow bring greenhouse-gas (GHG) emissions to zero tomorrow morning, the existing accumulation of CO_2 and methane in the atmosphere will disrupt life on this urbanizing planet for the rest of this century. Principal among these disruptions will be an increase in natural disasters resulting from a more energetic atmosphere, but growth of the earth's population will further intensify the effects of those disasters on humanity. By 2100 our planet will host perhaps 10 billion people, most of whom will live in cities; many of those cities will be exposed to major risks from extreme natural events. How will we cope with these disruptions?

One way to approach this question is to systematically examine how we have responded to natural and man-made disasters in the past, and to try to understand the social processes involved. As this chapter will show, the major challenge in preparing for climate-related incidents is the need to see them for what they are: phenomena created through the interaction of natural processes and human responses. That may sound straightforward, yet seeing disasters as they are is no simple undertaking. Understanding such massive events and their complex ramifications always requires social construction. Facts never can or do speak for themselves. Instead, they are filtered through and interpreted by models of social reality that emphasize the needs of observers over the needs of survivors. If we are to effectively address the challenges of climate change both for economic efficiency and social equity, it is important that we better understand the dynamics through which socially constructed interpretations evolve. In this chapter I review some of the most pressing challenges created by these dynamics, and suggest ways we might improve our understanding. In particular, I will focus on three topics: the role of media in the social construction of disaster; the social construction of estimates of deaths and injuries; and the interpretation of the economics of such massive events.

The evolving role of the media in the social construction of disaster

For the news media, disasters provide unparalleled opportunities for dramatic storytelling on a movie-like stage. Whether the story begins with so-called natural disasters – hurricanes, earthquakes, tsunamis – or with those described as man-made, such as the 2010 blowout of the BP *Deepwater Horizon* in the Gulf of Mexico, the drama of catastrophe is irresistible. Coverage typically begins with a description of the event itself, but drama dictates an almost overwhelming emphasis on immediacy. Television, for instance, might focus its resources on 'infographics' or high-altitude images to convey the scale of, say, a hurricane, but such overviews don't get much air time. Instead, TV crews rush to the scene so that a 'stand-up' reporter can read the story against a backdrop of palm trees bent over in powerful winds, seawalls breached by surf, roofs blown off houses, cars stranded, the flashing lights of emergency vehicles, buildings left in ruins. In man-made disasters, a conflagration may punch up the drama.

Until just a few years ago, video and even still photographs depicting disastrous events 'on the ground' were quite rare; the most common sources of such information were eyewitness accounts. Now cameras are everywhere – even if most of them are the relatively crude devices built into virtually every cell phone – and hardly any disaster goes unrecorded. And what reporters and bystanders miss, the now-ubiquitous security cameras capture. It is almost routine to see low-resolution, gray-toned videos, shot in the first moments of an earthquake, showing groceries shaken from supermarket shelves and frightened shoppers clutching whatever they can for balance or running from falling debris. In 2008, permanent outdoor cameras recorded the chaos in Sichuan, China, as buildings fell and people desperately sought safety.

Some of this dramatic coverage is useful to emergency managers and scientists in understanding the dynamics of such extreme events. There was, for instance, enough advance warning of the tsunami that devastated northern Japan in March 2011 that helicopters were ready to document the dreadful spectacle even before the wave came ashore. From the air, the wave is seen approaching the coast, then moving relentlessly inland over low-lying farmlands as it sweeps up cars, boats, homes and other buildings, some on fire. Other videos of the day usually stop short of showing victims dying, but they leave little doubt about the final outcome in the viewer's imagination. No tsunami has ever been observed more closely or more directly, and the videos give important details about how the devastation unfolded.

But contrast this record with the comparatively few scenes captured during the Boxing Day tsunami of 2004, as it inundated coastlines around the Indian Ocean. Most pictures came from terrified tourists vacationing in resort areas – just as many of the earliest reports of the tsunami were survival stories told by Europeans. The coverage made it easy for the outside world to imagine that somehow the tsunami had preferentially struck tourist locations – when in fact the greatest devastation and loss of life took place in villages and coastal settlements, well away from the resorts. The reason for the selective bias is obvious: villages and settlements are home to poor people for whom a video camera is an unimaginable luxury.

In fact, a selective bias in the images documenting disasters remains the rule rather than the exception. Earthquakes, for instance, can never be anticipated, so video coverage is opportunistic and extremely uneven. Even hurricane landfalls and the full impacts of floods are not comprehensively covered on the ground: people in their paths are usually warned to evacuate, and most actually do.

What is covered most comprehensively in disasters is their immediate aftermath, when few restrictions are in place and the news media are largely free to cover events as they please. Clearly, that statement has its caveats: some countries restrict access in the aftermath of a disaster. The most frequently cited case is the complete news blackout imposed by Myanmar following Cyclone Nargis. China was once known for restricting access after an earthquake, but of late the Chinese have been more open. Yet even where coverage is unrestricted, media distortion becomes greatest and storytelling departs most egregiously from reality in the days following a disaster, and with the most troubling consequences.

Disaster myths, media coverage and their consequences

The ways the media 'frame' a disaster story may have severe and telling consequences for the official responses to it, as well as for the lasting perceptions it leaves with the public. The leading example of media framing today is the coverage of Hurricane Katrina in New Orleans (see, for instance, Tierney *et al.*, 2006; Sun, 2011). Hurricane Katrina was predominantly an urban disaster. That is not to say that its impact outside New Orleans was trivial. Scores of people along the Mississippi Gulf Coast also lost their lives, and the storm surge there from the hurricane also destroyed homes and other buildings. But the damage was mostly limited to an area within two to three suburban blocks of the beaches, and, when the surge retreated a few hours later, it left devastation but few flooded regions. In fact, the story of Hurricane Katrina along the Gulf Coast – aside from its impact on New Orleans – was a fairly familiar one, little different from the stories of many hurricanes of the past. There were no rooftop rescues by helicopter, no reports of criminal activities and no masses of people huddling in shelters.

In New Orleans, though, the story was very different. Levees failed and the city was submerged. The water remained for days. Yet wind damage was not especially severe, and, for the most part, the Mississippi River was not responsible for the floods. So what went wrong? As it turned out, the levees that failed were not holding back the natural flow of waters in the Mississippi River. They had been constructed instead to serve as commercial shipping canals (the Industrial Canal, the Gulf Intracoastal Waterway and the Mississippi River Gulf Outlet, or MRGO) or to channel water away from the center of the city during heavy rainfall (the London Avenue Canal and the 17th Street Canal). The commercial canals, in particular, dated to the early part of the twentieth century and were cut through existing populated neighborhoods of New Orleans, placing the residents of the adjoining neighborhoods at grave risk in the event of levee failure. And sure enough, the most extensive damage and greatest loss of life occurred in the residential areas immediately adjacent to levee breaches on these commercial canals. Had these levees not failed at so many locations, the death toll would have been far smaller and the destruction from the storm much less severe (Jonkman *et al.*, 2008).

The levee failures were caused by a hurricane-generated storm surge that flowed from the Gulf of Mexico northwest across salt marshes and along the MRGO. Initially the levees broke at the junction of the MRGO and the industrial canals, where the water was funneled into a very narrow channel. These failures led to flooding across vast regions of the city, especially in poor, low-lying neighborhoods. The death toll exceeded that of any natural disaster in the U.S. since the Galveston Flood of 1900, and the flood displaced more people than any other disaster since the Dust Bowl of the mid- to late-1930s.

How did the media describe Hurricane Katrina in New Orleans? In what has become a common pattern of disaster coverage, the initial focus on urban search and rescue operations quickly turned to investigative reporting of criminal and other antisocial behavior. The latter was driven by several erroneous yet widespread assumptions – myths – about how people behave in disasters. Such myths, despite substantial evidence that they are indeed false (Dynes, 2007; Quarantelli, 2008, and references therein) determine not only how disasters are covered, but also how officials respond (Sun, 2011).

Two myths are typical: the looting myth (Barsky, 2006) and the myth of panic flight (Quarantelli, 2008). According to the looting myth, a disaster presents an irresistible opportunity for people (all people) to 'rob' stores and private homes left unprotected. Although not everyone might be tempted to rob a private home, the myth insists that we would all have a hard time restraining ourselves from grabbing, say, an iPad from an Apple Store whose doors were broken and ajar. People would, allegedly, rationalize that 'it's all covered by insurance anyway', and that the goods taken would get 'good and appropriate use'. Even more darkly, the myth asserts, in places where a large underclass lives close to a wealthy elite, the people of the underclass would take advantage of the disruption in normal law enforcement to rise up and steal whatever they could, simply to even the score against the upper classes. Mobs would form and roam the streets, destroying luxury goods or looting simply for selfish gain. As for the myth of panic flight, the name is descriptive: the idea here is that people caught in disasters lose their senses and race madly from the scene.

The effect of these myths is to make panic and lawlessness into constant themes sought out in media coverage of disasters. They surfaced quickly in descriptions of the 2010 earthquake in Haiti, even though actual, documented cases of looting and lawlessness were remarkably rare. Looting and antisocial behavior were apparently more common after the earthquake in Chile just a few weeks later, but that was generally reported with caveats of surprise. In Haiti, reporters described looting as more or less expected.

By a similar token, when disasters occur in places regarded as poorly governed, media coverage reflects that judgment. After Cyclone Nargis struck Myanmar, what was a genuinely poor response by the authorities again and again became a narrative of how a heartless military junta had callously disregarded the welfare of its people. In truth, the failure of the response was more likely a case of simple incompetence combined with lack of preparation. Also absent from the discussion was the role of aberrant nature: cyclones in the region typically trend north into the Bay of Bengal. Nargis, however, stalled midway into the Bay, then took a most unusual and rapid eastward turn along the southern Irrawaddy Delta. Certainly the Myanmar government failed to act effectively, but Cyclone Nargis would have caught any government flat-footed. In Haiti, too, no one expected an effective government response to the earthquake, and so the coverage focused on the challenges of getting foreign aid through unhelpful government red tape. A major subplot of the story, of course, was that plenty of corrupt officials were allegedly diverting funds and goods to their own benefit. Aid agencies faced massive challenges getting relief workers and materials to Haiti, but whether corruption was a major source of delays and inefficiencies is not proven.

Few people, after a moment's reflection, would regard commercial media coverage as a completely impartial portrait of any event, let alone a disaster. The dilemma lies in the media's codification of disaster myths, whereby social behavior observed during disasters is misrepresented and official response is shaped by a misconception of how events are unfolding. Sun (2011, pp1152–1153) identifies the following:

> First, disaster mythology may influence the scope and form of military involvement in disaster response by shaping official perceptions about whether the legal prerequisites for military intervention have been satisfied. More specifically, the mythology may make it more likely that the [U.S.] president will deploy federal troops in a law enforcement capacity by invoking the Insurrection Act, and – in the absence of that invocation, less likely that the president will be willing to commit federal troops to humanitarian missions. Second, belief in exaggerated reports

of looting and violence distorts implementation of response priorities outlined in disaster plans. Third, exaggerated fears of looting and violence lead public officials to implement restrictions on freedom and freedom of movement, many of which are authorized in state disaster laws, that may be counterproductive to relief efforts, including delaying return of evacuees to their homes. Such fears may also encourage excessive use of force by police.

The most troubling of these consequences is the militarization of disaster response and restriction of personal freedoms. Many decisions about how to respond to Hurricane Katrina in August 2005 in New Orleans appear to have been made on the basis of news reports repeating unverified stories of truly horrific developments (Sun, 2011). Among other misrepresentations of the actual situation, it was reported that babies were raped in the Superdome and that bodies by the score were piling up there, the victims of violence perpetrated by roving mobs (Sun, 2011). What is all the more puzzling is that seasoned journalists would – or should, in the skeptical environment of a newsroom – generally treat such stories as vicious rumors until proved otherwise. In the event, however, the clear suggestion was that local law enforcement had been overwhelmed or in some way was simply not up to the task. The myth of role abandonment by police bolstered by media reports of widespread lawlessness likely lead to the federalization of the National Guard and its deployment as agents of law enforcement in New Orleans, as permitted under the Insurgency Act.

No one actually died by violence in the Superdome. There were a few deaths: one suicide, one drug overdose, a couple of heart attacks and two respiratory failures. There were no deaths by gunshots and no stabbings. Evidence of rape is harder to verify, but the idea that rapists were marauding among innocent people confined to a horrid place is just not substantiated. Overall, it now seems that antisocial behavior and lawlessness in the aftermath of Hurricane Katrina were less frequent than they were before the storm. White groups of vigilantes and police officers are now known to have perpetrated some of the more troublesome incidents of violence, under the guise of protecting property. There is little doubt that some people took advantage of the situation, but the horrific narrative promulgated by the media is largely baseless.

One thing the media did show, without meaning to at all, was that the faces of those stuck in the Superdome and wading through the flooded streets of New Orleans did not look like the usual victims of disasters. No TV crew was interviewing a white middle-class male homeowner, shaking his head at the destruction that was his house, but also waiting impatiently for the insurance adjustor to arrive and make things whole again. The victims of Katrina who took shelter in the Superdome were mostly poor and black, not the stock characters in the media's portrayal of disaster, at least not in the U.S. They were waiting for help with the very basics of life: food, water, a place to defecate. None of them were expecting an insurance adjustor to arrive.

At bottom, the errors of fact and emphasis by the media reflect the misguided assumptions of persistent disaster myths. Why do we believe these myths? Is it simply in our nature to think the worst of others? By amplifying and sensationalizing disaster events (sensational enough without media exaggeration), and by constantly rearranging the storyline to fit the myths, the media perpetuate the myths themselves and so condition government responses to disasters. Any corrective reporting that might be done in the months and years after the event goes relatively unnoticed.

Death in disaster as a social construct

The reporting of death after a disaster would seem straightforward, yet it raises several fundamental and difficult issues. First is the most basic question of assessing mortality totals. How are the dead counted in a natural disaster? The death toll in Haiti from the earthquake in 2010 is a case in point.

Mortality in Haiti

Earthquake deaths result from a very small range of immediate consequences of the event itself, so there is little doubt in attributing a particular death to the disaster. People typically die from trauma associated with building collapse, often the collapse of their own homes. Injuries to survivors can outnumber fatalities by as much as ten to one, and they usually have the same or similar causes. Disease outbreaks from compromised sanitary conditions following any disaster are always feared, but they seldom materialize. People can die long after a disaster from injuries caused by the disaster event or from the exacerbation of pre-existing conditions. Earthquake mortality, in particular, is often greatest at night, when most people are inside their homes, or wherever people are densely concentrated in buildings. In the Sichuan earthquake of 2008, many children and teachers are thought to have been killed when school buildings collapsed. (The Chinese government has yet to release the demographic breakdown of deaths in that earthquake, so there is a residual concern that the media may have exaggerated the number of school collapses.)

Mass earthquake mortality is an urban phenomenon, and particularly so for rapidly expanding urban concentrations in developing and middle-income countries. In these settings the pace of new construction often exceeds the rate at which local governments can effectively enforce safe building standards, especially if governance is generally weak and subject to corruption. By the same token, disasters, especially earthquakes, that occur far from cities may have little economic consequence and cause few fatalities.

Many factors combined in Haiti in the March 2010 earthquake, which struck 20 kilometres west of the capital, Port-au-Prince, with a moment magnitude of 7.2. Earthquakes of this magnitude are not uncommon: 20 or more occur every year around the world. Early media reports put the number of deaths from the Haitian quake in the thousands; the first official estimate, announced on 14 January by President Rene Garcia Preval, gave a figure of between 30,000 and 50,000, but the president acknowledged then that the number could rise. Provisional statements of this general type are quite common, and they are often followed by upward revisions in death tolls. Of course, in the first few hours of a disaster event, or even after a day or so, it is very difficult to know how many have died. In serious events such as the Haitian quake, most morgues fail to function. In New Orleans, for instance, the U.S. Federal Emergency Management Agency (FEMA) established a mobile morgue in the town of Saint Gabrielle, a considerable distance from New Orleans, to compensate for the submerged and inoperative morgues in the city itself.

In the early days of the Haitian earthquake, the Red Cross estimated 50,000 dead, in accord with the initial estimate from the Haitian government. Several revisions followed, until the official death toll was put at 220,570 – though figures as high as 300,000 had been mentioned. The 200,000-plus estimate by the Haitian government was apparently derived from counts made of bodies brought to official burial sites. If correct, it exceeds the death toll from the 2004 Sumatran earthquake and tsunami, which affected a vast area around the Indian Ocean.

Two sources, however, have suggested the Haitian death toll may be much smaller than 200,000. Netherlands Radio Worldwide, in a report by Hans Jaap Melissen in 2010 titled 'Haiti quake death toll well under 100,000', claimed that by that date 'only' 52,000 people had been buried, though the government of Haiti was claiming a considerably larger figure. The article also asserted that the government reported 20,000 to 30,000 deaths in the coastal town of Leogane, whereas Leogane authorities said they had buried 3364. The article further reported that the government claimed 4000 dead in the town of Jacmel, whereas the French non-governmental organization (NGO) ACTED (a French acronym for Agency for Technical Cooperation and Development), whose workers were involved in burying the Jacmel dead, reported only 145 bodies. Jacmel authorities, the report went on to say, settled on a death toll of between 300 and 400. The government eventually raised its total count to 300,000. Most major relief agencies – Oxfam, Catholic Relief Services (CRS), *Medecins Sans Frontiers* (Doctors without Borders) and the like – adopted a figure closer to the earlier government estimate of 230,000, or else finessed the issue by stating that 'several hundred thousand' had died. On the first anniversary of the quake, the government put the death toll at 316,000.

The uncertainties and inconsistencies were further underscored in a 'post-disaster needs assessment' created by the Haitian government in the weeks after the earthquake.[1] There injuries were put at 300,000 and deaths at 220,000. A 3:2 ratio of deaths to injuries is actually quite low: typically, it is closer to 3:1 and may be much higher. If the injury figure is correct (and injury counts are somewhat easier to determine accurately, since they can be based on actual cases recorded by relief agencies), the more customary injury-to-death ratio implies a death toll closer to 100,000.

The second independent estimate of the death toll came from LTL Strategies, in a report to USAID on building assessment and rubble removal (BARR) (LTL Strategies, 2011, p32). LTL took a quite different approach to estimating mortality: the group surveyed some of the most heavily affected neighborhoods, asking the remaining residents for information about those killed or injured. Quoting from their report:

> The BARR survey specifically asked people how many of the residents in the building died, where the survivors went after the earthquake and the current location of the survivors. The survey focused on the hard hit area of lower Port-au-Prince, with a high concentration of yellow and red houses. With this data, they were able to make some inferences about the number of people killed, the total number of people who went to camps and the total living absentees from earthquake impacted houses, as well as the whereabouts of the absentees. Deaths per residence were calculated by using average occupancy per house and average death rate by yellow, green and red houses. The area impacted by the earthquake had an estimated population of 3 million people. An estimate based on the findings suggests that the number of people killed in the earthquake ranges between 46,190 and 84,961, much lower than commonly accepted estimates.

The LTL estimate is based on a cluster survey: based on the interviews, the analysts extrapolated from their samples to estimate the overall mortality. Estimates based on cluster surveys (including this one) are necessarily imprecise, but the authors of the LTL report do suggest that the discrepancy between their estimate and that of the Haitian government cannot be accounted for by factoring in all potential errors in their method.

The upshot is that an accurate death toll for this tragic event is unlikely ever to be resolved. An estimate of 300,000 is an outlier, much larger than usual for a quake of this magnitude. Figure 9.1 compiled by Bilham (2009) after an initial compilation by Hough and Bilham (2006, p321), suggests that the high estimate for mortality in Haiti places that earthquake well outside the expected range of deaths.

The plot also highlights how the Haitian tally compares with the relatively modest death toll of the much larger magnitude earthquake that

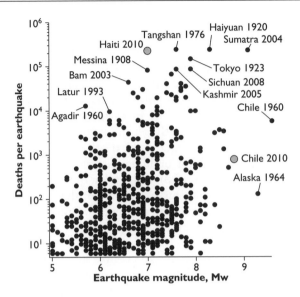

Figure 9.1 Gross earthquake disaster mortality versus earthquake magnitude. This compilation does not normalize for size of the exposed population.
Source: Bilham, 2009, after an initial compilation by Hough and Bilham, 2006.

struck Chile just a few weeks later (799 dead, according to sources quoted in Wikipedia)[2]. Other substantially larger recent earthquakes have not caused commensurately high death tolls. The 2008 Sichuan earthquake – which, at a moment magnitude of 7.9, released some ten times the energy of the Haitian quake and struck in a concentrated, rapidly expanding urban setting – caused 'only' about 70,000 deaths. If, however, the true Haitian figure is less than 100,000, the total looks far less like an anomaly among the death tolls for similar major disasters.

Disaster death tolls in context

Many observers have drawn attention to the broad range of death tolls from similar natural disasters, as reflected in data compiled by the United Nations Development Programme (UNDP, 2004) and the World Bank (Dilley *et al.*, 2005) in its Hot Spots report, as well as in the two Global Assessment Reports (GARs) (UNISDR, 2009, 2011) published by the UNISDR. One broadly agreed-upon factor is the influence of poverty on disaster mortality figures – poor countries almost always suffer substantially larger death tolls for disasters of a given 'size' than rich countries do (Mutter, 2005). The reasons may seem fairly obvious: for one thing, housing for the poor tends to be much more fragile than housing for the wealthy (even if the latter dwellings are not in any sense designed to resist extremes of nature). For another, the poor often live in much riskier settings, such as along river banks and on the steep slopes of the favelas that typify the slums around almost all Latin American cities. The poor also get little or no warning of impending disaster, and they have little means to escape even if they get a timely warning. The thousands who stayed put as Hurricane Katrina bore down on New Orleans did so for many reasons, but one significant factor was the scarcity of vehicles that might have offered them a way out.

Kahn (2005) has shown that 'economic development provides implicit insurance against nature's shocks [to built structures]', and that 'democracies and nations with higher-quality institutions suffer less death from natural disaster'. In other words, given that high mortality is typically an urban phenomenon, countries that have the institutional capacity to take on urban planning in a way that recognizes the safety risks of poor construction and of building on certain terrains, as well as the capacity to create and enforce building codes, will provide a greater measure of protection for their citizens. Lack of building codes is typically cited as the reason for the large death toll in Haiti. The failure to enforce such codes (along with an alleged failure to root out corruption) is often cited as the reason for the typically high mortality rates from earthquakes in China and Turkey. And comparative data show that these failures are unquestionably behind the excessive death tolls. Earthquakes of similar size in California have resulted in just a few tens of deaths. Strictly enforced building standards in Chile likely protected many people during the massive, moment magnitude-8.8 earthquake there in 2010.

It is worth noting that building fragility can lower mortality as well as raise it. Buildings in Port-au-Prince are typically low-rise, single-floor dwellings in sprawling slums. Although they are more likely to collapse than stronger buildings are, they are also less likely to kill. Typically they are cement-block constructions with heavy roofs for protection from the drenching rains. Both the block construction and the weight of the roofs make the structures dangerous to live in, and, when they do collapse, they cause deaths as well as many serious injuries. Unfortunately, collapses are common enough that the ratio of injuries to deaths is well known, and is relatively high: many people caught in such structural failures actually survive. And what this experience suggests, once again, is that, given the fairly high confidence that the number of injuries reported after the earthquake is accurate, the death toll could be substantially smaller than official government reports would have it, and closer to something like 100,000.

But there are many more factors determining disaster mortality risk than buildings and codes. The risks an individual faces in a natural disaster are at least as much socially constructed as physically determined, and that is especially so in urban settings (see Cutter et al., 2003 and Cutter, 2005, among other writings). The idea that vulnerabilities are socially constructed is often associated with the work of Ben Wisner (Wisner, 1993) and

Piers Blaikie (Blaikie *et al.*, 1994). Bankoff (2005) summarizes the ideas succinctly: 'Social systems generate unequal exposure to risk by making some people more prone to disaster than others and these inequalities are largely a function of the power relations (class, age, gender and ethnicity among others) operative in every society'. Both globally and locally, the hypothesis that class- and race-driven inequalities drive disparities of disaster outcome is persuasive. In Mutter (2010), I argued further that repeated disasters continually pry apart the divide between the rich and the poor, exacerbating differences that existed before the disaster, because the wealthy can better cope with the stresses through savings, risk transfer, mobility and insurance. Indeed, some significant component of the global and local inequalities in the world today can be attributed to 'disaster injustices' perpetrated by the conscious actions of the most powerful groups in society.

Death and transfiguration in New Orleans

New Orleans was a deeply divided city when Hurricane Katrina made landfall in late August 2005. The city lies in the poorest region of the country, and by virtually every indicator of social welfare New Orleans ranks at or near the bottom of all U.S. cities. As the result of decades of social change in New Orleans, relatively wealthy residents have come to live in inherently safer parts of the city: the higher ground. By contrast, socially marginalized people live on marginal lands far more subject to flooding than the business district, the tourist center of the French Quarter, or such residential areas as the Garden District, all of which suffered relatively little damage in Katrina. Of those who were displaced from New Orleans during and after the hurricane, people from the lowest income neighborhoods fared the worst. As I noted in Mutter (2010), the hurricane flushed out the poorest people. Of those who remained, almost without exception, the poorer neighborhoods have experienced the slowest repopulation and recovery of basic amenities such as schools, shops and petrol stations. In the poorest district of New Orleans – the Lower Ninth Ward – only about 24 percent of its former residents remain, whereas the population of the wealthy Central Business District has actually grown by 7 percent. Low-income African-American workers were seven times more likely to lose their pre-Katrina jobs than were higher-income white workers. And low-income people have found it harder than it was before the hurricane to obtain (and maintain) a basic, minimum standard of living, including good access to health care. In 2008, for instance, there were 38 percent fewer hospital beds available in New Orleans than before the storm (Quigley, 2010).

Katrina is not an anomaly, though it stands out as a singular point in U.S. disaster history with a death toll unmatched in almost 100 years. The blame for the tragedy can be laid in large part on the Army Corps of Engineers and its failure to maintain levee systems. But plenty of fault also lies with the long history of class conflicts and persistent social disparities that have plagued the city of New Orleans. And in that latter regard, New Orleans is an object lesson. Almost every other city in the U.S. – in fact, every large city on the globe – that is physically vulnerable to the extremes of nature also presents a social landscape of disparate vulnerabilities that could give rise to a Katrina-like event.

In the minds of many, the underlying assumption is that the poor are the most vulnerable citizens simply because they are poor. Their fate, according to this myth, is self-determined: to carry the greatest burden when disaster strikes, and there is no way to control the damage or to mitigate that burden. But the vulnerability of the poor to natural disasters is not inevitable; rather, it is constructed in large part by social processes that, though reversible, are seldom even recognized for their role in maintaining the most unjust disparity of all: the inequality of death.

Toward an economics of natural disaster

Natural disasters – and so, by extension, the effects of climate change that involve extreme events – have received relatively little attention in the academic literature of economics. There is no consensus theory of how (or even whether) the shock of a natural disaster propagates differentially into the economies of countries with differing economic composition or development status. Figure 9.2 schematically depicts how economists conceptualize the shocks of a natural disaster.

On the left a natural extreme event occurs at time T_e with magnitude A. If the event is an earthquake, A refers to its moment magnitude and T_e to the time of earthquake rupture, which can be determined to within a few seconds. If the event is a hurricane, the values of A refer to its strength on

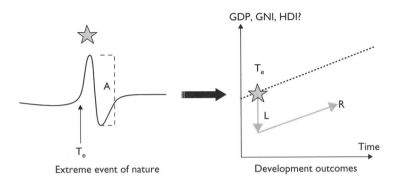

Figure 9.2 Stylized representation of the outcome of a natural extreme event (left side) on development (symbols are described in the text)
Source: Mutter. Note that this is an original figure developed by Mutter for this paper.

the Saffir-Simpson scale or perhaps to its Power Dissipation Index or peak wind speed; the time is the time of landfall. If the figure depicts drought, A is the Palmer Drought Severity Index, but the time is not a precise moment. Droughts are the longest lasting of natural disasters (drought conditions can precipitate famine quite rapidly, but here the diagram on the left refers only to the physical process). Flooding is similar to drought, in that the magnitude of flooding is hard to quantify and the timing is not as precise as the moment of earthquake rupture. (Of course the breaching of a river levee as part of a flood event can be accurately timed.)

The diagram on the right depicts the basic idea of socio-economic consequence – the disaster outcome. The dotted line represents the equilibrium growth of an economy in the absence of disasters. The welfare measure plotted on the vertical axis could be gross domestic product (GDP), gross national income (GNI), human development index (HDI) or any other relevant indicator. Here the welfare measure is assumed to be rising steadily. When the disaster occurs (time T_e), it generates a loss L. This is followed by a period of economic recovery along the growth line R. As depicted in this figure, the economy loses value as a result of the destructions of (some of) its capital stocks; then it merely resumes growing at its pre-disaster rate.

Much of the study of natural disasters by natural science focuses on determining the values and spatial distributions of T_e and A. The UNISDR's Global Assessment Reports and World Bank Hot Spot reports, mentioned earlier, include extensive maps, which give the distribution of various hazards, and multi-hazard maps, which show where various kinds of hazard overlap in the same geographic region. T_e and A are usually expressed in spatial and temporal probabilistic terms – the likelihood that events within a given range of sizes will occur in a given time interval in a specified region. The motivating idea is that, if one can estimate, within some reasonable bounds, the chances that some extreme natural event will occur, then one can take measures to reduce the losses L resulting from that event. Such approaches are referred to as disaster risk reduction (DRR).

Now consider Figure 9.3. The schematic diagram in panel A (top left) represents perhaps one of the worst possible outcomes of a disaster. A period of zero growth follows the loss caused by the disaster, as the economy is consumed with rebuilding the lost assets. By the time the total economy has returned to its pre-disaster state at T_R, the losses L_R have accrued and exceed the initial loss L by an amount $L_R - L$. That excess loss depends on the time the economy spends recovering at a rate slower than the pre-disaster growth rate. In the worst case scenario, the pre-disaster state is never restored (the slope of the recovery trajectory always remains gentler – less steep – than the dotted line). This would occur if the country hit by the disaster had little or no ability to support rebuilding, and if donors provided no external funds (equivalently, if the funds were provided but were not well spent). This

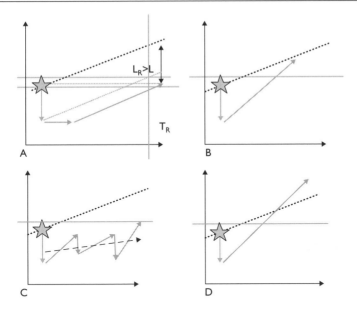

Figure 9.3 Four possible outcomes of a natural disaster on economic growth
Source: for panels A,B and C: Mutter; panel D derived from Hallegate and Pryzluski, 2011.
Note: panels A, B and C were developed by Mutter for this paper.

scenario is commonly assumed to be the most likely outcome of a disaster, especially in a relatively poor country.

In the second scenario (depicted in panel B, upper right), it is assumed that after the disaster only negligible time is lost before the economy begins recovering, so that in a relatively short time the level of the pre-disaster economy is regained. Note that the slope of the line that represents recovery is greater than that of the line representing the equilibrium economic growth trajectory of the pre-disaster economy. The implication is that the economy either has spare capacity, not fully utilized in support of current economic growth, that it can devote to recovery, or that capital from external sources such as the World Bank or donor nations provides enough inflow to fuel the accelerated economic growth. Here the resources devoted to recovery act in a sense like an economic stimulus package, because the economy grows faster after the disaster than it did in the pre-disaster period.

In the third scenario (panel C, lower left), recovery begins as it did in panel B, but, before it rejoins the pre-disaster growth trajectory, another disaster hits and there is a second asset shock. Recovery following the second shock may grow the economy more slowly than the first recovery did, but still faster than the nominal disaster-free rate. Then yet another shock strikes and the scenario repeats itself. The overall economic trajectory is depicted by the jagged saw-tooth pattern whose long-term average is represented by the dashed line. The slope of the dashed line shows that the average long-term growth is somewhat slower than growth would have been in the absence of disasters. Patterns of economic growth showing these features are quite common for many poor countries (Haiti in particular shows a pattern quite like this one, though not every downturn in Haiti's trajectory is associated with a natural disaster). Freeman (2000) presents essentially this notion of the effect of disasters on growth.

The fourth and final scenario (panel D, lower right) is the most optimistic one. It follows essentially the same trajectory as the one in panel B, except that there is an overshoot. The economy has been so stimulated in the post-disaster recovery phase that it continues to grow at that faster rate, exceeding the levels of capital growth that would have been achieved by the pre-disaster economy (Hallegatte and Przyluski, 2011).

One basic problem with this way of conceptualizing disasters is that the equilibrium growth rate of an economy – that is, its rate absent the effects of disasters – can never be measured. The steady line from which the asset drop occurs cannot be known. In all four scenarios in the diagram, the economy is always, nominally, operating under post-disaster conditions, and is consistently out of equilibrium as a result of those disasters.

Another difficulty is that there is no agreed-upon international standard for assessing the losses L, and so estimates could vary considerably by country. Gail *et al.* (2009) have suggested six sources of bias in estimating losses:

1   Hazard bias, which produces an uneven representation and distribution of losses among the various kinds of hazard.
2   Temporal bias, which makes it difficult to compare losses across time (because data on losses in past decades are less reliable than data on losses today).
3   Threshold bias, which results in an underrepresentation of minor and chronic events.
4   Accounting bias, which underreports indirect, uninsured and other losses.
5   Geographic bias, which generates a spatially distorted picture of losses because of over- or under-represented locales.
6   Systemic bias, which makes it difficult to compare losses across databases because of non-uniform estimating and reporting techniques.

The media often report losses very quickly, though they often refer only to the value of lost physical assets, and they typically count only insured property losses that can be fairly quickly assessed by insurance and re-insurance companies. These initial reports generally do not include the costs of publicly owned assets such as roads and bridges, or such critical public assets as schools and hospitals. Thus the initial loss L is not an economic loss per se (even though it is often referred to as an economic loss in media reports), but rather a capital-asset loss incurred at the time of the disaster. (For a discussion of this point, see Hallegatte and Przyluski, 2011.) A number of high-value elevated highways were destroyed in Kobe, Japan, as a result of the earthquake there in 1995, and parts of the Pan American Highway became impassable after the Pisco, Chile, earthquake in 2007. Although the value of L in the Chilean case was much smaller than it was for Japan, the economic losses were greater in Chile because there is no alternative to the Pan American Highway. In Japan, by contrast, many alternate routes remained open and passable through the Kobe region.

In relatively poor countries, most private property is either inadequately insured or not insured at all. Such property is also not generally valued as highly as capital assets are in wealthy countries, so it can seem as if wealthy countries suffer the greater losses. Furthermore, it is fairly obvious that measures of L should at least be expressed as a percentage of the total size of an economy. In assessing losses from global disasters, as well as in forecasting risks, the GAR (UNISDR, 2011) acknowledges this important point, though its simple logic often goes unmentioned in public discussions, which typically report only the absolute size of losses.

One would expect the make-up of an economy would also play a major role in how well a country can withstand nature's excesses and recover from them. Drought, for instance, mainly affects agriculture, and that sector is a far more important component of GDP in poor countries than it is in rich ones. Rich countries whose GDP comes primarily from the manufacturing and service sectors are inherently better insulated from nature in general and from nature's excesses in particular.

Geographic size matters, too. Earthquakes, hurricanes, floods and other such disasters, no matter how massive, all cause damage in relatively restricted areas. Consequently, unless the disaster makes a direct hit on an industry that is particularly critical to a country's economy, production in the rest of the country can often buffer the effect. The U.S. and China are both so big geographically, and their economies so large and diversified, that it is hard to imagine a natural disaster that would seriously affect the total economy of either country for very long. Albala-Bertrand (1993) makes that same point in a foundational paper. Most disasters, even the worst, he suggests, are spatially restricted, and so they could never have a catastrophic economic impact on a country's economy. Moreover, he argues, the investment needed to get an economy back on track is actually quite small. No disaster has ever seriously set back the economic growth of the U.S. Regional economies, of course, can be seriously affected – but even Hurricane Katrina and the Sichuan earthquake in China went relatively unnoticed in the national economies. The Japanese economy was not brought to a halt by the earthquake and tsunami of 2011, nor did the floods of 2010 seriously impede the economy of Pakistan, even though they had few historic precedents. Small countries can experience much greater impacts. The strike on Honduras by Hurricane Mitch in 1998 was so devastating that the Honduran president, Carlos Roberto Flores, claimed that economic progress in the country had been set back 50 years. That turned out not to be true, but Flores could hardly be blamed for thinking it might be, given the devastation of that event. Other small countries, including Fiji, Samoa, St. Lucia and Madagascar have undergone similar experiences. Large countries, and wealthier countries, have not.

The nonlinear consequences of natural disasters

All four of the simple scenarios depicted in Figure 9.3 assume for comparison purposes that the economic growth of a country is fixed, that each country begins growing from the same stage of development, and that the disaster shock is a perturbation to that fixed growth trajectory. It seems reasonable to suppose that the shock imposed by natural extremes of similar magnitude will act differently on countries in which the economic factors are different. Intuition might suggest that the poorest countries with the weakest governance might suffer the most from disasters and be least able to recover.

That intuition, however, is not borne out by several analyses. Kellenberg and Mobarak (2007, 2011); Hallegatte and Ghil (2008); Mutter (2008); Schumacher and Strobl (2008); Hallegatte and Dumas (2009); Padli and Habibullah (2009); and Hallegatte and Przyluski (2011) have all come to the same, seemingly counterintuitive conclusion that disaster losses may peak in middle-income countries. In other words, the poorest countries may not be the ones most severely affected. Countries traditionally described as the most vulnerable may, in fact, not be so vulnerable at all. At the other end of the economic spectrum, the ability of strong, developed economies with high GDPs, especially the ones associated with geographically large countries, to withstand the shock of a natural disaster is perhaps self-evident. The high levels of impact in middle-income countries may be related less to the absolute size of their economies than to their high growth rates and urbanization. The high death tolls from earthquakes in Port-au-Prince, Haiti, and Sichuan, China, can be ascribed to rapid urbanization, but that should not be taken to imply large economic losses. Mutter et al. (2009) found that the economic impacts of disasters were greatest in lower-middle-income countries, and could be negative in some countries and positive in others, seemingly similar to the first group.

What might account for the differences? On the one hand, an emerging economy may initially develop only in a few key sectors. A disaster that struck one of those sectors during this critical stage in development could, by sheer misfortune, have devastating and long-term consequences. On the other hand, a developing economy may benefit hugely from the stimulus provided by an injection of liquidity (Hallegatte and Dumas, 2009; Hallegatte and Przyluski, 2011). This possibility corresponds to the scenario sketched in Figure 9.3, panel D (see p187).

Skidmore and Toya (2002) first raised an intriguing special case of this scenario: the idea that outside capital mobilized in response to a disaster might actually lead to economic growth. In an empirical analysis they found that countries that were subject to the shocks of natural disaster at a relative high frequency actually grew faster than countries that suffered fewer disasters. This result, at first counterintuitive, is readily explained. If old and inefficient infrastructure (bridges, roads, port facilities) is washed away in a hurricane or destroyed in an earthquake, and if that is quickly replaced by much better infrastructure, the country's economy might reap a lasting benefit. That is particularly true if the replacement infrastructure is paid for with external aid, say, from the World Bank without acquiring national debt or depleting the national treasury. This kind of stimulus should not be confused with the short-term benefit that emergency reconstruction immediately following a disaster can bring to the local construction industry. Deep infrastructure replacement, in contrast, can confer a long-term benefit on a nation's production and commerce. Outside resources for infrastructure renewal in this sense are essentially the equivalent of an economic stimulus package that ultimately leads to the adoption of new technologies. Albala-Bertrand (1993; 2006) has argued that only a relatively small investment is needed to restore a disaster-struck economy to its pre-disaster growth rate. Any additional resources invested in the economy make it possible to grow even faster.

Bifurcation of disaster consequences

The schematic sketch in Figure 9.4 suggests how natural disasters might affect an economy at various stages of development.

In the initial stages of development (point A), losses to natural disasters are very low. In very poor economies there is little to be lost that can be measured by standard economic metrics such as GDP. Disasters are unlikely to substantially worsen the economic conditions of countries already mired in poverty. Such countries will suffer high losses of human capital, but those losses do not translate directly into the loss of productivity that would be captured in GDP. If, for instance, there are high death tolls among people primarily involved in the informal economy or subsistence farming, GDP cannot measure any negative outcome on those lives. Thus the relative so-called 'insensitivity of poor countries to disaster shocks' likely reflects the failure of GDP to detect the type of harm that disasters bring in these settings. (Indeed, the failures of GDP as a measure of welfare, particularly in poor countries, are now routinely criticized: see, for instance, section 1 of Chapter 2, p16, as well as the Commission on the Measure of Economic Performance and Social Progress's website.[3]

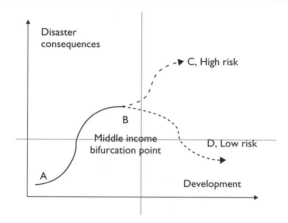

Figure 9.4 A proposed bifurcation model of how natural disasters affect development
Source: Mutter. Note that this is an original figure developed by Mutter for this paper.

As an economy develops along the path from point A to point B (Figure 9.4), welfare increases, but losses from disasters also increase until the economy grows into the range of middle-income, high-growth countries. But at point B the development path bifurcates, and the economy takes one of two possible and mutually exclusive trajectories. Societies taking the upper trajectory, C, suffer even higher losses in disasters, yet little enhancement in the welfare of their citizens. Societies taking the lower trajectory, D, reduce their economic vulnerability to disasters even as the welfare of their citizens continues to rise.

These bifurcating trajectories, I suggest, may help to explain the apparently contradictory findings reported in the literature. Some studies suggest that middle-income countries are the most vulnerable of all to the socio-economic shocks of a natural disaster. Other studies maintain that middle-income countries continue to absorb disasters with astonishing resilience. In fact, both kinds of studies may be right. Middle-income countries with high growth rates and high levels of urbanization may be responding to natural disasters by experiencing great losses and acquiring long-term penalties to economic production (Figure 9.3, panels A or C, and the path from B to C in Figure 9.4). Or, equally, they may be responding by taking advantage of the stimulus effect of recovery capital (Figure 9.3, panel D, and the path from B to D in Figure 9.4). What economic conditions determine which path is taken are hard to predict, given our current state of analytical understanding, but it is clear that the trajectory will vary by economic sector, growth within that sector and the nature and size of the disaster. Disasters such as droughts and some floods that do less damage to built infrastructure than hurricanes or earthquakes do may be less likely to trigger the stimulus effect. By the same token, countries whose governance is viewed as untrustworthy by the international donor community typically receive less donor assistance, and so a disaster may lead to a decline in welfare for a substantial period. After the most devastating disasters, countries that have only recently emerged from poverty via growth in a single sector may slide back into poverty if that sector is damaged.

Finally, the stable growth trajectory to D and beyond describes what disasters do to the most advanced economies. Although they may suffer large financial losses, their strength enables them to absorb large shocks with little lasting effect on production.

Concluding remarks

Extremes of nature have brought misery to human societies throughout recorded history. Yet a rigorous understanding of how these extreme events imperil the progress of societies toward improved welfare is still lacking. Misconceptions and myths distort the public understanding of disasters and may lead public officials to take inappropriate and even potentially harmful actions during and after a disaster. The economic consequences of the shock of a natural disaster are not well understood at a theoretical level, and empirical analyses lead to incomplete and conflicting conclusions about the effects of disasters on the prospects for development. What is known at present can seem puzzling and counterintuitive. Disasters often seem to have far less impact than one might expect.

What message does this hold for a future in which we can no longer live in the climate we have become accustomed to? If, as I noted at the beginning of this chapter, climate change is inevitable, then adaptation to climate change is equally inevitable. Adaptation may come about through thoughtful planning, or it will happen willy-nilly, via dynamic social forces that play out a stage of vast global inequalities. The analysis done here suggests that climate change may be an agent for inequality, a means whereby the world will become even more divided than it is today. If some societies can, even by accident, actually benefit from a disaster event, then the urgent need is to understand how that can come about. Is there some still-undiscovered formula that can be applied to all societies, not just to the wealthy or the lucky? Is it possible to imagine that we can do better than merely adapt? Can we, perhaps, actually learn to prosper in our new world?

Acknowledgment

I have greatly benefited from discussions with students in the Ph.D. program in Sustainable Development at Columbia University's School of International and Public Affairs. I have also greatly benefited from many fruitful discussions with Sonali Deraniyagala of University of London's School of Oriental and African Studies and Columbia's School of International and Public Affairs.

Notes

1   See http://siteresources.worldbank.org/INTLAC/Resources/PDNA_Haiti-2010_Working_Document_EN.pdf
2   See http://en.wikipedia.org/wiki/2010_Chile_earthquake#cite_note-860
3   See http://www.stiglitz-sen-fitoussi.fr/en/index.htm

References

Albala-Bertrand, J. (1993) *Political Economy of Large Natural Disasters*, Oxford University Press, New York

Albala-Bertrand, J.M., (2006) 'The unlikeliness of an economic catastrophe: Localization and globalization', Working paper 576, Queen Mary, University of London, School of Economics and Finance http://ideas.repec.org/p/qmw/qmwecw/wp576.html, accessed March 30, 2012

Bankoff, G. (2005) 'The tale of the three pigs: taking another look at vulnerability in the light of the Indian Ocean tsunami and Hurricane Katrina', Understanding Katrina: Perspectives from the Social Sciences, Social Sciences Research Council, http://understandingkatrina.ssrc.org/Bankoff, accessed March 30, 2012

Barsky, L. (2006) 'Disaster realities following Katrina: revisiting the looting myth', in *Learning from Catastrophe: Quick Response Research in the Wake of Hurricane Katrina*, Natural Hazards Center, University of Colorado, Boulder, CO

Bilham, R. (2009) 'The seismic future of cities', *Bulletin of Earthquake Engineering*, September, DOI 10.1007/s10518-009-9147-0

Blaikie, P., Cannon, T., Davis, I. and Wisner, B. (1994) *At Risk Natural Hazards, People's Vulnerability and Disaster*, Routledge, London and New York

Cutter, S.L. (2005) 'The geography of social vulnerability: race, class, and catastrophe', Understanding Katrina, Perspectives from the Social Sciences, Social Sciences Research Council, http://understandingkatrina.ssrc.org/Cutter, accessed March 30, 2012

Cutter, S.L., Boruff, B.J. and Shirley, W.L. (2003) 'Social vulnerability to environmental hazards', *Social Science Quarterly*, vol 84, no 1, pp242–261

Dilley, M., Chen, R.S., Deichmann, U., Lerner-Lam, A.L., Arnold, M., Agwe, J., Buys, P., Kjekstad, O., Lyon, B. and Yetman, G. (2005) *Natural Disaster Hotspots: A Global Risk Analysis*, Disaster Risk Management Series No 5, World Bank, Washington, DC

Dynes, Russell (2007) 'Panic and the vision of collective incompetence', *Natural Hazards Observer*, vol 31, no 2, pp5–6

Freeman, P.K. (2000) 'Estimating chronic risk from natural disasters in developing countries: a case study on Honduras', presented at the World Bank's Annual Bank Conference on Development Economics-Europe-Development Thinking at the Millennium, June, Paris

Gail, M., Borden, K.A. and Cutter, S.L., (2009) 'When do losses count? Six fallacies of natural hazards loss data', *Bulletin of the American Meteorological Society*, vol 90, no 6, pp799–809, doi: http://dx.doi.org/10.1175/2008BAMS2721.1

Hallegatte, S, and Dumas, P. (2009) 'Can natural disasters have positive consequences? Investigating the role of embodied technical change', *Ecological Economics*, vol 68, pp777–86

Hallegatte, S. and Ghil, M. (2008) 'Natural disasters impacting a macroeconomic model with endogenous dynamics', *Ecological Economics*, vol 68, pp582–92

Hallegatte, S. and Przyluski, V. (2011) 'The economics of natural disasters: concepts and methods', Policy Research Working Paper 5507, World Bank, Washington, DC

Hough, S. Elizabeth and Bilham, R.G. (2006) *After the Earth Quakes: Elastic Rebound on an Urban Planet*, Oxford, New York

Jonkman, S.N., Maaskantl, B., Boyd, E. and Levitan, M. (2008) 'Loss of life caused by the flooding of New Orleans after Hurricane Katrina: a preliminary analysis of the relationship between flood characteristics and mortality', presented at 4th International Symposium on Flood Defence: Managing Flood Risk, Reliability and Vulnerability, Toronto, Ontario, Canada, May 6–8

Kahn, M.E. (2005) 'The death toll from natural disasters: the role of income, geography and institutions', *Review of Economics and Statistics*, vol 87, no 2, May, pp271–284

Kellenberg, D.K, and Mobarak, A.M. (2007) 'Does rising income increase or decrease damage risk from natural disasters?', *Journal of Urban Economics*, vol 63, no 3, pp788–802

Kellenberg, D.K. and Mobarak, A.M. (2011) 'The economics of natural disasters', *Annual Review of Resource Economics*, vol 3, pp297–312

LTL Strategies (2011) 'Building assessments and rubble removal in quake-affected neighbourhoods in Haiti; BARR survey final report', prepared for USAID http://pdf.usaid.gov/pdf_docs/PNADY468.pdf, accessed March 30, 2012

Melissen, H.J. (23 February, 2010) 'Haiti quake death toll well under 100,000', http://www.rnw.nl/english/article/haiti-quake-death-toll-well-under-100000, accessed March 30, 2012

Mutter, J.C. (2005) 'The Earth sciences, human well-being and the reduction of global poverty', *Eos Transactions*, April 19, http://eesc.columbia.edu/courses/v1003/lectures/sustainable_development/mutter-eos.pdf, accessed March 30, 2012

Mutter, J.C. (2008) 'The preconditions of disaster: premonitions of tragedy', *Social Research: An International Quarterly of the Social Sciences*, vol 75, no 3, pp691–724

Mutter, J.C. (2010) 'Disasters widen the rich-poor divide', *Nature*, vol 466, no 26, August

Mutter, J.C., Archibong, B. and Pi, D. (2009) 'When is a natural disaster a development disaster? When is a natural disaster not a disaster?', *Eos Transactions*, Fall annual meeting AGU (American Geophysical Union)

Padli, J. and Habibullah, M.S. (2009) 'Natural disaster death and socio-economic factors in selected Asian countries: a panel analysis', *Asian Social Science*, vol 5, no 4, April

Quarantelli, E.L. (2008) 'Conventional beliefs and counterintuitive realities', *Social Research: An International Quarterly of the Social Sciences*, vol 75, no 3, Fall, pp873–904

Quigley, B. (2010) 'Katrina Pain Index 2010 New Orleans – Five years later', http://www.huffingtonpost.com/bill-quigley/katrina-pain-index-2010-n_b_673383.html, accessed March 30, 2012

Schumacher I. and Strobl, E. (2008) 'Economic development and losses due to natural disasters: the role of risk', *Work. Pap. hal-00356286*, *Dep. Econ.*, Ecole Polytechnique, Paris

Skidmore, M. and Toya, H. (2002) 'Do natural disasters promote long-run growth?', *Economic Inquiry*, vol 40, no 4, pp664–87

Sun, L.G. (2011) 'Disaster mythology and the law', *Cornell Law Review*, vol 96, no 4, pp1131–1208

Tierney, K., Bevc, C. and Kuligowski, E. (2006) 'Metaphors matter: disaster myths, media frames, and their consequences in Hurricane Katrina', *Annals of the American Academy of Political and Social Science*, vol 604, no 1, March, pp57–81

UNDP (2004) 'Reducing disaster risk: a challenge for development', Bureau for Crisis Prevention and Recovery, http://www.unisdr.org/2005/mdgs-drr/undp.htm, accessed March 30, 2012

United Nations International Strategy for Disaster Reduction Secretariat (UNISDR) (2009), *Global Assessment Report on Disaster Risk Reduction: Risk and Poverty in a Changing Climate*, UNISDR http://ideas.repec.org/p/qmw/qmwecw/wp576.html, accessed March 30, 2012

UNISDR (2011) *Global Assessment Report on Disaster Risk Reduction 2011: Revealing Risk, Redefining Development*, UN International Strategy for Disaster Risk Reduction, http://www.preventionweb.net/english/hyogo/gar/2011/en/home/index.html, accessed March 30, 2012

Wisner, B. (1993) 'Disaster vulnerability: scale, power and daily life', *GeoJournal*, vol 30, no 2, pp127–140

Chapter 10

Urbanization of climate change

Responding to a new global challenge[1]

William Solecki, Cynthia Rosenzweig, Stephen Hammer and Shagun Mehrotra

Cities and climate change

Cities find themselves on the front lines of climate change.[2] The direct effects of a warming earth will exacerbate many longstanding urban ills, such as rapid population growth, sprawl, poverty and pollution, and, in general, climate change will stress the urban environment along multiple pathways (Rosenzweig *et al.*, 2011a; UN-Habitat, 2011). Its indirect impacts and feedbacks will also be most keenly felt in cities, simply because of their concentrated and integrated economic activities, their highly complex systems of infrastructure and social services, and their multilayered governance. Cities will need to find new ways to protect their citizens and assets, to determine how to set investment priorities for strengthening or replacing infrastructure, and to assess how climate change will affect their plans for long-term growth and development.

Cities must also be recognized as crucial elements in any global responses to climate change (Rosenzweig *et al.*, 2011a). Cities generate as much as 70 percent of global greenhouse-gas (GHG) emissions (International Energy Agency, 2008), and so they are obvious targets for mitigation efforts. But they also demand the special attention of policy-makers because of several factors, overlooked in early climate research, that make cities extremely vulnerable to climate change. First, most people on the planet now live in cities, and urban growth is projected to continue well into the twenty-first century, nearly doubling to some 6.3 billion people by mid-century (UN, 2010). Second, cities are hubs of economic activity; they often support a larger metropolitan region or even the national economy. That, of course, also gives cities an advantage as well as a vulnerability – since, as centers of wealth and innovation, they often have the best tools and greatest resources for tackling the challenges of climate change. Third, nearly all cities have grown up (and continue to be built up) along coasts or riverbanks, exposing them to some of the most potentially damaging effects of climate change. For example, increases in sea level and large storm surges will threaten critical infrastructure. More frequent and intense floods and droughts will put even greater demands on water supplies that are often scarce already. Fourth and finally, cities have outsize effects on their own environment: among their other environmental impacts, they create so-called urban heat islands (UHIs) and pollute their own air and water.

A generalized vulnerability and risk-management paradigm is emerging that provides a useful framework to city decision-makers for mitigating and adapting to climate change (Mehrotra *et al.*, 2009; Rosenzweig *et al.*, 2011). City managers are increasingly recognizing that the environmental conditions of the past do not provide a particularly useful forecast of future environmental conditions. Instead, managers are depending increasingly on risk-based protocols for dealing with climate change (Yohe and Leichenko, 2010). Frameworks for assessing climate-change vulnerability and risk are typically developed out of three sets of indicators, on the basis of readily available data:

1   The climate hazards a city faces, such as more frequent and longer duration heat waves, more frequent heavy downpours and more frequent and expanded coastal flooding.
2   Demographic and geographic features related to vulnerability, such as the size and density of a city's population, its topography, the portion of its population living in poverty and the fraction of the national gross domestic product (GDP) that the city generates.
3   Indicators of adaptive capacity – in other words, data relevant to the ability of a city to act: What information about climate change is readily available? How many resources can be allocated for mitigation and adaptation? What institutions, governance bureaus and change agents are present and likely to be effective in helping the city to adapt?

Current and future climate hazards in cities

The scientific basis for action and policymaking by city decision-makers and other stakeholder groups comes from existing, city-specific climate data and down-scaled projections from global-climate models. Those models project that by the 2050s temperatures will increase around the world, on average, by between 1 and 4 Celsius degrees (Rosenzweig *et al.*, 2011a). Cities, of course, will not be exempt from those increases.

But the urban environment and the activities it supports will amplify those baseline effects. For one thing, cities are already hotter than their surrounding suburban and rural areas, both because concrete and other building materials absorb heat and because the landscape no longer benefits from the natural evaporative cooling of the trees and other vegetation that streets and buildings have displaced. The result is the now-familiar phenomenon of the UHI. Climate change will exacerbate UHI conditions in cities by intensifying summer heat waves, making them both hotter and longer than usual.

Those heat waves in turn can lead to health crises and other negative effects on individuals, power shortages arising from increased use of air conditioning and other cooling technologies, and stress on machinery and other mechanical systems.

The concentration of residential, commercial, industrial and transportation systems (the last including roads, automobiles and railroads) in cities causes intense air pollution and its associated hazards to the health of urban residents. The warmer temperatures associated with climate change will aggravate those problems as well, producing greater amounts of secondary air pollution (e.g. oxides of nitrogen, NOx, and sulfur, SOx). Warmer temperatures also lead to greater energy use by heating, ventilation and air conditioning (HVAC) cooling systems and less-efficient machine functioning, further increasing the amount of primary and secondary air pollution.

Major contributors to weather and climate variability, such as tropical and extratropical storm systems, as well as shifts in such global climate systems as the El Niño–Southern Oscillation and the North Atlantic Oscillation, affect climate extremes in cities. How the frequency of these events and systems will be altered, if at all, by anthropogenic climate change is still to be determined. What is clear, however, is that the greater the shift in a city's environmental baseline, the greater will be the impact of climate extremes. Higher rates of sea-level rise, for instance, will lead to more severe coastal flooding. Changes in precipitation patterns are also projected to amplify local variability: the intensity of rain storms is expected to increase, causing more floods, but the time intervals between storms are expected to lengthen as well, leading to more droughts in many cities and regions.

Climate change and urban sectors and services

As climate change emerged as an issue of global concern, cities focused on mitigation efforts to reduce energy consumption and carbon output. More recently, the emphasis has shifted to adaptation and resilience to climate change as well as to mitigation.[3] That shift makes it particularly important to understand how climate change will affect the ways urban systems operate within specific sectors and services: energy, water and wastewater, transportation and public health. Increased flooding, for instance, will degrade materials used in construction and infrastructure, which will particularly affect the energy and transportation sectors (Wilby, 2007). Most impacts will be negative, as in the example of materials degradation, but not all: the demand for heat in the winter will likely decline. The take-home lesson is that analyzing how climate change is likely to affect specific sectors and services is critical if cities are to realistically consider their policy alternatives and develop effective strategies for adapting to (as well as mitigating) urban climate risks (Rosenzweig et al., 2011a). Here we briefly detail some of the most significant impacts across several sectors and services.

Energy

The effects of climate change on the energy sector will be felt on both supply and demand. Power plants are frequently located along bodies of water, hence are susceptible to both coastal and inland flooding – as the March, 2011, inundation of Japan's Fukushima Daiichi Nuclear Power Station made abundantly clear. As for hydropower, the projected changes in intensity and frequency of precipitation will increase the variability in both quantity and timing of the water available for conversion to energy. The likely increase in heat waves will lead to more peak load demands, which stress energy distribution systems and increase the chances of brownouts and blackouts. These interruptions of service will have negative effects both on local health and the local economy. As we suggested earlier, climate change will generally reduce energy demand in cooler seasons, and it will increase demand in warmer seasons – but the overall impact will depend on the balance of seasonal effects. For any given city, analyses are needed to determine that balance; in general, the data recorded for such seasonal shifts show that the increased GHG emissions from increased cooling demands outweighed the GHG reductions from lower heating demands.[4]

For the energy sector, adaptation and mitigation strategies often overlap, and it is critical to emphasize both to help reduce the inevitable impacts of climate change. For example, programs for managing demand to cut peak load blend elements of both adaptation and mitigation. So do projects for updating power plants and energy distribution networks, which aim to increase resilience to flooding, wind storms and extremes of temperature. A third example is diversifying the mix of fuels, including an increased share of renewable energy sources, that generate a city's power.

Seoul's Energy Declaration of 2007 well illustrates these parallel (and, at times, competing) sets of interest. The declaration focuses on improving the city's energy self-reliance, its use of alternative energy sources and its commitment to demand-side management, as well as on building and enhancing strategies to cope with climate change (Kim and Choi, 2011). Yet in the cities affected by the declaration, climate-related concerns often take a back seat to the goals of reducing poverty, promoting economic development and improving social institutions by scaling up access to modern energy services. Adopting these mitigation measures could bring greater reliance on renewable sources of energy (including biomass-based fuels for cooking and heating), making cities even more vulnerable to climate change. After all, many sources of renewable energy are subject to changing climate regimes.

Water and wastewater

Cities are constantly trying to cope with water: maintaining supplies of fresh drinking water, managing excess water from flooding, controlling wastewater and sewerage flow.[5] Climate change will put all these systems under great stress. Both the quantity and quality of the water supply will be significantly affected by the projected increases in both floods and droughts (Aerts *et al.*, 2009; Case, 2008; Kirshen *et al.*, 2008). Although precipitation is expected to increase in some areas, particularly in the mid and high latitudes, water availability is projected eventually to decrease in many regions, including cities whose water is supplied primarily by meltwater from mountain snow and glaciers.[6] The gap between water supply and demand will likely increase, as drought-affected areas expand (particularly for cities in the lower latitudes) and as floods intensify (Kamai-Chaoui, 2009).

Within cities, impervious surfaces and increased precipitation intensity can overwhelm drainage systems. In cities within developing countries, more than half the people rely on vendors, who make up an informal water-supply system (see Chapter 8). As climate continues to change, both these informal services and the formal urban water supply will be highly vulnerable to drought, extreme precipitation and sea-level rise. Long-term planning for the impacts of climate change on the formal and informal water-supply and wastewater-treatment sectors in cities is required, and plans should be monitored, reassessed and revised every five to ten years as climate science progresses and data improve.[7]

Several adaptation and mitigation strategies – often with co-benefits – are available for the water and wastewater sector, which make these systems more resilient in the face of increased supply and operational stress (Kirshen *et al.*, 2008; Nelson *et al.*, 2009). In the immediate future, programs for effective leak detection and repair, as well as for managing demand, should be undertaken in formal and, to the extent relevant, informal water-supply systems (Rosenzweig *et al.*, 2007). Demand can be managed, in part, through stronger water-conservation measures – beginning with low-flow toilets, shower heads and other fixtures. Higher temperatures also bring higher evaporative losses, thereby both increasing demand for water and reducing its supply. Under those circumstances, among others, water reuse (e.g. the use of graywater) can play a key role in enhancing water-use efficiency, especially for landscape irrigation in urban open spaces.[8] Citywide water marketing through the informal private sector can also increase water-use efficiency, improve the robustness of the delivery system and help encourage water usage across various sectors of the economy in some urban circumstances, such as water-supply shortages. Where water is already becoming increasingly scarce, such as in Santiago, Chile, the capability of the water market to distribute water equitably – and thereby to resolve water conflicts – is expected to become increasingly important.[9] Water banking (whereby water collected during wet years is stored for use in dry years) is a way of hedging against uncertainties, and it, too, can improve system robustness. Capturing rainwater instead of pumping groundwater can substantially reduce the use of energy.[10]

Transportation

Because so many urban residents, particularly the urban poor, rely every day on transportation systems, any effects of climate change on urban transportation systems could have dramatic consequences for daily life (Revi, 2008).[11] Transport-related climate risks depend on the complex mix of transportation options unique to that city (Wilby, 2007), but certain broad distinctions among cities have outsize importance. Cities tend to be built around either mass transit or the individually owned vehicle. And transportation systems may be built at ground level, underground or as elevated roads and railways. The potential impact of the various consequences of climate change, particularly flooding, evidently depends on those factors (Prasad *et al.*, 2009). Tunnels, vent shafts and ramps are clearly at risk. The possibility of flooding requires that large and numerous pumps be ready for use throughout these systems, and that a city maintain the capability to quickly remove debris and repair or replace such key infrastructure as motors, relays, resistors and transformers.

In addition to their vulnerability to rising sea levels and storm surges, transportation systems are particularly vulnerable to excessive heat. Overheating can cause buckling of steel rails, throwing them out of alignment, which can lead to train derailments.[12] Concrete roadways can also buckle or 'explode' and asphalt roads can melt. Excessive heat can also reduce the expected lifespans of train wheels and automobile tires. Whether a city's transportation system moves mainly people or goods also affects the risks – particularly the heat risks – associated with climate change. Climate impacts on power and telecommunication systems can pose further risks in the transportation network; one of the most direct, and perhaps surprising, consequences of excess heat is that overhead wires can sag so low from expansion that they risk shorting out electrically.

Although urban transportation systems are exposed to many serious risks, they also have a key role to play in climate-change mitigation. We only scratch the surface of this role by highlighting such measures as adopting energy-efficient taxis and enhancing public transportation to reduce the use of individual vehicles.

Several basic adaptation and mitigation strategies have been outlined for the urban transportation sector (Revi, 2008):

• Adopt a mix of technical and ecosystem-based approaches.
• Strengthen and build levees.
• Install or remove dams.
• Limit flood damage by pumping.
• Improve drainage to protect transportation assets.
• Elevate equipment to reduce flood risk.
• Temporarily move rolling stock in advance of storms to protected locations.
• Diversify options among the various modes of transport.

It is critical that climate considerations be incorporated into the plans, construction and management of transit systems, even as existing transportation assets are being retrofitted.

Public health

Cities are subject to serious health risks from climate change, since a large and high-density population amplifies the potential for negative outcomes.[13] Climate change, for instance, is likely to exacerbate existing health risks in cities and to create new ones. The growth in the populations of urban poor and elderly compounds the threats of heat and vector-related diseases (that is, diseases transmitted by organisms, including humans, in the environment; Bartlett et al., 2009). Cities with limited existing water services are also at greater risk of drought and vector-related diseases (Reid and Kovats, 2009). Other critical health-related issues can surface with rising sea levels and increased flooding of coastal zones (McGranahan et al., 2007).

Because the infrastructure for health protection is already overburdened in many cities in developing countries, climate-change adaptation strategies need to focus on the most vulnerable urban residents. Adaptation and mitigation strategies associated with public-health issues in cities must be integrated with strategies for other sectors and services (Frumkin et al., 2008; World Health Organization, 2009). Such strategies need to promote 'co-benefits', such as reducing existing health hazards, particularly among those who bear the brunt of them, as well as helping to reduce people's health vulnerability to climate-change (Bell et al., 2007).[14] For example, efforts to ease the effects of UHIs via such passive approaches as tree planting and installing green roofs and permeable pavements not only will save energy (e.g. by reducing the need for air conditioning), but also promote better public health (Bell et al., 2007). Other strategies for adapting to climate change with minimal impact on public health include:

- improving and increasing water and energy service;
- regulating the growth of settlements in flood plains; and
- expanding health surveillance and early warning systems through technology and social networking.

Strategies for disaster risk-reduction also connect directly with strategies for maintaining public health (Solecki et al., 2011). As we noted earlier, climate change is associated with extreme events, and such events have both direct and indirect implications for health. Cities in developing countries as well as in the developed world are actively working to link their climate-change adaptation and disaster risk-reduction strategies, in hopes of enhancing resilience to climate change and adaptive capacity. In Pune, India, for example, the Pune Municipal Corporation recently began a comprehensive disaster management-planning effort, focused on linking the resources of the city with those of regional management agencies. The resulting plan became the vehicle for a series of local adaptation-related activities, such as improved flood control and the development of early warning systems.[15]

Cross-cutting issues

It is entirely possible, of course, for inappropriate zoning, uninformed urban planning and general (mis)management of resources, combined with unchecked population growth, to exacerbate the effects of climate change. It is also possible (and clearly preferable) for cities to mitigate and adapt to it. City governments have many ways to strengthen their decision-making and take the latter course: through effective leadership, science-based policy-making, efficient and innovative financing, jurisdictional coordination – especially in cases of cross-boundary issues – and citizen participation and engagement (Bai, 2007). We focus here on two points of discussion that deserve special attention: urban land-use planning and governance.

Urban land use and planning

The vulnerability of a city to climate change is not a fixed and unmanageable predicament. Rather, through the intelligent use of urban land, whatever vulnerability is present can be modified and, often, at least partly remedied. The remedies stem from an awareness of a city's natural setting, an understanding of how the design of urban form intentionally (or not) gives rise to the built environment, and an active effort to reduce the effects of UHIs (Blanco and Alberti, 2009).[16] Adapting to climate change through urban land management involves many moving parts: the legal and political systems, planning departments, zoning regulations, infrastructure and urban services, land markets and fiscal arrangements. Planning and managing an effective response to climate change is highly dependent on coordinating these parts – the more so because many metropolitan areas with seemingly common interests are politically fragmented. Cities in the Global South also have the additional disadvantages of lacking not only the extensive human and capital resources of their Northern counterparts, but also the traditional institutional mandate to implement and control local land use and development (Parnell *et al.*, 2009).

Several adaptation and mitigation strategies have been identified that reduce risk exposure, or vulnerability; promote reductions in energy use; or both (McEvoy *et al.*, 2006). Some of the strategies include relatively small-scale adjustments to existing building codes and land regulations that would bring big reductions in the hazards of climate change: elevating buildings in flood-prone areas, reducing energy use for heating and cooling, increasing the space planted in trees and vegetation to reduce the heat-island effect

(Condon *et al.*, 2009). Other strategies would require more transformative shifts, many of which have been described in the hazard-mitigation literature: reducing sprawl by increasing the densities of people and of buildings; mixing land uses to reduce automobile traffic and increase the reliance on public transit; and restricting land use in areas subject to such predictable climate-change impacts as sea-level rise and riverine flooding.

Governance

Yet despite the abundance of good ideas in the literature, it is hard to over-state the many challenges local governments must face if their cities are to mitigate and adapt to climate change.[17] For any city, climate is just one of many issues on the local agenda. Governments must make trade-offs between current priorities and long-term risks. Often the uncertainties about the local impacts of climate change affect how a community sets priorities for investments and actions. Local authorities can be constrained by policy and fiscal limitations. One of the most significant issues is how to finance climate-change action. Jurisdictional conflicts can also be a major challenge to local governments and the inclusion of multiple stakeholders adds a level of complexity that can prove hard to overcome. Yet despite all these difficulties, decision-makers and stakeholders in many cities are actively working on the challenges of implementing mitigation and adaptation strategies.

Urbanization and the environmental crisis of climate change

Although cities may now find it daunting to respond to climate change, it is important to recognize that they have met environmental challenges in the past similar to the ones embodied in the risks of climate change. The responses of cities, furthermore, have been quite dynamic, and their residents have shown tremendous adaptive capacity. In many ways – as urban historian Thomas Bender notes – cities remain 'unfinished', and they are constantly being built and re-built, both literally and figuratively. It is during this constant process of renewal that the opportunities for responding to past environmental challenges and promoting resilience can be seized.

As cities grow, both resources and the capacity for continued expansion become limited. These limits occur frequently in a variety of contexts: environmental (e.g. limits on water and energy supply); societal (e.g. constraints imposed by ethnic and racial conflicts); political (e.g. limits of governance); and economic (e.g. limits on opportunity and employment). These limits can develop into crises that must be resolved if the city is to continue to grow. The resolution of these crises often leads to fundamental transformations in the city, which are punctuated by transitions.

There are several root causes of environmental crises in cities. Many have to do with the natural setting and resources of the city (e.g. the lack of a natural supply of drinking water). Others derive from significant shifts in the character and structure of the connections between human and natural systems: a new and extensive reservoir system for supplying water, for example, or a major environmental disaster that alters the pattern of every-day life. Still other transformations are more explicitly societal in origin: a shift to a new mode of production and social reproduction, for example, as in the historical shift from a port-oriented, trading center to a production and manufacturing center.

Many drivers of environmental transitions and transformations have been documented, including the emergence of new technology, rapid population growth, the growth of poverty, the accumulation of wealth, the appearance of large-scale environmental hazards, the emergence of resource limitations involving local relative or absolute deficits of critical items such as water and energy, and dramatic shifts in institutional capacity and capability. But in all these cases, the role of crises is critical for understanding how the transitions occur.

Transitions emerge when systems come under extreme stress. Three basic kinds of system transitions (see Figure 10.1) have been identified (Scheffer, 2009). Two involve sudden shifts down the length of a line representing a system in equilibrium. In these cases, system recovery involves movement back up the line toward a higher system state. For example, a major flood might dramatically alter the structure and function of an ecosystem in a wetland meadow or an electrical distribution grid, but with time the system would recover and return to its earlier condition. The third kind of transi-tion, however, can include a 'phase change' or a 'regime shift', in which movement to another equilibrium point of the system is nonlinear. These transitions are associated with system-level tipping points, and they are hard for the system to recover from without substantial outside intervention. A critical question is, What kind of system transitions will result from the effects of climate change on cities?

What kinds of crises can drive transitions in cities? The list includes virtually any stress to which cities have been subjected: scarcity of ecologi-cal resources (water supply, food and energy); shifts in land use (e.g. the collapse of a peri-urban, agricultural community); demographic changes (e.g. ethnic and racial population shifts); socio-economic factors (e.g. war, civil disturbance, gentrification, capital disinvestment and reinvestment); and urban spatial development (e.g. congestion and lack of mobility). These crises and transitions have also been described and analyzed by virtually every conceivable scholarly subspecialty, including political economy, politi-cal ecology, environmental history and conservation biology; studies have focused on issues of resilience, vulnerability, environmental transformation, sustainability and adaptive management (Solecki and Murphy, 2012).

The history of any city often includes many environmental crises and their associated transitions, each emerging over time and often overlapping

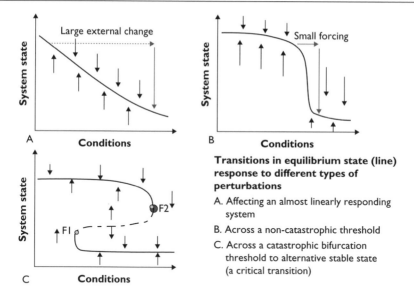

Figure 10.1 Transitions in equilibrium state: Response to different types of perturbations
Source: adapted from Scheffer, et al., 2009.

with other crises and transitions. Crises often come to a head after several failed attempts to resolve an issue, during which time the issue deteriorates. When eventually the issue develops into a full-blown crisis, the economic stability, continued growth and future habitation of the city can come into question. In these situations, tipping points and thresholds are frequently passed and transitions occur. And that is not the end of the complications: the resolution of a crisis often leads to new conditions that contribute to future crises – at other spatial, temporal and social scales.

Environmental crises and transitions in New York City

The pattern of environmental crisis and transition can be documented from the developmental history of New York City. This case study shows how a series of profound environmental crises and their resolutions led not to smooth evolutionary growth but rather to a punctuated history of development.

By the early 1800s, New York City – founded as the Dutch colonial outpost in the early 1600s – had become the largest city in the U.S., and remains so to this day. Since its beginnings, New York has been continually recast: from minor frontier settlement to port city, from port city to manufacturing hub, from manufacturing hub to financial center and, eventually, to a de facto world capital. Although each shift (i.e. transformation) was associated with tension (i.e. crises) and change (i.e. transition), probably the most profound shift was its transition from a relatively compact, late nineteenth-century city clustered around its port to the sprawling city it became in the early twentieth century, spreading into places that were long considered its hinterlands (Scobey, 2003).

Throughout its history since 1800, New York has also undergone several environmental crises and associated transitions. In general, these have mirrored the growth of the city as a modern metropolis. Most of the crisis-transition pairs were characterized by a series of lead-up events, early attempts at solution, increasingly heightened levels of concern and eventual resolution. These resolutions also precipitated unintended consequences, which themselves led to further environmental change, degradation and other crises (see Table 10.1).

A key lesson from this history is that past decisions have significant implications for the scope and likely success of sustainability practices today (Solecki and Leichenko, 2006). By analogy, one can look at events today and speculate about their future impact on resilience and sustainability generally, and on climate-change adaptation in particular. From this temporal perspective, one can look both backward and forward to suggest how best to link current environmental policies, along with demands for enhanced economic growth, infrastructure development and human livelihood, with future sustainability. From those links come the best options we can devise for adapting to climate change.

Climate-change adaptation in an urban context: The latest crisis for New York City

The most important environmental challenge for New York City in the first decades of the twenty-first century is climate change. It is projected to have wide impacts on the city's critical infrastructure through higher temperatures, more intense flooding events and sea-level rise. Dealing with a crisis of such magnitude requires long-term strategic planning. Because the city was early to recognize the risks of climate change, and because it has made a commitment to mitigation of GHG emissions as well as to adaptation, New York has become a national and international leader in responding to the threat.

A decade of response

Current climate-change adaptation efforts in New York City build on previous assessments and studies (see Table 10.2). For example, the Metropolitan East Coast Regional Assessment of Climate Variability and Change (MEC) (one of the regional components of the U.S. National Assessment of the Potential Consequences of Climate Variability and Change) (Rosenzweig and Solecki, 2001) investigated potential risks of climate variability and change, identified key vulnerabilities to the stresses that climate change is

Table 10.1 New York City environmental crises and their resolutions

Crisis	Problem	Time Frame	Transition	Positive Impact	Negative Impact
Water quality and supply	No stable supply of safe drinking water	1790s–1830s	Completion of first large-scale reservoir systems – Croton System	Stable and robust water-supply system	Increased demand for water; accelerated urban growth
Open space and recreation	Lack of open space in rapidly developing neighborhoods	1830s–1850s	Central Park development and playground movement	Passive and active outdoor recreation opportunities	Property value shifts/rise in urban inequity
Public health and sanitation	Solid and liquid wastes in the streets	1860s–1880s	Professionalization of waste and trash management	Elimination of waste on city streets	Pollution of waterways/distant dumping
Mobility and congestion	Difficult to move on city streets because of the volume of traffic	1890s–1920s	Regional plan and Robert Moses; highway construction	Promote mobility via a system of major and minor arterial roads	Automobile dependency and sprawl
Urban renewal/loss of community	Development without taking local interests into account	1940s–1960s	Environmental impact statements and historical preservation	Landmarks protection and community-based planning	Property value shifts/investment delays
Air and water pollution	Public health and ecology risks from pollution	1940s–1960s	State and federal pollution-control legislation	Reduced risks and enhanced amenity values	Transfer of polluting facilities out of the region

Table 10.2 Climate change studies on the New York City Metropolitan Region

Year	Title	Agency
2011	New York State ClimAID Adaptation Assessment	New York State Energy Research and Development Authority
2011	Economic Vulnerabilities of New Jersey to Climate Change	New Jersey Department of Environment Protection
2010	New York City Panel on Climate Change	NYC Office of Long-Term Planning and Sustainability
2010	New York State Sea Level Rise Task Force	New York State Department of Environmental Conservation
2009	Rising Waters; Long Island Shore Study	The Nature Conservancy
2008	NYCDEP Climate Change Program Assessment and Action Plan	New York City Department of Environmental Protection
2007	August 8, 2007 Storm Report	Metropolitan Transit Authority
2007	Confronting Climate Change in the U.S. Northeast: Science, Impacts, and Solutions	Union of Concerned Scientists
2001	Climate Change and a Global City: The Potential Consequences of Climate Variability and Change[a]	U.S. National Climate Assessment and Columbia Earth Institute
1999	Hot Nights in the City: Global Warming, Sea-Level Rise and the New York Metropolitan Region	Environmental Defense Fund
1996	The Baked Apple? Metropolitan New York in the Greenhouse	New York Academy of Sciences

[a] As one of the regional components of the U.S. National Assessment of the Potential Consequences of Climate Variability and Change, the MEC (Rosenzweig and Solecki, 2001) investigated potential risks of climate variability and change, identified key vulnerabilities to the stresses that climate change is likely to introduce, and examined feasible adaptation strategies. It also drew attention to the need to mitigate atmospheric GHG concentrations in order to reduce climate risks.

likely to introduce, and examined feasible adaptation strategies. It also drew attention to the need to mitigate atmospheric GHG concentrations in order to reduce climate risks.

Also germane to ongoing climate-adaptation efforts are lessons learned from responding to recent extreme-weather events that have stressed the infrastructure. Within the metropolitan region, leading scientists, agency representatives and members of non-governmental organizations (NGOs) have studied issues related to climate extremes and climate change for more than a decade. In 2004, a climate-change adaptation initiative was launched by the city's Department of Environmental Protection (NYCDEP). The NYCDEP is responsible for the New York City water and wastewater systems, which supply and drain water for nine million people. Part of the initiative was the creation of the NYCDEP Climate Change Task Force, whose mission was to ensure that all aspects of departmental planning:

1   take into account the potential risks of climate change on the city's water supply, drainage and wastewater management systems, and
2   integrate the management of GHG emissions to the greatest extent possible.

The major product of the NYCDEP Task Force was the Climate Change Assessment and Action Plan for the agency (NYCDEP, 2008). Since many climate-change adaptations identified through this process help to increase the robustness of current systems managed by the NYCDEP, the recommendations by the NYCDEP Task Force also had the immediate benefit of improving responses to present-day climate variability. For example, the Task Force recommendations showed how best to deal with episodes of intense precipitation in the upstate reservoirs. The work of the Task Force became the benchmark and exemplar of work soon to be carried on by other city agencies.

Benchmark climate events

Although no single weather-related event can be attributed to climate change, New York City has experienced climate extremes in its recent history that have brought attention to the potential risks posed by climate change to the city's critical infrastructure. Recent extreme climate-related events include Hurricane Irene in August 2011, which led the city for the first time to activate its storm-surge evacuation plan and its associated risk-reduction planning activities on a broad scale (e.g. shutting down the public-transit system). Although the flooding caused by the storm surge was not as severe as expected, city agencies were able to test their emergency-planning protocols.

The summers of 2010 and 2011, which were exceedingly hot and stormy, are also regarded as recent weather extremes. The summer of 2011 was particularly intense – July was one of the hottest months on record for New York City, and August was one of the wettest. These events and others, which resulted in large social and economic costs, provide valuable insights into the impacts climate change could have in the future. They also high-light the need, even without climate change, to improve the city's resilience to environmental stressors. In many cases, linking the efforts to adapt to climate change tomorrow with risks faced by the city today is an effective adaptation strategy.

Current actions

In 2006, New York's Mayor Michael Bloomberg created the Office of Long-Term Planning and Sustainability, with the goal of developing a comprehensive plan to create a greener, more sustainable city. That agency has significantly strengthened the planning for climate change in New York, as well as in the surrounding region. Mitigating and adapting to climate change were also central goals of the city's comprehensive sustainability plan, PlaNYC 2030, released in 2007. One of the earliest actions by PlaNYC was to set an ambitious goal of reducing GHG by 30 percent of 2005 levels by 2030. A year later, in 2008, Bloomberg announced a long-term action plan to reduce energy consumption and GHG emissions from the city's municipal buildings and operations, also to 70 percent of current levels, by 2017, 13 years earlier than the citywide goal set by PlaNYC. The reductions in emissions from municipal operations will cut the city's annual GHG output by nearly 1.7 million metric tons and reduce peak demand for electricity by 220 megawatts (New York City, 2007).

Also in 2008, the PlaNYC's portfolio expanded as it created an inter-agency Climate Change Adaptation Task Force, charged with identifying climate-change risks and opportunities for the city's critical infrastructure,[18] and then developing coordinated adaptation strategies to address those risks. The Task Force was made up of some 40 city, state and federal agencies, regional public authorities and private companies that operate, maintain or regulate critical infrastructure related to energy, transportation, water and waste, natural resources and communications in the New York Metropolitan region. To support the Task Force, the city convened a panel of climate-change and environmental-impact scientists, along with legal, insurance and risk-management experts, known as the New York City Panel on Climate Change (NPCC). Its purpose was (and is) to provide technical advice to the city on climate-change science, the potential impacts of climate change and the kinds of adaptation best suited to the city's critical infrastructure.

A crucial component of the NPCC's work was to examine the effectiveness of current regulations and design standards in mitigating the effects of sea-level rise, storm surge, heat waves and inland flooding. The most important aspect of this work for the city is to adjust its current building codes so as to maintain the current low level of risk. In other words, how do you build buildings that can withstand the increased frequency and intensity of precipitation, flooding events, heat waves and extreme winds?

Another project, and product, of the NPCC is the Adaptation Assessment Guidebook (AAG), which describes to stakeholders how to create an

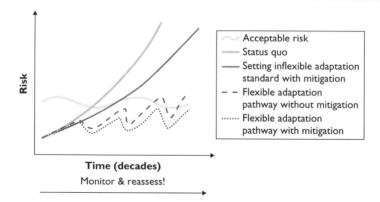

Figure 10.2 Adaptive urbanization climate-risk management in cities, flexible adaptation pathways and interactive mitigation and adaptation
Note: graphic adapted from Lowe *et al.*, 2008.
Source: Rosenzweig and Solecki, 2010a.

inventory of their at-risk infrastructure, and how to develop adaptation strategies that can address those risks. The steps outlined in the AAG are intended to become integral parts of ongoing risk management, maintenance and operation, and capital planning of the agencies and organizations that manage and operate critical infrastructure.

The NPCC fosters an approach to climate change known as Flexible Adaptation Pathways (FAP). FAP was originally developed by the London Thames Estuary 2100 project (TE2100) as an approach that can be adjusted and modified over time to reflect the dynamic and ongoing evolution in the scientific understanding of climate change (see Figure 10.2). FAP was also intended to take account of current local, national and global economic and social conditions. NPCC's multidimensional approach to managing the climate-change risk to infrastructure can be helpful in planning climate-change adaptation in other sectors besides infrastructure, as well as in other cities and metropolitan regions.

Cities act: Local, national and global climate-change adaptation initiatives

New York City is not alone in planning for climate-change adaptation. Cities around the world are highly vulnerable to climate change, but they, too, have great potential to lead in both adaptation and mitigation. And despite the economic and political constraints that many cities face, they are serving as important laboratories for climate-change action. Numerous examples exist in the more developed countries, but even in developing countries cities as diverse as Durban, South Africa; Maputo, Mozambique; Mexico City; Quito, Ecuador; and Taipei, Taiwan, have been actively working on climate initiatives (see Rosenzweig *et al.*, 2011b for more discussion). These initiatives are designed to facilitate the development of climate-action plans and to build the adaptive capacity of local institutions – and to make sure that both are linked with ongoing urban development. The Mexico City government, for instance, has dramatically accelerated its focus on climate change with innovative decision-making and research tools. Mexico City's Virtual Center on Climate Change (CVCCCM)[19,20] exemplifies the government's commitment.

Many cities have begun to interact and connect with national or transnational programs and projects designed to enhance urban adaptive capacity. These programs and projects provide opportunities for sharing tools, strategies, lessons learned and best practices. Selected cities in the least developed countries (LDCs) have interacted, for instance, under the auspices of a project known as CLACC (Capacity Strengthening in LDCs for Adaptation to Climate Change). CLACC's objective is to strengthen the capacity of organizations in low-income countries and support their initiatives in sustainable development and climate-adaptation planning.[21]

Thanks to the efforts of many cities, ample information on climate risk and response is available for effective action. Yet this information and data need to be more widely disseminated. To effectively address the challenges presented by climate change, cities need to bring climate science, adaptation strategies and mitigation actions into the mainstream of their daily decision-making, as well as their long-term plans and investments. The best resources for doing so are often home-grown: many cities in both developing and developed countries host research communities who are willing and able to help to develop plans for assessing and acting on climate change.

Even among the cities developing long-term action plans, many still would like to update their plans with the latest scientific estimates of the changing character of global and local climate risks. Recent assessments of the impacts of climate change on cities, along with efforts by the Organization for Economic and Cooperative Development (OECD), UN-Habitat, the World Bank, the Urban Climate-change Research Network and ICLEI (Local Governments for Sustainability) aim to bring ongoing knowledge and cutting-edge research to urban policy-makers, and thus to build capacity for city climate action. Policy discussions on climate change that once focused almost exclusively on mitigation have begun to stress the importance of adaptation along with mitigation – and they are highlighting the role of cities in adaptation.

In the U.S. several authoritative, recent studies of climate-change adaptation are now available. America's Climate Choices is an initiative of the national academies (National Academy of Science and the National Academy of Engineering), stemming from the Department of Commerce

Appropriations Act of 2008. A study released in October 2009 by the U.S. Government Accountability Office highlights the actions cities are taking to promote climate resilience in the U.S. This work is now being fully updated by the U.S. National Climate Assessment being conducted by the U.S. Global Change Research Program, and is due to be released in 2013.

At the international level, the Climate Summit for Mayors was hosted by Durban in December 2011, in conjunction with the 17th Conference of the Parties (COP17) to the United Nations Framework Convention on Climate Change (UNFCCC). The goal of the summit was to highlight the important role of cities in both mitigating and adapting to climate change. The C40 initiative, a partnership of the Clinton Climate Initiative and the Large Cities Climate Leadership Group, of which New York City is a charter member, was started in 2005 to promote the role cities can play in responding to climate change.

Another global organization, ICLEI, has brought together more than 1100 city and local government associations to work on enhancing the role of cities in international responses to climate change. Much of ICLEI's work has focused on mitigation efforts. Its Cities for Climate Protection Campaign is designed to help cities and local governments to adopt GHG-reduction strategies via quantifiable measures while enhancing urban quality of life. In addition to such mitigation efforts, ICLEI has also begun to recognize the need for cities to adapt to climate change, and it has launched adaptation initiatives in Australia, Canada, Europe and the U.S.

Numerous other international organizations and partnerships have also made significant contributions to promoting the local adaptive capacity of cities. Under the Sustainable Urban Development Network (SUD-Net), the Cities in Climate Change Initiative of UN-Habitat works to raise awareness, develop tools and build capacity for adaptation and mitigation projects in cities of developing countries. In Kampala, Uganda, for instance, this initiative has promoted energy- and water-focused climate-action projects as well as links between the national and local response capacities.[22]

Urbanization and keys to climate success

Other municipalities and urban areas can draw from New York and other leading-innovator cities in devising their own decision-making support strategies and protocols for addressing climate change. Listing the elements that contribute to success is simple and straightforward: strong leadership; broad involvement among government, private sector and scientific communities; establishment of clear goals; creation of targeted tools to support the planning efforts; development of mechanisms for evaluating (and re-evaluating) the results; and creation of a knowledge network. As always, taking action that integrates all these elements is the hard part.

Ongoing assessments of climate change by cities themselves is critical if cities are to successfully adapt to climate change. By 'owning' such assessments, cities can point to a process and cite a foundational knowledge base that confers the legitimacy, credibility and salience they need to assert their place at the table in global climate-change negotiations (Cash *et al.*, 2002). Legitimacy and credibility come about through interactions with scientific experts and city leaders (from both developed and developing countries); through membership in city associations such as ICLEI, C40, United Cities and Local Governments (UCLG) and Metropolis; through links with international development agencies such as Cities Alliance, the United Nations Environment Programme (UNEP), UN-Habitat and the World Bank; and through the support of nation states themselves. We specifically include nation-states in this list, because it is vital for nations to recognize and support the role of cities as key partners in mitigation and adaptation.

The salience of urban climate assessments arises from the growing realization that cities are the 'first responders' to climate change, both in mitigation and in adaptation. The close connections between city leaders and their constituents – compared with the more distant relationships between national leaders and their citizens – make cities the appropriate level of government for a great many climate-change actions. That is not to say that other levels of government can stand aside: all government levels – local, provincial, national and international – are needed to respond to the immense challenges of climate change.

The assessments of urban climate should be responsive to the special needs for practical and timely information by decision-makers in cities of both the developed and the developing world. At the same time, such assessments will serve a critical benchmarking function, giving cities the feedback they need to learn what happens – what works and what doesn't work – as climate change and the responses to it unfold. And assessments will help to strengthen the understanding of how to continue promoting urbanization in an era of climate change.

A final ingredient for success in responding to climate change is the need for close connection with the highest levels of city governance. In New York and London, for instance, a crucial element to successful 'mainstreaming' of climate change has been high-level 'buy-in' by city officials. The mayors of each city were champions of the climate-change issue for their city. In New York, the mayor's engaged leadership was essential in setting and meeting the climate-change goals. At the commissioner level, the groundbreaking work on how to deal with the impact of climate change on the New York City water system was actively initiated and supported by NYCDEP commissioners. There is ample (and even inspiring) precedent for such visionary support. Those responsible for creating the upstate water system for New York in the late 1830s and early 1840s had a planning horizon of

100 years. In the present day the mayor and his commissioners are taking actions whose benefits will continue to be appreciated for at least another 100 years.

Notes

1 Portions of this chapter were adapted from Rosenzweig *et al.* (2011a), Rosenzweig *et al.* (2010b) and Rosenzweig and Solecki (2010a).

2 We define 'cities' here in the broad sense to be urban areas, including metropolitan and surrounding suburban regions. We conceptualize urbanization as ongoing and continuous system-level processes that take place in all cities, whether they be older, more established cities such as London and Tokyo or rapidly developing and growing cities such as Dkaha or Mumbai.

3–4 Hammer, S.A., Keirstead, J., Dhakal, S., Mitchell, J., Colley, M., Connell, R., Gonzalez, R., Herve-Mignucci, M., Parshall, L., Schulz, N. and Hyams, M. (2011) 'Climate change and urban energy systems', in Rosenzweig *et al.* (2011a).

5–8 Major, D.C., Omojola, A., Dettinger, M., Hanson, R.T., and Sanchez-Rodriguez, R. (2011) 'Water and wastewater', in Rosenzweig *et al.* (2011a).

9 Barton, J. and Heinrichs, D. (2011) 'Santiago de Chile: adaptation, water management, and the challenges for spatial planning', in Rosenzweig *et al.* (2011a).

10 Major, D.C., Omojola, A., Dettinger, M., Hanson, R.T., and Sanchez-Rodriguez, R. (2011) 'Water and wastewater', in Rosenzweig *et al.* (2011a).

11 See also Mehrotra, S., Lefevre, B., Zimmerman, R., Gercek, H., Jacob, K., Srinivasan, S. and Salon, D. (2011) 'Climate change and urban transportation systems', in Rosenzweig *et al.* (2011a).

12 Mehrotra, S., Lefevre, B., Zimmerman, R., Gercek, H., Jacob, K., Srinivasan, S. and Salon, D. (2011) 'Climate change and urban transportation systems', in Rosenzweig *et al.* (2011a).

13 Barata, M., Ligeti, E., De Simone, G., Dickinson, T., Jack, D., Penney, J., Rahman, M. and Zimmerman, R. (2011) 'Climate change and human health in cities', in Rosenzweig *et al.* (2011a).

14 See also Barata, M., Ligeti, E., De Simone, G., Dickinson, T., Jack, D., Penney, J., Rahman, M. and Zimmerman, R. (2011) 'Climate change and human health in cities', in Rosenzweig *et al.* (2011a).

15 Penney, J. (2011) 'Disaster risk management in Pune, India', in Rosenzweig *et al.* (2011a).

16 See also Blanco, H., McCarney, P., Parnell, S., Schmidt, M. and Seto, K. (2011) 'The role of urban land in climate change', in Rosenzweig *et al.* (2011a).

17 McCarney, P., Blanco, H., Carmin, J. and Colley, M. (2011) 'Cities and climate change: the challenges for governance', in Rosenzweig *et al.* (2011a).

18 For the Task Force, critical infrastructure is defined as systems and assets (excluding residential and commercial buildings, which are handled by other efforts) that support activities so vital to the city that the diminished functioning or destruction of such systems and assets would have a debilitating impact on public safety and/or economic security.

19 Conde, C., Martinez, B. and Estrada, F. (2011) 'Mexico City's virtual center on climate change', in Rosenzweig *et al.* (2011a).

20   See the organization's website at http://www.cvcccm-atmosfera.unam.mx/
cvcccm
21   Dodman, D. (2011) 'Urban vulnerabilities in the least developed countries', in
Rosenzweig et al. (2011a).
22   Lwasa, S., Mabiliirzi, F., Njenga, C., Mukwaya, P., Koojo, C. and Sekimpi,
D. (2011) 'Adaptation and mitigation of climate change impacts in Kampala,
Uganda', in Rosenzweig et al. (2011a).

References

Aerts, J., Major, D.C., Bowman, M., Dircke, P. and Marfai, M.A. (2009) Connecting
Delta Cities: Coastal Cities, Flood Risk Management, and Adaptation to Climate
Change, Free University of Amsterdam Press, Amsterdam
Bai, X. (2007) 'Integrating global concerns into urban management: the scale
argument and the readiness argument', Journal of Industrial Ecology, vol 11,
pp51–92
Bartlett, S., Dodman, D., Hardoy, J., Satterthwaite, D., Tacoli, C. (2009) Social
Aspects of Climate Change in Urban Areas in Low- and Middle-Income Nations.
World Bank Fifth Urban Research Symposium – Cities and Climate Change:
Responding to an Urgent Agenda
Bell, M.L, Goldberg, R., Hogrefe, C., Patrick, L.K., Knowlton, K., Lynn, B.,
Rosenthal, J., Rosenzweig, C. and Patz, J.A. (2007) 'Climate change, ambient
ozone, and health in 50 U.S. cities', Climatic Change, vol 82, pp61–76
Blanco, H. and Alberti, M. (2009) 'Building capacity to adapt to climate change
through planning', in H. Blanco and M. Alberti (eds) Hot, Congested, Crowded,
and Diverse: Emerging Research Agendas in Planning, Progress in Planning,
vol 71, pp153–205
Case, T. (2008) 'Climate change and infrastructure issues. AWWA Research
Foundation, drinking water research', Climate Change Special Issue, vol 18,
pp15–17
Cash, D., Clark, W.C., Alcock, F., Dickson, N.M., Eckley, N. and Jäger, J. (2002)
'Salience, credibility, legitimacy and boundaries: linking research, assessment and
decision making.' KSG Working Papers Series RWP02-046, Harvard Kennedy
School, Cambridge, MA
Condon, P.M., Cavens, D. and Miller, N. (2009) 'Urban planning tools for climate
change mitigation', Policy Focus Report, Lincoln Institute of Land Policy,
Cambridge, MA
Frumkin, H., Hess, J., Luber, G., Malilay, J. and McGeehin, M. (2008) 'Climate
change: the public health response', American Journal of Public Health, vol 98,
pp435–445
International Energy Agency (IEA) (2008) 'Energy use in cities', in World Energy
Outlook, IEA, Paris
Kamai-Chaoui, L. (2009) 'Competitive cities and climate change: an introductory
paper', in OECD Regional Development Working Papers No. 2, OECD, Paris
Kim, K.-G. and Choi, Y.-S. (2011) 'Seoul's efforts against climate change', in
C. Rosenzweig, W.D. Solecki, S.A. Hammer and S. Mehrotra (eds) Climate
Change and Cities: First Assessment Report of the Urban Climate Change
Research Network, Cambridge University Press, New York

Kirshen, P., Ruth, M. and Anderson, W. (2008) 'Interdependencies of urban climate change impacts and adaptation strategies: a case study of Metropolitan Boston USA', *Climatic Change*, vol 86, issue 1–2, pp105–122

Lowe, J., Reeder, T., Horsburgh, K. and Bell, V. (2008) 'Using the new TE2100 science scenarios', U.K. Environment Agency, unpublished PowerPoint presentation

McEvoy, D., Lindley, S. and Handley, J. (2006) 'Adaptation and mitigation in urban areas: synergies and conflicts', *Proceedings of the Institution of Civil Engineers*, vol 159, no 4, pp185–191

McGranahan, G., Balk, D. and Anderson, B. (2007) 'The rising tide: assessing the risks of climate change and human settlements in low elevation coastal zones', *Environment and Urbanization*, vol 19, pp17–37

Mehrotra, S., Natenzon, C., Omojola, A., Folorunsho, R., Gilbride, J. and Rosenzweig C. (2009) 'Framework for city climate risk assessment', World Bank Commissioned Research for Urban Research Symposium 5, World Bank, Washington, DC

Nelson, K.C., Palmer, M.A., Angermeier, P.L., Glenn, E., Moglen, G.E., Angermeier, P.L., Hilderbrand, R.H., Dettinger, M. and Hayhoe, K. (2009) 'Forecasting the combined effects of urbanization and climate change of stream ecosystems: from impacts to management options', *Journal of Applied Ecology*, vol 46, no 1, pp154–163

New York City (2007) *PlaNYC: A Greener, Greater New York*, Office of the Mayor, New York, http://nytelecom.vo.llnwd.net/o15/agencies/planyc2030/pdf/full_report_2007.pdf, accessed April 4, 2012

NYCDEP (New York City Department of Environmental Protection) (2008) *Assessment and Action Plan: A Report Based on the Ongoing Work of the DEP Climate Change Task Force*, New York City Department of Environmental Protection Climate Change Program, New York.

Parnell, S., Pieterse, E. and Watson, V. (2009) 'Planning for cities in the global south: an Afrocam research agenda for sustainable urban settlements', in H. Blanco and M. Alberti (eds) 'Shaken, shrinking, hot, impoverished and informal: emerging research agendas in planning', *Progress in Planning*, vol 72, pp233–241

Prasad, N., Ranghieri, F. and Shah, F. (eds) (2009) *Climate Resilient Cities*, World Bank, Washington, DC

Reid, H. and Kovats, S. (2009) 'Special issue on health and climate change', *TIEMPO: A Bulletin on Climate and Development*, vol 71

Revi, A. (2008) 'Climate change risk: an adaptation and mitigation agenda for Indian cities', *Environment and Urbanization*, vol 20, no 1, pp207–229

Rosenzweig, C. and Solecki, W.D. (eds) (2001) *Climate Change in a Global City: The Impacts of Potential Climate Variability and Change in the New York Metropolitan Region*, Columbia Earth Institute, New York

Rosenzweig, C. and Solecki, W. (eds) (2010a) *Climate Change Adaptation in New York City: Building a Risk Management Response: New York City Panel on Climate Change 2010 Report*, Annals of the New York Academy of Sciences, vol 1196, New York Academy of Sciences, New York

Rosenzweig, C., Solecki, W., Hammer, S.A., and Mehrotra, S. (2010b) 'Cities lead the way in climate-change action', *Nature*, October 21, vol 467, pp909–911

Rosenzweig, C., Solecki, W., Hammer, S.A. and Mehrotra, S. (eds) (2011a) *Climate Change and Cities: First Assessment Report of the Urban Climate Change Research Network*, Cambridge University Press, New York

Rosenzweig, C., Solecki, W.D., Blake, R., Bowman, M., Faris, C., Gornitz, V., Jacob, K., LeBlanc, A., Leichenko, R., Sussman, E., Yohe, G., Zimmerman. R. (2011b) 'Developing coastal adaptation to climate change in the New York City infrastructure-shed: process, approach, tools, and strategies', *Climatic Change*, vol 106, issue 1, pp93–127

Rosenzweig, C., Major, D.C. and Demong, K. (2007) 'Managing climate change risks in New York City's water system: assessment and adaptation planning', *Mitigation and Adaptation Strategies for Global Change*, vol 12, no 8, pp1391–1409

Scheffer, M. Bascompte, J., Brock, W.A., Brovkin, V., Carpenter, S.R., Dakos, V., Held, H., van Nes, E.H., Rietkerk, M. and Sugihara, G. (2009) 'Early-warning signals for critical transitions', *Nature*, vol 461, September 3, pp53–59

Scobey, D.M. (2003) *Empire City: The Making and Meaning of the New York City Landscape (Critical Perspectives on the Past)*, Temple University Press, Philadelphia

Solecki, W.D. and Leichenko, R. (2006) 'Urbanization and the metropolitan environment: lessons from New York and Shanghai', *Environment*, vol 48, pp8–23

Solecki, W. and Murphy, C. (2012) 'Transition theory and understanding urban water supply systems in the context of climate change', submitted to *Global Environmental Change.*

Solecki, W., O'Brien, K. and Leichenko, R. (2011) 'Disaster risk reduction and climate change adaptation strategies: convergence and synergies', *Current Opinion in Environmental Sustainability*, vol 3, pp135–141

UN (United Nations) (2010) *World Population Prospects: 2009 Revision*, UN Department of Economic and Social Affairs, New York

UN-Habitat (United Nations Human Settlements Programme) (2011) *Cities and Climate Change: Global Report on Human Settlements 2011*, Earthscan, London

Wilby, R.L. (2007) 'A review of climate change impacts on the built environment', *Built Environment*, vol 33, p1

World Health Organization (WHO) (2009) *Protecting Health from Climate Change: Connecting Science, Policy and People*, WHO, Geneva

Yohe, Gary and Leichenko, Robin (2010) 'Chapter 2: Adopting a risk-based approach', in Cynthia Rosenzweig and William Solecki (eds) *Climate Change Adaptation in New York City: Building a Risk Management Response: New York City Panel on Climate Change 2010 Report*, Annals of the New York Academy of Sciences, vol 1196, pp29–40, New York Academy of Sciences, New York

Index

accountability 85, 89, 91, 98
Accra 28
Adaptation Assessment Guidebook (AAG) 212–13
advertising 27–8
advocacy 140
affordable housing 49, 103, 136
Africa: coastal areas 34; floods 35; informal sector 44–5, 104; participatory budgeting 165; rental sector 107–8; shelter finance 104, 144; 'urban penalty' 51; urbanization 1; water and sanitation systems 153, 155; water stress 36
agriculture 33, 36, 189
Ahmedabad 113, 115
air pollution: climate change 199; fuel regulation 98; health transitions 19; London 15; New York City 209; respiratory infection 29; urban environmental-risk transition 20, 21, 22
Albala-Bertrand, J. 189, 191
alcohol disorders 53
alcohol tax 96
Alliance for Healthy Cities (AHC) 87, 92–3
Alma-Ata Declaration on Primary Health Care (1978) 16, 42
Alvarinho, Manuel 35
Angola 105, 107, 109
Argentina 165
Asia: health issues 9–10, 82–102; informal economy 104; shelter finance 104, 111, 144; urbanization

1, 2; water and sanitation systems 155
Asian Coalition for Housing and Rights (ACHR) 89
Asian Development Bank (ADB) 112–13
Asian Forum on Corporate Social Responsibility (AFCSR) 94
Asian Infectious Disease Project (AIDF) 93
avian influenza 93, 94, 95, 100

Baan Mankong Programme 129, 134–6
Baker, Judy 46
Bangalore 93
Bangkok 53, 120
Bangladesh 34, 35, 43, 82, 86, 109
banks 105, 117, 123n6, 131, 162
Belo Horizonte 2, 9, 65–75, 76, 79
Bender, Thomas 205
best practices 75–7, 78
Bhutan 86
Blaikie, Piers 183–4
Bloomberg, Michael 212
Bolivia 165
Boonyabancha, Somsook 90, 121, 122
Botswana 106
Brazil: Belo Horizonte 2, 9, 65–75, 76, 79; favelas 17, 65; health inequalities 55; home ownership 107; incremental housing development 123n2; infant mortality 52; mortgage finance 112; participatory budgeting 9, 66–70, 71, 72, 74–6, 165; political